Reinhard Brandl

Cost Accounting for Shared IT Infrastructures

GABLER EDITION WISSENSCHAFT

Reinhard Brandl

Cost Accounting for Shared IT Infrastructures

With a foreword by Prof. Dr. Martin Bichler

GABLER EDITION WISSENSCHAFT

Bibliographic information published by Die Deutsche Nationalbibliothek
Die Deutsche Nationalbibliothek lists this publication in the Deutsche Nationalbibliografie;
detailed bibliographic data is available in the Internet at <http://dnb.d-nb.de>.

Dissertation Technische Universität München, 2007

1st Edition 2008

All rights reserved
© Betriebswirtschaftlicher Verlag Dr. Th. Gabler | GWV Fachverlage GmbH, Wiesbaden 2008

Softcover re-print of the Hardcover 1st edition 2008

Editorial Office: Frauke Schindler / Anita Wilke

Gabler-Verlag is a company of Springer Science+Business Media.
www.gabler.de

Cover design: Regine Zimmer, Dipl.-Designerin, Frankfurt/Main
Printed on acid-free paper

ISBN 978-3-8349-4647-8

Für meine Eltern

Foreword

During the past few years, determining the "value of IT" has ranked high on the agenda of IT managers and Chief Information Officers (CIOs). The rather broad and abstract topic has been intensively discussed in the Information Systems literature for many years. It turns into a very tangible problem in the field of IT cost accounting. Nowadays, corporate information systems are distributed systems. A detailed measurement of resource demands of IT services on a distributed IT-infrastructure and respective accounting and cost allocation turns out to be very expensive and impractical in most cases. The large proportion of indirect costs and the difficulty of finding adequate allocation rates are a significant problem in practice, regularly leading to free-rider problems. This problem has largely been ignored in the academic literature so far. Dr. Brandl proposes a method to derive estimators for the resource demand of service requests in a distributed IT infrastructure. This estimator is based on a set of load tests and respective measurements as they are often performed during the deployment phase of new information systems. Cost allocation keys can now be determined based on the number of service invocations per user or per department and the respective estimators.

While these measurements provide a lean method for the determination of usage-based cost allocation keys, it is not obvious that the estimators have sufficient accuracy, in particular concerning different types of services and volatile workloads. Although it is not possible to provide tangible results for all types of information systems, Mr. Brandl performs a large number of experiments for typical multi-tiered information systems as they are in widespread use today. Queuing network models are used to validate the results for different workloads and multiple types of services. The experiments shows that resource consumption in heterogeneous environments can be predicted with high accuracy. Overall, this leads to a viable solution for the cost accounting of distributed information systems.

Dr. Brandl makes an important contribution to a largely neglected field. The book provides practical advice for IT managers for a very timely topic. I therefore hope and expect that the book will be well received not only among academics, but in particular among practitioners in cost accounting and IT controlling.

Prof. Dr. Martin Bichler

Preface

The provision of central IT infrastructure components, such as servers, storage, and networking equipment, accounts for a considerable proportion of the IT budgets of larger organizations. Typically, such components are shared among multiple applications and internal customers. Objective measurements of their respective resource consumption are technically difficult and incur high costs. In practice, infrastructure cost allocation is regularly based on simplified allocation keys which cause multiple free-rider problems and discontent among the stakeholders.

This thesis proposes a method to estimate the expected resource consumption of customer-oriented services across the components involved. The estimates are determined in a load test prior to the roll-out of an application system and then combined to so-called resource profiles. By means of these resource profiles, costs can be allocated to services or service invocations. During regular operations, consumption measurements at the different components can be omitted. The estimates therefore need to be unbiased even in cases of varying system workloads and in heterogeneous environments. Furthermore, they should support IT Capacity Planning and bridge the gap between business forecasts and IT resource planning.

The concept was implemented in a software toolkit and evaluated in a set of experiments with multi-tier database applications in a data center of the BMW Group. Queuing Network Models were used to validate the resource profiles under different system workloads. In the experiments, a surprisingly high accuracy of consumption estimates as well as of Queuing Network Model predictions could be determined. Besides the experimental validation, it was analyzed how the approach could be integrated into existing IT processes at the BMW Group.

The work presented in this thesis would not have been possible without the great support of two persons: Prof. Dr. Martin Bichler and Dr. Michael Ströbel. They gave me the opportunity to work on this topic and provided continuous feedback, inspiration, and encouragement. I am deeply grateful to both of them.

During my time as a doctoral candidate, I was employed by the BMW Group. I greatly appreciated the pleasant working atmosphere and the kind support from all my colleagues. In particular, I would like to thank my managers Harald Raufer, Alexander Pauli, and Bernhard Huber, who gave me the freedom to pursue my research activities and provided me with interesting and responsible tasks to collect valuable business experiences far beyond the dissertation project. At the BMW Group, I was given access to all the relevant information and data center resources. However, without the technical expertise of Volker Smuda and Alexander Pochivalow, it would not have been possible to conduct more than 500 load tests during the development and evaluation phase of the software toolkit. Furthermore, I am particularly thankful to my colleagues Dr. Markus Greunz and Hartmut Liefke for their numerous comments on the viability of my approach.

I would also like to thank Prof. Dr. Helmut Krcmar who readily accepted to act as the second reviewer of the thesis and provided me with valuable advice regarding future steps.

Finally, I am deeply indebted to my family for enabling me to go this way and providing continuous support, patience, and understanding throughout my whole life.

Dr. Reinhard Brandl

Contents

List of Figures

List of Tables

Chapter 1

Introduction

1.1 Problem Statement

In recent decades, industrial data centers have been subject to many technological changes. Until the mid-90s, central mainframe architectures dominated. They provided homogeneous environments for applications and users, high Quality-of-Service and elaborate workload management for an effective resource usage. Then the rise of client/server technologies initiated a move toward distributed, multi-tier systems running on low-cost, and often heterogeneous, hardware. Over the years more or less independent hardware silos, each dedicated to a distinct enterprise function or application, became commonplace (Foster and Tuecke, 2005). However, along with this shift, the average server utilization decreased to 25 % and lower (Schmitz, 2005). Today, client/server principles are still standard, but along with advances in virtualization technologies (see for instance Xen, University of Cambridge, n.d.) there is a trend toward sharing IT infrastructure among multiple applications and service customers.

Regarding today's IT budgets, the largest portion (28 %)[1] is spent on salaries of full-time IT staff (see figure 1.1). The second largest cost pool is computer hardware (21 %), which accounts together with Networking and Communications hardware (14 %) for more than one-third of an average IT budget. In times of rising budget pressure, IT managers are typically required to provide not only such a cost type classification, but to allocate the costs to the business processes or the business units[2] that caused them.

---

[1] Between September and December 2005, Forrester Research surveyed 270 IT executives at European enterprises (> 1,000 employees, different industries) on their IT budgets and spending for 2006 (see Bartels, 2006).

[2] In the following referred to as the *customers* of IT services.

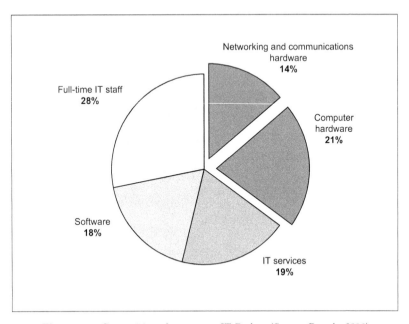

Figure 1.1: Composition of an average IT Budget (Source: Bartels, 2006)

The technological changes described above have also affected cost structures of data centers and approaches to determine appropriate cost allocation keys. Mainframes traditionally provide accounting mechanisms that are tightly coupled with the operating system and enable an apportionment of resource usage to specific applications or users (see for instance Fujitsu Siemens, n.d.; IBM, n.d.b). By means of the consumption shares, infrastructure costs (e.g., amortization, maintenance, licenses) can be subdivided among the customers. In distributed client/server environments, as depicted in figure 1.2, the determination of such usage-based allocation keys is by far more challenging (Bertleff, 2001, p. 63). If the hardware is dedicated to specific customers, the incurred costs can be treated as direct costs (see example of client 1 in figure 1.2). The actual resource consumption (e.g., CPU time or number of I/O operations) is not a relevant cost driver and can be ignored. However, more and more IT infrastructure is nowadays shared among multiple applications and business units. In such environments, the resource consumption of applications is a major driver for new investment decisions. An average application server in an industrial data center (e.g., 4 processors, 16 GB memory) can easily host dozens

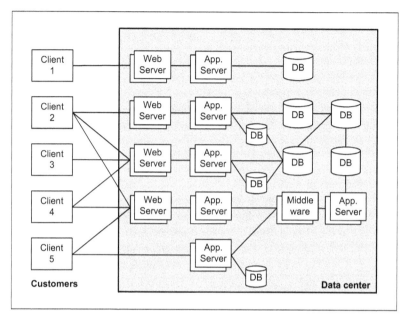

Figure 1.2: Example: Shared and dedicated Data Center Resources

of light-weight applications, whereas in other workload scenarios, the same server may be fully utilized by one or two applications. If the costs for such a server are treated as indirect costs and are apportioned via flat rates or fixed percentages, the IT management, as well as the concerned business units, has only a few possibilities for cost controlling and planning. The creation of cost transparency is further complicated as servers are usually not offered as a standalone product, but as part of larger IT systems. A request in a three tier database application, for example, comprises a web server, an application server, and a database server, which are all typically used by different applications (see figure 1.2). Tracking resource consumption is one of the toughest but most critical parts of a successful cost transparency program (Appel et al., 2005, p. 13).

Besides the improvement in cost transparency, the allocation of IT costs is also an IT Governance instrument, which can encourage desired behavior on the supply and demand side. However, a simplified cost allocation mechanism, based for instance on the number of employees in a business unit, may lead to multiple free-rider problems and political tensions. Business owners of application systems might not consider the resource requirements when selecting off-the-shelf software. Also, the owners of "light-weight" applications might have to bear a very high share of the costs for a particular application or database server, which in turn makes it more difficult to finance these applications. Obviously, a consumption-based model, where IT infrastructure costs can easily be allocated to application owners or even to users directly, increases cost transparency and would have a number of advantages. A technical possibility would be to determine cost allocation keys through detailed monitoring and metering of each service request. This would require assigning a unique identifier for each user to each database request and each thread running on an application server in order to determine exactly how much of the resources a service customer has consumed. It would force the adaptation of the entire IT infrastructure, cause a huge monitoring and metering overhead, and is typically not viable. Furthermore, business customers probably would not accept technical accounting metrics such as the processor times of different servers. As they cannot directly correlate such metrics with their business activities, they can hardly plan or control cost allocation. In mainframe environments, with one single resource, this might have been possible, but the concept cannot be transferred to client/server infrastructures. The use of customer-oriented cost allocation keys (e.g., number of executed business transactions) shifts the problem to the IT units, which must then translate their resource-oriented cost sheets (e.g., per server, per stored gigabyte) into metrics reflecting business operations. This challenges internal IT units in particular. External outsourcing providers have a greater flexibility to adapt their accounting metrics to the needs of their customers and, for instance, are not required to determine fair cost shares.

Regarding the technical complexity and the potential overhead, it is not surprising that IT Cost Accounting and Chargeback is often based on simplified cost allocation keys (Gadatsch et al., 2005; Syskoplan, 2002). Practitioners, however, regularly report discontent, conflicts, investment setbacks and distorted use of IT services due to internal cost allocation. IT analysts at Gartner even estimate that through 2008, 50 % of chargeback initiatives implemented by IT organizations will be seen as failures on the part of the business, the IT organization or both (Gomolski, 2005, p. 2).

Summing up, in shared and distributed IT infrastructures the determination of accurate usage-based cost allocation keys is often fraught with technical problems and unreasonable overheads. Simplifications, however, may lead to organizational problems such as free-rider behavior, political tensions or biased management decisions.

1.2 Research Approach

Most research on the design of IT Cost Accounting and Chargeback systems stems from behavioral science (see for instance McKinnon and Kallman, 1987; Ross et al., 1999; Verner et al., 1996). Basically, researchers study a number of real world cases to identify chargeback approaches and processes that are appropriate to achieving organization-level objectives. A second prominent category of publications evaluates the viability of different costing methodologies (e.g., activity-based costing vs. traditional costing) for IT units (see for instance Fürer, 1994; Funke, 1999; Gerlach et al., 2002; Mai, 1996). Although these research approaches provide valuable results on organizational and human phenomena and on the appropriateness of cost management methods, they do not address the fundamental, technical problems. In this thesis we therefore follow a design-science approach (see for instance Hevner et al., 2004; March and Smith, 1995; Simon, 1996). In particular, we focus on the following question:

How can IT Service providers determine usage-based cost allocation keys for shared IT infrastructures?

The purpose is to develop a new cost allocation approach that should help to avoid the technical and organizational problems described above. We limit the scope to operational, interactive systems for Online Transaction Processing (OLTP), as those systems are typically shared among multiple customers and the determination of cost allocation keys is particularly difficult. From the existing literature on IT Cost Accounting and Chargeback we derive that, from a customer perspective, services such as the execution of a business transaction or the access to an information system would be an appropriate basis for cost allocation. However, instead of measuring the resource consumption during regular operations, we propose to determine, during standard load tests prior to the roll-out of an application system, estimates for the expected resource consumption of such services. The consumption estimates at the different resources are combined to a *resource profile* per service. The resource profile then could constitute the basis for the allocation of costs per service or per service invocation. Deriving such profiles, however, is not a trivial task. We consider four basic requirements:

1. **Accuracy** The resource profiles should be unbiased, in the sense that on average they should not over- or underestimate the true resource consumption.

2. **Consistency** The estimation of resource profiles should be in the same manner applicable to various kinds of hardware and software resources.

3. **Capacity Planning** The resource profiles should enable a translation of the customers' forecasted service usage into IT resource requirements and thus support the IT Capacity Planning.

4. **Operating Efficiency** The estimation should cause little extra work and integrate well with existing IT Service Management processes.

The concept is based on the hypothesis that the resource consumption increases linearly with the number of service invocations. To validate this hypothesis and to evaluate the concept regarding the above requirements we create the following artifacts: First, a process to derive resource profiles from load test measurements (method) and, second, a software toolkit implementing the process (instantiation). The evaluation then is based on three separate approaches:

1. **Experiments: Resource Profiles** We verify in several experiments the precision of measurement and analysis instruments, the repeatability of the process and the effect of parameter changes on resource profiles (*Requirements 1, 2 and 4*).

2. **Experiments: Analytical Models** The resource profiles should be unbiased, even in situations with multiple concurrently active services and varying workloads. We simulate such conditions in load tests and use consumption estimates from the resource profiles to parametrize analytical performance models. We then compare the model predictions with experimental results. Thus, we can verify the hypothesis on the linear increase of resource consumption and the appropriateness of resource profiles for Analytical Capacity Planning. We claim that if the resource profiles can be readily used for capacity planning, their accuracy is also sufficient for cost allocation (*Requirements 1 and 3*).

3. **Proof of concept: BMW Group** The experiments take place in a data center of our industrial partner, the BMW Group. Thus, we can evaluate the practicability of the approach and analyze how it could be integrated into professional IT Service Management processes (*Requirements 2 and 4*).

The research presented in this thesis aims to contribute a viable alternative to existing cost allocation methodologies and should constitute a basis for further studies on the organizational and technical design of IT Cost Accounting and Chargeback systems.

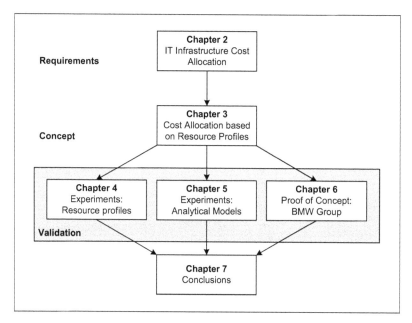

Figure 1.3: Structure of the Thesis

1.3 Overview of the Thesis

The thesis is organized along the research approach described above (see figure 1.3):

Chapter 2 The chapter starts with an overview of IT Cost Accounting and Chargeback and a brief introduction to basic terms and processes (section 2.1). We then focus on appropriate cost allocation approaches for today's client/server infrastructures. Based on a survey of literature (section 2.2), we describe major objectives and requirements of the involved stakeholders and point out the dilemma between customer-oriented and resource-oriented approaches (section 2.3). In section 2.4 we present a classification of cost allocation methods and illustrate why they often do not achieve the major objectives of IT Cost Accounting and Chargeback. The chapter concludes with a brief discussion on the future relevance of the problem against the background of today's organizational and technological trends (section 2.5).

Chapter 3   In this chapter we present the idea of allocating costs using customer-oriented services and their estimated resource consumption. We first define the scope of our considerations (section 3.1) and then detail the concepts of services, resource profiles and the cost allocation process (section 3.2). The underlying hypotheses on resource consumption are formalized in section 3.3. We then derive four major requirements on resource profiles and the profiling process that we consider as critical to the practical success of the approach (section 3.4). In section 3.5 we present the process for the determination of resource profiles and the software toolkit developed to validate the concept. Section 3.6 gives an overview of the validation presented in the subsequent chapters. Section 3.7 compares the concept to related approaches.

Chapter 4   We present the results of several experiments conducted with the software toolkit introduced in section 3.5. In sections 4.1 and 4.2 we provide an overview of the test infrastructure, the example application systems and the test series. In section 4.3 we then detail the experimental results. For the experiments we have set the following three objectives: First, we try to verify if the model describing the total resource consumption holds in the example environment. Second, we test the precision of the measurement and analysis tools. Third, we analyze the effects of parameter changes during the profiling process and compare the experimental results with the model predictions. The results are summarized in section 4.4.

Chapter 5   The motivation for the model-based validation approach presented in this chapter is twofold. First, it should enable a validation of the accuracy of the consumption estimates in situations with multiple concurrently active services and varying workloads. Second, by means of analytic performance models we try to demonstrate the appropriateness of resource profiles for Capacity Planning. That motivation is detailed further in section 5.1. In section 5.2 we provide an overview of IT Capacity Planning methods. We chose Queueing Network Theory as the mathematical basis for our performance models. In section 5.3 we introduce major concepts of Queueing Network Theory and then present the software tools developed for the analysis and verification of respective models (section 5.4). We continue the experiments presented in chapter 4 and use consumption estimates from the resource profiles as input parameters for a performance model. In section 5.5 we first describe the experimental setting and then detail the performance model. We evaluate the predictive accuracy of the model with services including single and multiple client requests. The experimental results are summarized in section 5.6. As standard of comparison we introduce in section 5.7 published results of a related experiment. The findings are summarized in section 5.8.

Chapter 6 In this chapter, we describe the results of a proof-of-concept conducted in cooperation with our industrial partner, the BMW Group. We first detail our motivation (section 6.1) and discuss whether the general considerations on requirements, objectives and practiced approaches are in accord with the situation at the BMW Group (section 6.2). We then focus on Java/J2EE-based application systems, report experiences of the tests in a data center of the BMW Group and propose an integration of resource profile determination into the existing IT Service Management Processes (section 6.3). Section 6.4 summarizes the results of the proof-of-concept.

Chapter 7 The thesis concludes with a summary of results (section 7.1) and a brief outlook onto future areas of research (section 7.2).

Chapter 2

IT Infrastructure Cost Allocation

2.1 IT Cost Accounting and Chargeback

2.1.1 Classification

There are several possibilities to structure the field of IT Cost Accounting and Chargeback. In the present context, the Management Accounting and Information Management perspective are of particular relevance. In the following, we briefly introduce both perspectives and provide references for further reading.

Management Accounting supports managers in planning and controlling their operations. In contrast to Financial Accounting, which addresses the needs of external parties (e.g., investors, creditors and tax authorities), the focus of Management Accounting lies inside the organization. The objective is to motivate and to assist managers in attaining their organizational objectives in a timely, efficient and effective manner (Kaplan and Atkinson, 1998, p. 1). Management Accounting is not constrained by external reporting requirements and can be designed according to an organization's needs. Relevance is more important than objectivity and auditability. Nevertheless, the data used must be defensible and transparent to internal participants (Kaplan and Atkinson, 1998, p. 1). One of the most important input types for Management Accounting is cost information. Costs arise from the acquisitions and use of organizational resources, such as people, equipment, materials and facilities (Kaplan and Atkinson, 1998, p. 13). *Cost Accounting* tracks, records and analyzes this information and reports costs associated with products or activities of the organization back to the management. Therefore, traditional costing systems implement a two-stage process. First, costs are assigned to *cost centers* (e.g., departments, subsidies) and, second, to *cost objects* (e.g., products produced by a department). Accordingly, costs can be categorized into direct and indirect costs. *Direct costs* are incurred by and can be directly traced to a cost center or a cost object. Examples of direct costs are direct raw materials or direct wages. *Indirect costs* or *overhead costs* cannot be fully traced back, because they are incurred by a number of cost centers or cost objects (Owen and Law, 2005, p. 211). Costs can be further categorized into variable and fixed costs. *Variable costs* change in direct proportion to the production or sales volume, while *fixed costs* remain constant over a certain period of time. Direct and indirect costs can either be fixed or variable. Costing systems differ by the cost categories they take into account. In a *full-cost approach*, fixed and variable costs are allocated to the cost object. In a *variable-cost approach*, only direct costs plus variable overhead costs are allocated (Owen and Law, 2005, p. 252). The reported product costs are meant to reflect the marginal costs of manufacturing (Cooper and Kaplan, 1987, p. 205). However, not all departments (cost centers) directly produce or distribute the organization's output (cost objects). Typically, two different types of departments can be distinguished: *production departments* and *service departments*. The costs of service departments should be assigned to production departments to promote cost control and efficiency by (Kaplan and Atkinson, 1998, p. 62):

- providing incentives for efficient performance by the managers of the service departments.

- motivating prudent use of the outputs from service departments by the managers of production departments.

Furthermore, managers of the consuming departments, who are charged for the services on a quantity and quality basis, will (Kaplan and Atkinson, 1998, p. 63):

- exercise more control over the consumption of that output in their departments.

- compare the costs of using the internal service department with the costs of comparable services purchased outside the firm.

- attempt to communicate to the service department the quality level of services desired, including showing their willingness to pay more to receive higher-quality service or to accept lower quality in order to pay less.

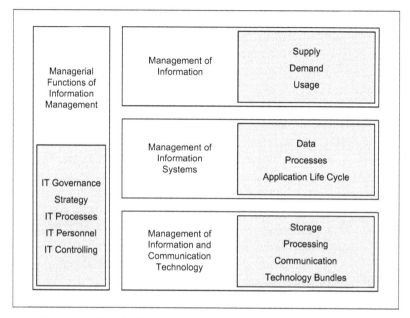

Figure 2.1: Model of Information Management (adapted from Krcmar, 2004, p. 47)

IT departments are typical examples of service departments. Their costs are mostly fixed as they do not vary with the actual level of production. IT costs are partially direct and can be assigned to departments incurring the costs (e.g., costs for dedicated servers or desktop computers). Indirect IT costs, such as costs for a shared data center infrastructure, are incurred by multiple departments or even for the whole company and cannot be directly attributed. Depending on the costing system, these indirect costs are or are not allocated to production departments. If the costs are apportioned, the challenge is to define appropriate allocation keys (e.g., per usage, per revenue share, per employee). Arbitrary allocation bases may lead to distorted product costs and biased management decisions. The optimal design of Management Accounting and Cost Accounting systems is the subject of a broad range of literature. In particular, we refer the interested reader to Kaplan and Atkinson (1998) and Horngren et al. (2005) (United States perspective), Reichmann (2006) and Horváth (2006) (German perspective), and Spitta (2000) (focus on IT costs).

Management Accounting and Cost Accounting focus on the provision of decision support information for managers. As mentioned above, the allocation of costs and the collection of internal charges for the usage of Information Systems intentionally changes users' behavior. Planning and controlling those effects falls under the realm of *Information Management*. According to Krcmar (2004), Information Management includes overall managerial functions as well as the *Management of Information*, *Management of Information Systems* and the *Management of Information and Communication Technologies* (see figure 2.1). The objective of Information Management is to ensure, with regard to business objectives, the best possible use of the resource information. Information Management is a management as well as a technology discipline, and is an integral part of corporate management (Krcmar, 2004, p. 49). Above mentioned tasks of planning and controlling users' or departments' behavior are fulfilled by the overall managerial functions. *IT Governance* specifies "the decision rights and accountability framework to encourage desirable behavior in the use of IT" (Weill and Woodham, 2002 cited by Krcmar, 2004, p. 288). *IT Controlling* coordinates the use of the resource information, the lifecycle of the Information Systems (*Portfolio*, *Project* and *Product Controlling*) and the IT infrastructures (*Infrastructure Controlling*) (Krcmar, 2004, p. 421). The allocation of costs and the collection of charges are powerful instruments of Product Controlling and Infrastructure Controlling. They can encourage necessary behavior, but can also lead to political tensions, investment setbacks and distorted use of IT services (Blosch et al., 2003b, p. 6). In the following sections we focus on identifying appropriate cost allocation approaches to avoid those conflicts.

Concerning further reading on Information Management, we refer the interested reader to Biethahn et al. (2004); Heinrich (2002) and Krcmar (2004). Teubner and Klein (2002) provide a comparative book review. Furthermore, IT Cost Accounting and Chargeback is typically addressed in literature on IT Controlling (see for instance Gadatsch and Mayer, 2006; Heilmann, 2001; Kargl, 1999; Krcmar et al., 2000; von Dobschütz et al., 2000). Schauer (2006) provides a comparative review of books published in Germany and the United States.

2.1.2   Definition of Terms

Before we focus on how IT Cost Accounting and Chargeback can be realized, several terms with potentially ambiguous meanings are introduced. The definitions correspond, as far as possible, with the terms used in the IT Infrastructure Library (see Office of Government Commerce, n.d.).

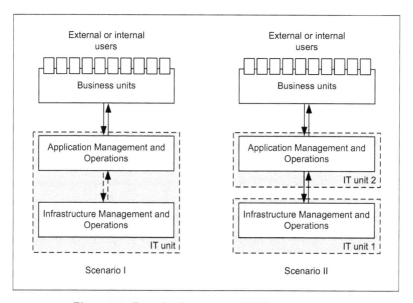

Figure 2.2: Example: Organization of IT Service Provision

In the following, we refer to a *company* if an organization is meant as a whole and to *business unit* or *IT unit* if an organizational subunit (e.g., department, division, subsidiary) is described. The outputs of IT units are IT services. An *IT service* is based on the use of Information Technology and supports the customer's business processes. An *IT infrastructure service* is not directly used by a business unit, but is required for the provision of another IT service. *Customer* is used to refer to the business or IT unit that is receiving a service. The *user* is the person who makes day-to-day use of the service. An *application* is a piece of software that provides functions that are required by an IT service. An *application system* is a combination of one or more applications that provides one or more IT services.

Concerning the organization of IT service provision, we differentiate between infrastructure-related IT functions such as operations of servers, storage and networks, and application-related functions such as application maintenance, operations and support. Figure 2.2 illustrates the concept with two example scenarios. In the first scenario all functions are integrated in one IT unit. Single customers for IT services are the business units. In the second scenario the functions are separated. The IT unit managing the

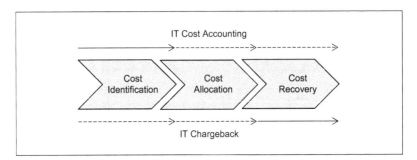

Figure 2.3: IT Cost Accounting and Chargeback Processes (adapted from Blosch et al., 2003b, p. 7)

applications is on the one hand a customer of the IT infrastructure services and on the other hand the IT Service Provider for the business units.

2.1.3 Overview of Processes

IT Cost Accounting and Chargeback can be divided into three major processes (Blosch et al., 2003b): *Cost Identification*, *Cost Allocation* and *Cost Recovery* (see figure 2.3)[1]. Whether and how these processes are implemented depends primarily on the funding of the IT units. Three basic funding models can be distinguished (adapted from Bertleff, 2001, p. 58 and Office of Government Commerce, 2001, ch. 5.3.2):

- **Fixed IT budget** and no charges for business units

- **Cost recovery** with charges based on actual costs

- **Self-funding** with an autonomy in setting prices

The funding models can be combined according to management objectives, overall Cost Accounting guidelines and organizational needs. For instance, a self-funding profit center can be created with the business objective of making a profit, breaking even or operating with a subsidy (Office of Government Commerce, 2001, ch. 5.3.2). The three IT Cost Accounting and Chargeback processes then can be described as follows.

---

[1]   The IT Infrastructure Library proposes a related process structure: *Budgeting, Accounting, Charging* (Office of Government Commerce, 2001, ch. 5)

Cost Identification focuses on achieving cost transparency inside the IT units. The objective is to identify actual costs for the different IT services and thus control the efficiency of their provision. This process is mandatory, whether or not the costs are further allocated to the business units (Blosch et al., 2003b, p. 8). The underlying costing approach (e.g., full-costing, variable-costing) typically depends on overall accounting guidelines.

Cost Allocation then distributes the costs to the business units. The objective is to enable business and IT managers to control what the money is spent on (e.g., cost share per business unit, cost share per process). In a typical company more than half of the IT costs are spent on shared services (e.g., data center operations, network management, telecommunications) (Blosch et al., 2003a, p. 14). For these services the chosen cost allocation keys[2] are decisive. Arbitrary cost allocations may distort the determined cost shares and bias management decisions.

Cost Recovery actually charges the accounts of the business units for their usage of IT services. The focus lies on changing customer behavior. To a certain degree and according to management objectives, market mechanisms can be used to regulate supply and demand of IT services. Charges may be dependent on costs or on market prices, for instance. However, Cost Recovery can also lead to political tensions and to suboptimal use of IT services. Thus, credible cost identification and allocation mechanisms are required.

Benefits and potential problems of the processes are summarized in table 2.1. Cost Allocation and Cost Recovery are optional processes. In the literature the term IT Cost Accounting sometimes applies only to Cost Identification, and sometimes also to Cost Allocation and Cost Recovery. IT Chargeback is used to describe the three processes or, at least, Cost Recovery. To avoid misunderstandings, we refer in the following to IT Cost Accounting *and* Chargeback if all three processes are meant. Alternatively, we could have used *IT Financial Management*, but this term may also include additional aspects such as budgeting or investment appraisal.

---

2   An overview of common cost allocation keys is given in section 2.4.

Process	Benefits	Potential problems
Cost Identification	Makes IT unit's costs visible	Costs hidden in multiple budgets
	Allows IT services to be costed	IT unit accounts don't match Finance's
	Provides the basis for cost control	Chart of accounts is not detailed enough
Cost Allocation	Allows assessment of BU performance	Disagreements over the choice of method
	Improves forecasting, decision making	Focus on IT service cost rather than value
	Spreads best practices across BUs	IT unit is not resourced to administer methods
Cost Recovery	Strongly influences BU behavior	BUs attempt to use external service providers
	Improves IT discipline in BUs	The trust and credibility of IT unit plunge
	Creates financial discipline in IT unit	The wrong behaviors are encouraged

Table 2.1: Benefits and Problems of IT Cost Accounting and Chargeback (adapted from Blosch et al., 2003b, p. 7)

2.1.4 Cost Allocation for IT Services

A major difficulty of IT Cost Accounting and Chargeback is that IT units perform various kinds of tasks. An overview with examples of 30 IT functions is provided in figure 2.4[3]. Typically, outputs of several IT functions are bundled to IT services, which then support the business processes of customers. Desktop-related IT services, represented by the light-gray boxes in figure 2.4, can be particularly well specified (e.g., the configuration of a desktop computer with office applications and network access, see Bertleff, 2001, p. 62 for an example) and incurred costs clearly allocated to the business units (e.g., per desktop computer, per telephone line). By far more complex is apportioning costs for the provision of central business application systems, represented by the dark-gray boxes in figure 2.4. This is because, firstly – in contrast to standardized desktop-related services – each application system has its own infrastructure, application and support requirements and, secondly, because a single instance of an application system is typically used concurrently by various customers. In the literature (see for instance Spitta, 2000; Spitta and Becker, 2000) and in practice (see section 2.4) application systems are often considered as internal IT cost objects. Incurred costs are first allocated to the application system and then

---

[3] The following abbreviations are used in figure 2.4: *HR* Human Resources, *PSA* Professional Services Automation, *CRM* Customer Relationship Management, *R&D* Research and Development, *DC* Data center.

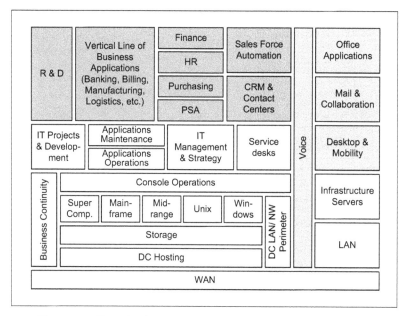

Figure 2.4: Example: Overview of IT Functions (adapted from Barton, 2006)

apportioned among the customers or attributed to a single business owner. For instance, the costs for HR, Finance and Purchasing systems can be attributed to the business units fulfilling these tasks. This approach has several difficulties. First, in cases where such single business owners do not exist, additional cost allocation keys must be determined (e.g., per employee, per transaction or per login). Second, apportioning fixed labor costs might require a time recording system (see Spitta and Becker, 2000 for a discussion of possible problems) and, finally, determining usage shares of shared IT infrastructure resources could become technically complex.

Major functions required for the provision of an application system, their relative cost shares[4] and possibilities to allocate these costs to customers are depicted in figure 2.5. Under the assumption that an appropriate time-recording system exists, costs for external

---

[4] The percentage rates indicate the share of *Total Costs of Ownership* (TCO). The TCO concept was initially developed by Gartner, Inc. to assess the total lifecycle costs of an IT investment (see Redman et al., 1998).

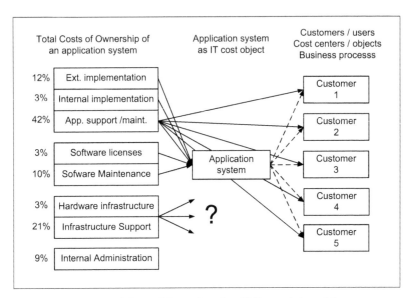

Figure 2.5: Total Costs of Ownership of an IT System (adapted from Spitta, 2000; Spitta and Becker, 2000; Ziehm, 2004)

and internal implementation services can be assigned to the concerned application systems. Cost for application support and maintenance can be either assigned to customers (e.g., per help-desk call, per change request) or to the application system. Software licenses and maintenance refers to server software, such as database server and application server software. Incurred costs can be assigned to the applications system. The same is possible for costs of dedicated infrastructure resources. However, if infrastructure resources are shared by multiple applications systems, the question of appropriate cost allocation keys arise. In contrast to costs for internal administration, the infrastructure costs are associated with a certain capacity level. The resource consumption of applications is a major cost driver. From a Cost Accounting perspective a usage proportional distribution of costs, either to applications or to customers, would be reasonable[5] (see for instance Horngren et al., 2005, pp. 532-535 or Horváth, 2006, p. 713). The literature on IT Controlling predominantly recommends the use of technical consumption metrics, such as

---

[5] For a fundamental discussion of "reasonable" cost allocation principles we refer the interested reader to Riebel (1994, p. 67-79).

processor time, number of Input/Output (I/O) operations and stored Gigabytes (see for instance Gadatsch and Mayer, 2006, p. 180, Spitta, 2000, p. 282 or Kargl, 1999, p. 122). In a mainframe environment the allocation of resource consumption is supported by comprehensive accounting mechanisms such as the *System Management Facility* (SMF) of IBM (see IBM, n.d.b) or the *"Rechenzentrum-Abrechnungsverfahren"* (RAV) of Fujitsu-Siemens (see Fujitsu Siemens, n.d.). In the context of today's distributed and heterogeneous client/server infrastructures such an approach has flaws (Bertleff, 2001, p. 63). On the IT side, metering and consolidating consumption data from distributed and heterogeneous components is elaborate and cost-intensive. On the customer side, diverse technical metrics, such as processor times from different servers, are difficult to comprehend and to control.

Overall, the diversity of IT functions requires differentiated Cost Accounting and Chargeback methods. Particularly in shared client/server environments usage-based cost allocation seems to be difficult. The necessary efforts for the determination of accurate cost allocation keys could potentially outweigh their benefits. These problems have motivated a closer analysis of appropriate cost allocation approaches for today's client/server infrastructures. Before we provide in the following sections an overview of literature (section 2.2), overall objectives and requirements (section 2.3) and practiced approaches (section 2.4), we specify the term *IT infrastructure*.

2.1.5   IT Infrastructure Services

In section 2.1.2 an *IT infrastructure service* was defined as a service which is not directly used by a business unit, but required for the provision of another IT service. More general, prior to installation and operation of business applications, technical and organizational conditions must be fulfilled, i.e. an infrastructure must be provided (Krcmar, 2004, p. 211).

> **Infrastructure** consists of the hardware and software for communication, computing and storage which is required by an application (technical infrastructure) as well as of human resources and services necessary for setup and usage (organizational infrastructure) (Krcmar, 2004, p. 211).

Accordingly, *IT infrastructure costs* include all costs related with the provision of the infrastructure (e.g., utility, hardware, personnel). The technical infrastructure consists of

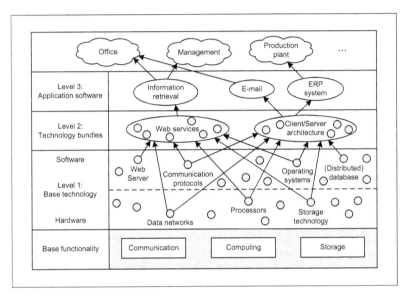

Figure 2.6: Information and Communication Technology (adapted from Krcmar, 2004, p. 212)

hardware and software infrastructure entities, in the following referred to as *base technology*, which provide the *base functionalities* communication, computing and storage. Only specific combinations of base technologies are reasonable. Those application-independent combinations are called *technology bundles*. The concept is summarized in figure 2.6. Infrastructure comprises levels one and two. The exact delineation between software infrastructure entities and applications might not be clear-cut. Software infrastructure is application-independent, such as operating systems, server software, database management systems and application integration software. However, applications suites, which bundle multiple applications, e.g., for Enterprise Resource Planning (ERP) or Customer Relationship Management (CRM) often also contain software infrastructure entities. For instance, SAP platform software such as SAP NetWeaver (see SAP, n.d.a) belongs to software infrastructure (level 1), whereas the ERP solution built upon is part of the applications (level 3).

2.2   Survey of Literature

For the following survey of literature, we set two objectives. First, the establishment of an overview of scientific work in the domain and current practices in industry. Second, the identification of overall objectives and requirements on IT Cost Accounting and Charge-back as guidelines for the development of alternative approaches. We therefore focus on four different types of sources:

1. Scientific work on IT Cost Accounting and Chargeback (section 2.2.1)

2. Empirical studies on the state-of-the-practice (section 2.2.2)

3. IT Service Management Reference Models (section 2.2.3)

4. Guidelines from Commercial Research Companies (section 2.2.4)

In each section we present one to three prominent publications in detail and provide references to further reading.

2.2.1   Scientific Work

From our investigation on scientific work in the domain, three major research branches have emerged: First, the adoption of Activity-based costing approaches to data centers to overcome the limitation of traditional cost accounting systems (section 2.2.1.1); second, IT Controlling in distributed environments (section 2.2.1.2); and third, the optimal design of chargeback systems and practices to achieve organization-level objectives (section 2.2.1.3).

2.2.1.1   Process and Activity-based Costing

Traditional cost center/cost unit costing is primarily designed to determine costs for end-products with a high proportion of variable production costs. Fixed overhead costs are either not allocated (variable costing), or apportioned among the cost centers, for instance by using fixed percentages, production volumes or measured usage rates (full costing)[6]. However, if overhead costs dominate, the per-unit cost information is likely to

---

[6]   For an overview of traditional IT Cost Accounting, we refer the interested reader to Mai (1996), who discusses the applicability and the optimal design of three traditional Cost Accounting approaches (Full Costing based on actual/budgeted costs and Variable Costing based on budgeted costs) for IT infrastructures with shared resources.

be biased. A possible solution to this problem of traditional Cost Accounting systems is the *Activity-based costing* approach. It was first developed in the United States (see Cooper and Kaplan, 1987, 1988; Miller and Vollmann, 1985) and later operationalized and adapted to the German *Process costing* (see Horváth and Mayer, 1989). Instead of apportioning overhead costs among cost centers, they are first allocated to the activities (processes) which actually cause the costs and then, in a second step, to the end-products depending on their usage of these activities (processes). Data centers are typical examples of environments where costs do not vary directly with production volumes. At least in the short term, most costs are fixed. The determination of cost shares per IT product produced would be a suitable case for Activity-based costing approaches (Kargl, 1999, p. 131). However, the concept was originally developed for production environments with physical goods. A number of authors (see for instance Fürer, 1994; Funke, 1999; Gerlach et al., 2002; Gerlinger et al., 2000) have proposed a transfer to data centers. We present below the studies of Fürer (1994) and Funke (1999), as they focus in particular on shared data center infrastructures.

The concept of **Fürer (1994)** can be briefly summarized as follows. First, the data center services are divided into three activity centers (Processing, Storage, Output). Then, the author analyzes the workload and the scare resources, i.e. the potential bottlenecks, and selects out of them for each activity center one cost driver (Fürer, 1994, p. 153):

- **Processing**: number of I/O operations

- **Storage**: size of reserved space

- **Output**: number of printed pages

The total budgeted operating costs for an activity center divided by the forecasted usage results in a cost share per cost driver unit (e.g., costs per I/O operation). On the process side, the author starts with applications and divides them into transactions which he considers as business sub-processes. For each transaction he determines, by the analysis of historical data, the average number of consumption units of the cost-driving resource. Thus, he derives cost portions per transaction and, by forecasted or measured quantities, the costs for business processes (Fürer, 1994, p. 137 et seqq.). The concept is illustrated by examples of mainframe infrastructures at major banks in Switzerland.

Besides the costing approach, a major contribution is the in-depth evaluation of stakeholders and objectives of IT Cost Accounting (see Fürer, 1994, p. 38-55).

Funke (1999) goes in his work even a step further. In the same manner as Fürer (1994), he divides the data center into the three activity centers: Processing, Storage and Output. Additionally, he considers during the allocation of costs to processes not only the technical resource consumption, but also end-user requirements, such as response time or Quality-of-Service. The definition of an IT service is based on the specifications of DIN 66273-1[7] (see DIN 66273, 1991).

Excursion: The DIN standard 66273-1 considers an IT system, including all software and hardware components, as black-box. A *service* is defined as a successful response to a request or, more precisely, as the fulfillment of a user job within a predefined response time and in accordance with certain functional and non-functional quality and quantity standards. Correspondingly, *performance* is defined as the number of successfully fulfilled jobs within a unit of time. Based on the different performance requirements of end-users, the standard describes a process for the determination of load profiles, e.g., for performance tests (see Dirlewanger, 1994, for a detailed description).

In the context of Cost Accounting, the advantage of this approach is that the metrics are customer-oriented and multiple cost-driving factors can be integrated. So, for instance, to high-priority jobs with tight response-time requirements and peak load profiles a higher a cost share could be allocated, even if their total resource consumption is equal to other jobs with lower priorities (Funke, 1999, p. 202-206).

The two studies bridge the gap between business processes and IT resource consumption by conversion tables (Funke, 1999, p. 201) and average resource consumption values (Fürer, 1994, p. 163). The focus of both lies on Cost Accounting. The authors neither go into technical details nor provide experimental results to demonstrate how these tables or values are determined.

---

[7] The national standard DIN 66273 had been transferred to the International Organization for Standardization and was published as ISO 14756 in 1999 (see ISO 14756, 1999).

2.2.1.2 IT Controlling of Distributed Systems

IT Cost Accounting and Chargeback is typically addressed in the mostly practice-oriented literature on IT Controlling (see for instance Gadatsch and Mayer, 2006; Heilmann, 2001; Kargl, 1999; Krcmar et al., 2000; von Dobschütz et al., 2000). Earlier publications usually come from mainframe-oriented data centers with one central resource and do consider the situation of shared client/server environments.

Aurenz (1997) was one of the first authors, who analyzed how the ongoing technical and organizational decentralization of IT systems affects IT Controlling. For his considerations, he structures IT Controlling according to Krcmar and Buresch (1994) in Portfolio Controlling, Project Controlling, Product Controlling and Infrastructure Controlling. IT Cost Accounting is part of IT Infrastructure Controlling (see section 2.1.1). However, from his 1997 perspective, the determination of usage-based cost allocation keys is less problematic, as on the one hand, hardware and software in distributed environments is mostly dedicated to business units (Aurenz, 1997, p. 355) and on the other hand, future accounting software will provide user-oriented accounting metrics (Aurenz, 1997, p. 357).

Current literature on IT Controlling mostly proposes technical metrics to allocate costs of shared client/server infrastructures (see for instance Gadatsch and Mayer, 2006, p. 180) and does not provide clear answers how internal IT Service Providers should meet the demand for customer-oriented accounting metrics. However, we identified an interesting approach by **Scheeg (2005)**. His primary purpose is not cost allocation, but forecasting future operations costs. In the planning phase of a client/server-based IT system, decision-makers often face multiple implementation alternatives, relying on different technologies and infrastructure resources. At that time the (short-time) implementation costs are very transparent. However, the Total Costs of Ownership are dominated by future operations costs (see also figure 2.5). This claim is underpinned by an empirical analysis of life cycle costs of 30 applications in three different organizations. As a solution, the author proposes the use of cost tables, which integrate implementation and operations costs. So, total costs of solution alternatives can be evaluated and compared already during the planning phase. To enable the estimation and comparison of operations costs, the author abstracts from the technical view on applications and introduces IT products, which are defined as "business process support services" (Scheeg, 2005, p. 139). By means of the customer's forecasted demand for IT products and standard performance benchmarks such as TPC-C (see TPPC, n.d.b) and SAPS (see SAP, n.d.b), the IT planners should estimate the required capacity and resource costs for the different alternatives (Scheeg, 2005, p. 157).

Basically, the same business process support services and performance benchmarks could be later used to allocate the operations costs to the customers. However, the focus of Scheeg (2005) lies on overall aspects of IT Controlling. He does not provide any experimental validations or real-world examples for this part of his study.

2.2.1.3 Organizational Objectives and Chargeback Systems

Mainly in the United States, behavioral science focuses on the question of which chargeback approaches and processes are appropriate for achieving organization-level objectives (see for instance McKinnon and Kallman, 1987; Ross et al., 1999; Verner et al., 1996). As a representative of this research branch, we present in the following the frequently cited contribution of **Ross et al. (1999)**. Their paper addresses the question, "What chargeback practices lead to effective managerial decisions on information technology investment and use?" The authors first propose a model of IT Chargeback (see figure 2.7) to analyze relationships between chargeback policies and practices and three outcomes: First, business unit IT investment and usage decisions; second, performance evaluations of business unit managers and, third, business unit assessments of IT performance. Based on this model they surveyed the situation in 10 US-based, Fortune 500-sized companies through multiple telephone interviews (09/1995-01/1996).

As the most common outcome of IT Chargeback, evident in all 10 firms, the study identified "reduced resource consumption". Charges help business units to identify less expensive ways to accomplish their objectives. However, only in four cases did the respondents confirm that chargeback had an impact on major IT investment decisions. Interestingly, business managers from these four firms characterized core IT as business-focused and claim that they receive "good" value from IT, while in the other six companies the interview partners described the value added by IT services as "questionable". A further analysis of these relationships revealed that the four companies with positive outcomes intensively used the administrative chargeback processes to encourage communication between IT and business (e.g., through regular negotiations about rates and services, communication of total costs and charges). This supported a mutual understanding of costs and requirements and resulted in an enhanced business-IT partnership. According to the authors, "this is the (largely) untapped potential of IT chargeback".

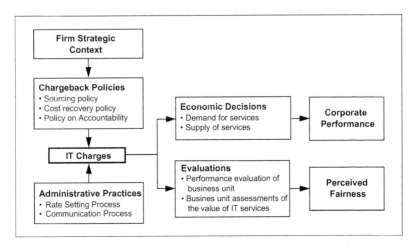

Figure 2.7: Model of IT Chargeback (Source: Ross et al., 1999)

2.2.2 Empirical Surveys

We present three empirical surveys, each with a different focus. Hübner et al. (1999) analyze IT Cost Management in centralized and decentralized environments. Gadatsch et al. (2005) focus on the overall state-of-the-practice of IT Controlling. Syskoplan (2002) examines IT Asset Management and the cost allocation methods. All three studies analyze the situation in Germany, respectively in German-speaking countries. For a survey of the international situation we refer to IT Governance Institute (2006) and Drury (1997).

The comprehensive study of **Hübner et al. (1999)** focuses on IT Cost Management in the German banking sector. At that time (1997-1999) the rise of client/server technologies and new business models, like direct banking, changed the systems architectures in data centers and the underlying cost structures. The study consists of four major parts. First, characteristics of client/server systems and of Cost Accounting in the banking sector are introduced. In an empirical part, the effects of the developments mentioned above on IT Cost Management are analyzed. The results are based on 44 questionnaires filled out by 44 German banks in 1997. Finally, the authors derive implications and recommendations for the practice. Although client/server technologies and system architectures have advanced in the meantime, general results from the empirical survey on the objectives, requirements and difficulties of internal IT Chargeback approaches are still of interest.

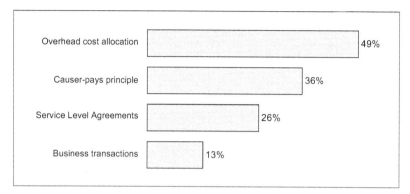

Figure 2.8: IT Cost Allocation in Germany (Source: Frisch, 2002 cited by Gadatsch and Mayer, 2006, p. 154)

Selected results concerning internal IT Chargeback approaches:

- Major objectives: "Cost Transparency" and "Cost Consciousness" (Hübner et al., 1999, p. 75)

- Major requirements: "Fairness", "Transparency" and "Accuracy" (Hübner et al., 1999, p. 79)

- Major difficulties: "Overhead costs", "Metering resource consumption" and "Acceptance" (Hübner et al., 1999, p. 82)

Gadatsch et al. (2005) present the results of a survey on the state of IT Controlling in the German-speaking countries conducted in 2004. The analysis is based on 40 questionnaires, predominantly filled out by executives from IT and Controlling departments. The sample comprises companies from different industries and size (6 - 250,000 employees, median: 930 employees). The study reveals that a large proportion of companies do not make use of major IT Controlling instruments.

Selected results:

- 51.3 % of the companies conduct no internal chargeback for IT services.

- 51.3 % make no use of IT Asset Management systems.

- 23.7 % conduct no cost benefit analysis for IT investments

Unfortunately, the analysis does not take into account the heterogeneity of the sample (e.g., company size, industry size). Further differentiations would raise the significance of the results.

The IT market research company IDC analyzed in July 2002, on behalf of Syskoplan AG, the state of IT Asset Management in Germany (**Frisch, 2002; Syskoplan, 2002**). The survey is based on interviews with IT managers from 51 German companies with more than 500 employees. The results (see figure 2.8) concerning IT Cost Accounting support the findings of Gadatsch et al. (2005). 49 % of the companies make no use of IT Chargeback systems and allocate their IT costs as overheads.

The fundamental finding of Syskoplan (2002) and Gadatsch et al. (2005) that most companies in German(-speaking) countries make only limited use of IT Controlling instruments is confirmed by related surveys (see for instance Controller Verein, 2004; Paul-Zirvas and Bereszewski, 2004; Son and Gladyszewski, 2005).

2.2.3   IT Service Management Reference Models

Overall, IT departments face the challenge of evolving from a technology- and resource-centered applications and infrastructure provider to a customer-oriented service provider (Hochstein et al., 2004, p. 382). In the context of these change processes several organizations have developed reference models, which should serve as guidelines for the analysis and improvement of the IT Service Management (ITSM) processes[8]. In the following, we briefly present the advice on IT Cost Accounting and Chargeback of two wide-spread models, namely the *Information Technology Infrastructure Library* (ITIL) and the *Control Objectives for Information and related Technology* (CobiT).

Information Technology Infrastructure Library   ITIL is a structured collection of best-practices for the realization of a cost-efficient IT organization and for the provision of high-quality services (Häusler et al., 2005, p. 16 et seqq.). In the first half of this decade it has emerged as a de-facto standard and has gained an enormous popularity (Häusler et al., 2005, p. 6 et seqq.). ITIL can be divided into seven core parts (see figure 2.9).

---

[8]   For a comprehensive overview and comparison of different models, we refer to Häusler et al. (2005).

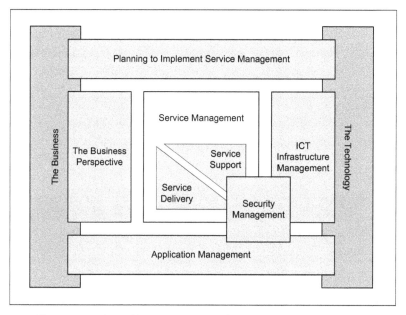

Figure 2.9: ITIL Publication Framework (Source: Office of Government Commerce, 2002b, ch. 1.4)

IT Financial Management is a core process of *Service Delivery* (Office of Government Commerce, 2001, ch. 5). ITIL defines the objectives of IT Financial Management as follows (ch. 5.1.4)[9]:

1. to provide cost-effective stewardship of the IT assets and resources used in providing IT services.

2. to be able to account fully for the spend on IT services and to attribute these costs to the services delivered to the organization's customers

3. to assist management decisions on IT investment by providing detailed business cases for changes to IT services.

---

[9] The following chapter citations refer to the ITIL book "Service Delivery" (Office of Government Commerce, 2001, ch. 5.x.x).

In analogy to the three IT Cost Accounting and Chargeback processes presented above
(see section 2.1.3), ITIL divides IT Financial Management into *Budgeting*, *IT Accounting*
and *Charging*. All three processes are discussed and guidelines for their implementation
are provided. Concerning IT Accounting, ITIL recommends a simple, fair and accurate (if
possible) cost model (ch. 5.3.7). For allocating costs of shared resources, ITIL recommends
to establish, during the annual planning, standard unit costs for each IT resource (e.g.,
per processor time, per stored GB). The expenditures per cost center are then monitored
and determined on a monthly basis (ch. 5.3.14). If the business units are charged for
their usage of IT services, the chargeable items should be as close as possible to the
organization's business deliverables.

> "Only a lack of information should force Charging to be directly based on
> resource usage; this lack of information must be overcome and it is important
> that in the analysis phase, steps are taken to ensure the future vailability of
> information" (ch. 5.4.4).

On the other hand, business deliverables are often not suited for chargeback, mainly
because the allocation of resource consumption would require unacceptably high measurement efforts (ch. 5.4.4). ITIL does not provide a complete answer to this dilemma.
The benefits must be weighed against the cost of implementation and operation of the
charging and monitoring system from case to case.

Control Objectives for Information and related Technology   CobiT is a framework for IT governance and control practices. It does not explicitly describe how ITSM
processes can be realized, but provides a structured overview of what should be done. CobiT is complementary to ITIL. In practice it is often used for auditing processes which have
been realized according to the ITIL guidelines (Hochstein and Hunziker, 2003, p. 51). The
4th edition of CobiT (IT Governance Institute, 2005) is organized into four domains (*Plan
and Organize, Acquire and Implement, Deliver and Support* and *Monitor and Evaluate*),
34 high-level objectives and 215 control objectives. IT Cost Accounting and Chargeback falls within the domain of Deliver and Support and the high-level objective *Identify
and Allocate Costs* (DS6). Four control objectives are therefore defined (IT Governance
Institute, 2005, p. 124):

1. **Definition of Services** Identify all IT costs and map them to IT services to support
   a transparent cost model. IT services should be linked to business processes such
   that the business can identify associated service billing levels.

2. **IT Accounting** Capture and allocate actual costs according to the defined cost model. Variances between forecasts and actual costs should be analyzed and reported on, in compliance with the enterprise's financial measurement systems.

3. **Cost Modeling and Charging** Based on the service definition, define a cost model that includes direct, indirect and overhead costs of services and supports the calculation of chargeback rates per service. The cost model should be in line with the enterprise's cost accounting procedures. The IT cost model should ensure that the charging for services is identifiable, measurable and predictable by users to encourage proper use of resources. User management should be able to verify actual usage and charging of services.

4. **Cost Model Maintenance** Regularly review and benchmark the appropriateness of the cost/recharge model to maintain its relevance and appropriateness to the evolving business and IT activities.

Additionally, CobiT provides performance indicators and a process maturity model, which support an audit of the processes. However, it does not provide any details about how the Cost Allocation should be realized.

2.2.4 Commercial Research

In the present context, valuable contributions and insights into current and future developments stem from commercial analysts and consulting companies. We therefore integrated into this survey the viewpoint and the recommendations of Gartner, Inc., one of the leading IT research companies worldwide.

The fundamental positions of Gartner on IT Chargeback and the ways it can support the cost-effective delivery and use of IT services are summarized in one comprehensive report[10] (see Blosch et al., 2003a). Subsequent publications (e.g., Gomolski, 2005; Heine, 2006) are mainly based on this document.

For Gartner IT Chargeback is primarily a governance mechanism that can be used to create desirable behavior of users or business leaders in the use of IT services (Blosch et al., 2003b, p. 2). They distinguish three steps: Cost Identification, Cost Allocation and Cost Recovery (see figure 2.3 and table 2.1). For Cost Allocation the perception of

---

[10] A summary of the document is freely available (see Blosch et al., 2003b).

Method	Allocation Base	Areas Where Suited
Market-based pricing	per measured unit of service	For defined, end-to-end services, often available on the market
Negotiated flat rate	projected service usage	Well-defined projects
Tiered flat rates	service accessibility, whether used or not	Help desks, application maintenance, data centers
Measured resource usage	measured consumption of resources	Storage, e-mail, telecoms
Direct cost	dedicated resource ownership	Application development, dedicated projects
Low-level allocation	specific IT service costs, based on user size (e.g., employees, revenue)	Desktops, IT overhead, strategy, IT architecture
High-level allocation	overall IT costs, based on user size (e.g., employees, revenue)	All of IT is consolidated under High-level allocation

Table 2.2: Overview of Cost Allocation Methods (adapted from Blosch et al., 2003b, p. 37 and Gomolski, 2005)

Chargeback as governance mechanisms implies that the method and the allocation bases must be oriented toward the need of customers. They assume that business managers use the following four criteria for the evaluation of different approaches (Blosch et al., 2003b; Gomolski, 2005):

1. **Simplicity** Business units seek a billing method that is easy to manage, and invoices that are easy to understand. Simplicity tends to be the dominant driver when the magnitude of IT costs is low, cost-effectiveness is the primary consideration in managing the chargeback system or the IT organization is highly trusted.

2. **Fairness** Business units want to pay only for their own usage and adamantly avoid the cross subsidization of other clients. This is the dominant driver when there are poor relations between the IT organization and business units, when business units suspect that the IT organization's costs are out of control, or when the enterprise is decentralized.

3. **Predictability** Business units seek assurance that there will be little or no variation between their budgets for IT services and their actual invoices. This is dominant when IT cost variances would jeopardize the business units' performance targets (such as government or low-margin business units).

4. **Controllability** Business units seek a cost structure that will enable them to actively manage their IT costs. This is prevalent when there is a dramatic shift in

Legend: ◯ High, ○ Medium, ∘ Low

	Simplicity	Fairness	Predictability	Controllability
Market-based pricing	Low	Medium	Low	Medium
Negotiated flat rate	Medium	Medium	High	High
Tiered flat rates	High	Medium	High	Low
Measured resource usage	Low	Medium	Low	Medium
Direct cost	Medium	Medium	Low	Medium
Low-level allocation	Medium	Low	Medium	Low
High-level allocation	Medium	Low	Medium	Low

Figure 2.10: Strengths and Weaknesses of Cost Allocation Methods (Source: Blosch et al., 2003a, p. 37)

business results (revenue collapse or strong growth) or uncertainty about the business unit's future performance, or when the business unit's primary objective is flexibility.

Selecting a cost allocation method for an IT service depends on what behavior should be encouraged, the needs of the business units and the administrative capabilities of the chargeback team. Gartner has identified seven common methods, ranging from *Market-based pricing*, which requires well-defined end-to-end service definitions and directly enables a benchmark with external service providers, to *High-level allocation*, which distributes total IT costs by simple business parameters, such as number of business units' employees or revenue share. In table 2.2 the different methods, their allocation bases and the areas where suited are summarized. In figure 2.10 the methods are assessed against the requirements presented above.
The publications of Gartner and related companies have a strong strategic orientation and focus on a management audience. For advice on more practical aspects of IT Chargeback,

we refer to the books of Jochen Michels (see for instance Michels, 2003a,b,c, 2004) and to
the publications of the IT Financial Management Association (see ITFMA, n.d.).

2.3 Requirements and Objectives

In the previous section we analyzed the domain of IT Cost Accounting and Chargeback
from different literature perspectives. Although the backgrounds of the works were different, we identified a consensus on three general requirements for IT Cost Allocation
methods: **Simplicity**, **Fairness** and **Accuracy** (Blosch et al., 2003b; Hübner et al.,
1999; IT Governance Institute, 2005; Office of Government Commerce, 2001).

> "The simpler the allocation method, the better" (Blosch et al., 2003b, p. 8)

> " [...] apportionment should be firstly simple, secondly fair and thirdly accu-
> rate (if possible)." (Office of Government Commerce, 2001, ch. 5.3.7)

Beyond the general requirements, the determination of a Cost Allocation method
depends on a company's overall objectives on IT Cost Accounting and Chargeback. Typically, this situation is not clear-cut, due to the three different groups of stakeholders
involved (see figure 2.11). First, the Executive Management, which sets standards and
objectives, not only for IT but for all managerial accounting activities. Second, the business units as customers and, third, the IT units as providers of IT services (see figure 2.11).
Each group has its own objectives which are partially shared and partially opposed or
contrary to the overall requirements of Simplicity, Fairness and Accuracy. Figure 2.12
provides an example overview of consisting and conflicting objectives[11].

The primary challenge for the establishment of an IT Cost Allocation system is to define
accountable items, which balance out these objectives and requirements. For many IT
services accountable items are self-suggesting, e.g., per desktop computer, per help desk
call, per dedicated server and so forth. However, when it comes to shared infrastructures a
dilemma between resource-oriented (e.g., per processor second, per transferred byte) and
customer-oriented (e.g., per business activity, per business transaction) cost allocation
arises.

---

[11]   The objectives and their relationships are discussed by Fürer (1994, p. 38-55).

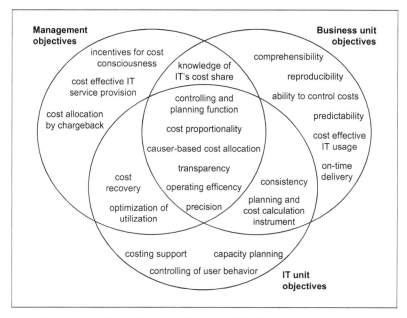

Figure 2.11: Stakeholders and Objectives of IT Cost Accounting (adapted from Fürer, 1994, p. 48)

If business units are charged for their usage of IT services, a customer-oriented approach seems to have considerable advantages. At the business units cost allocation for instance per business transaction enables a better controlling of IT usage (including predictability, comprehensibility, reproducibility and ability to control costs) and an alignment of business forecasts with IT budget planning. Furthermore, cost transparency is increased as such an approach facilitates the determination of IT cost shares per produced product, per business process or for other company-wide cost objects. However, there are two essential difficulties associated with customer-oriented approaches: First, the identification of business activities, appropriate for IT cost allocation and, second, the determination of adequate cost shares for the different activities. As most IT costs are not directly related to the actual usage of IT services, a methodology for allocating fixed or step costs to the accountable business activities is required. Finally, if cost allocation keys are biased, they may encourage suboptimal behavior and cause free-rider problems (see Wheatley, 2003, for illustrative examples).

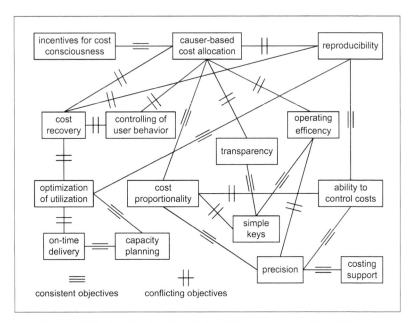

Figure 2.12: Consistent and conflicting Objectives (adapted from Fürer, 1994, p. 50)

"I'm saving money, even though it must be costing the company more - anomalies in the charging system will be exploited by businesses." (Office of Government Commerce, 2001, ch. 5.4.2)

These problems do not occur for resource-oriented approaches. Typically, standard cost accounting determines costs per resource (e.g., for a particular server) or at least per resource pool (e.g., for all Unix servers). These costs can be either directly attributed to a single business owner or apportioned by some form of usage-based cost allocation key (see next section). Business transactions typically involve multiple resources. Measuring and consolidating their total resource consumption is mostly not possible or associated with unreasonable efforts. On the other hand, allocating costs by various technical consumption metrics neglects most of the positive controlling potential of IT charges. Against this background, the purpose of chargeback for shared client/server and network infrastructures is seriously questioned (see for instance Liebmann, 1996; Oleson, 1998; Wheatley, 2003).

"[...] But a rigorous chargeback methodology - one that will earn respect - requires IS management to develop, administer and maintain what can become a Byzantine method of data collection. Worse, a rigorous cost accounting system is often prohibitively expensive. Worst of all, the data needed to make such a system work, particularly in the client/server environment, is almost impossible to gather because of the degree of detail needed to make a cost accounting system accurate." (Oleson, 1998)

Beyond the above considerations, this fundamental dilemma of IT Cost Accounting and Chargeback approaches has been subject of extensive discussion in literature (e.g., Quinlan, 1989, p. 78; Fürer, 1994, p. 44; Funke, 1999, p. 74; Ross et al., 1999; Office of Government Commerce, 2001, ch. 5.4.4; Michels, 2003b, ch. 4.1.1).

2.4 Practiced Approaches

The second objective of the literature study was to get an overview of practiced approaches to IT Infrastructure Cost Allocation. Besides approaches that are based on non-IT allocation keys (e.g., cost allocation per employee or per revenue share), we identified five basic concepts for apportioning infrastructure costs. These concepts are briefly introduced in the following (see figure 2.13 for an overview).

Direct cost allocation   Where a hardware resource is dedicated to a specific application or a business function, the costs of the assets can be directly attributed. This procedure is transparent and easy to implement. It is not IT-specific. However, the underlying assumption – that there is a single business owner of a resource – is mainly limited to application server and storage infrastructure. Other resources, like network components or middleware for application integration, are usually shared.

(Tiered) flat rate per application   If the application, rather than the infrastructure, is dedicated to a single business owner, costs can be allocated by a flat rate. The actual resource consumption is not considered. The BMW Group uses such flat rates for applications on its J2EE infrastructure (see chapter 6). Gartner recommends tiering the flat rates according to functionality, expected usage (e.g., number of registered users) and service levels (see Blosch et al., 2003a; Heine, 2006). This approach is particularly easy to implement, as no explicit differentiation of resource costs and no metering is required.

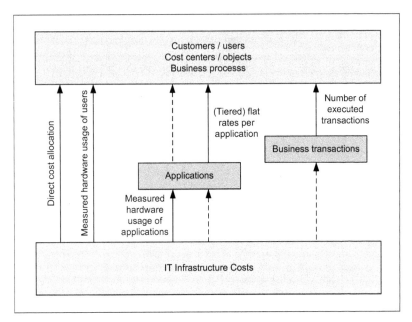

Figure 2.13: Classification of practiced Approaches

The accompanying lack of transparency may be accepted if the applications are of a similar nature (complexity, workload, etc.) and are predominantly used by a single business unit.

Measured hardware usage of end-users   A widespread approach to allocating costs of a shared infrastructure is a proportional breakdown to the business units according to their resource consumption. Measured usage is commonplace for disk storage and telephony services. However, when it comes to client/server computing, a single request usually involves multiple heterogeneous components (e.g., web server, application server and database server). Measuring and allocating resource consumption directly to business units is associated with two fundamental problems.

1. From a user perspective, diverse technical metrics are difficult to comprehend and to control. Let us consider a business manager, receiving an account statement, based on the processor times of multiple servers. As he cannot directly correlate

the charges with his (business) activities, it is difficult for him to plan or control resource consumption. In mainframe environments, with one single resource, this might have been possible, but the approach cannot be transferred to client/server infrastructures.

2. Due to performance and security reasons, the original business context of a transaction (e.g., user, business activity) is mostly not available in the backend. User names are not further transmitted after a successful authorization and connection pools are used for database access. A SQL statement, for instance, does not contain any information about the actual user of the application who submitted the query. Modern DBMS support the allocation of resource consumption (processor time, query runtime, etc.) to the connection pools of the application servers, but they cannot reconstruct the original user.

For centrally controlled, scheduled and monitored batch jobs these problems can be partially overcome. However, for interactive workload a clear assignment of resource consumption – and thus of costs – to users is often not possible.

Measured hardware usage of applications   Metering and allocating resource consumption to applications or databases is supported by most operating systems and server software. It is also the domain of professional accounting and billing tools (see for instance Econet, n.d.; IBM, n.d.a; Nicetec, n.d.; USU, n.d.)[12]. Their strengths are the collection of accounting data by custom agents or by log files analysis, the consolidation of this information and the generation of reports for chargeback and management information. However, in client/server environments they are also facing the problems described in the previous paragraph. Thus, they mostly provide only a per-application and not a per-user or a per-department view on resource consumption. Accordingly, they assume either a single business owner per application or use external data from the application or the organization to derive cost portions for the business units:

"Once you know the cost of an application as a whole, you can determine the cost of functional metrics produced by the application. For example, if you knew that "Payroll" cost \$10,000 and that it produced 1,000 paychecks then the average cost of a paycheck is \$10.00. Then, you could allocate the

---

[12]   An overview of commercial accounting and billing tools is provided by Siebertz (2004, p. 49).

cost of payroll to the departments and business units based on the number
of paychecks they received." (Excerpt from the CIMS System Description
Manual: CIMS Lab, n.d.)

Business transactions There may be two very different motivations behind using business transactions for the allocation of IT costs. On the one hand, it could be considered as a form of simple overhead cost allocation, similar to costs per employee or cost per revenue share. On the other hand, it could be intentionally used for enabling an effective controlling of IT usage and costs by the business units (see section 2.3). In practice, the situation is often not as clear-cut as in the payroll example described above. Applications could provide different services and the usage intensity of the services may not be dependent on business figures such as the number of employees. Furthermore, if the accountable transactions and their cost shares are not carefully determined, they might also encourage suboptimal behavior and cause free-rider problems.

Outsourcing providers have recognized the potential of customer-oriented accounting metrics. In the context of on-demand and utility computing scenarios, the industry provides solutions which enable a detailed metering of business transactions for accounting purposes. As a representative example, we briefly present in the following excursion the concept of the utility metering service of the IBM Universal Management Infrastructure (see Albaugh and Madduri, 2004).

Excursion: The *Universal Management Infrastructure* (UMI) is a collection of software and architectures supporting the management and operations of hosted infrastructures and applications at IBM's utility computing data centers (IBM, 2004). Major functionalities of the UMI are metering, monitoring, auto-provisioning, SLA management, portal, billing, ordering, reporting and help desk/change management (Albaugh and Madduri, 2004). The utility metering service supports usage metering and billing for on-demand services on the infrastructure as well as on the application level (e.g., end-user billing for the usage of specialized supply management applications). The architecture of the metering service allows the integration of third-party applications. Additionally, IBM has set up a process (see Chang et al., 2004), which should enable independent software vendors to adopt their applications and offer them as on-demand services to their customers.

The utility metering approach of IBM requires the UMI as the proprietary infrastructure environment and is not directly transferable to internal data centers. Furthermore, it solves only half of the problem, namely metering and allocating the usage of services. It does not directly provide an answer to how the step costs for the infrastructure should be apportioned among the provided services. In outsourced environments this is less relevant, as rate setting follows different objectives than in internal cost-centers (e.g., profit maximization vs. fairness, competitiveness of price model vs. cost transparency, etc.).

With regard to the overall objectives for IT Cost Accounting and Chargeback (see section 2.11), all of the approaches presented above have flaws. Direct cost allocation and measured hardware usage of end-users are hardly applicable to shared infrastructures. Both application-oriented approaches implicitly rely on single business owners for the applications, which might not be the case. An allocation of costs using the number of executed business transactions could support an effective controlling of IT usage and costs by the business units. However, it is difficult to establish a transparent link of business transactions to the infrastructure costs.

2.5 Discussion

Starting point for the considerations of the previous sections was the question of what are appropriate cost allocation approaches for today's client/server infrastructures (see section 2.1.4). We surveyed the literature (section 2.2), pointed out the dilemma between customer-oriented and resource-oriented allocation methods (section 2.3) and described why practiced approaches often do not achieve major objectives of IT Cost Accounting and Chargeback (section 2.4). In the following, we briefly discuss the future relevance of the question against the background of today's organizational and technological trends.

> "After pouring millions of dollars into in-house data centers, companies may soon find that it's time to start shutting them down. IT is shifting from being an asset companies own to a service they purchase." (p. 67 Carr, 2005)

Although the hypotheses of Carr (2003, 2005) about the future role of IT are the subject of controversial discussions (see for instance Harvard Business Review, 2003), it seems quite clear that internal IT organizations are undergoing a transformation from resource-centered applications provider to customer-oriented service providers (see for instance Brenner, 2004). The Society for Information Management surveyed in 2003, 2004 and 2005 the management concerns of IT executives. The top-ranked issue in all three reports was *IT and business alignment*, defined as "applying IT in an appropriate and timely way, in harmony and collaboration with business needs, goals, and strategies" (Luftman et al., 2006). As top enablers of IT and business alignment, the respondents of the 2005 survey indicated: *IT understands the firm's business environment* (Luftman et al., 2006). Business managers drive IT to focus on cost-effective support of business processes rather than on technologies. IT managers, in turn, are forced to justify their budgets and thus try to increase cost transparency by allocating their costs as far as possible to the businesses.

Concerning today's technological trends, the variety of terms, such as *service-oriented architectures*, *grid*, *on demand*, *utility computing*, *software as a service* or *virtualization* might be confusing at first glance. However, according to the analysis of Foster and Tuecke (2005) these and other related terms "represent different perspectives on the same overall goal — namely, the restructuring of enterprise IT as a horizontally integrated, service-oriented architecture". This "overarching trend" (Foster and Tuecke, 2005) means, on the one hand, that distributed hardware resources are pooled together (e.g., by virtualization technologies) and then managed and allocated in a common and automated manner. Thus, overall utilization can be improved and operating costs reduced (Foster and Tuecke, 2005). On the other hand, the goal implies that the interfaces between application components, workload management systems, and physical resources are standardized so that the different components can be assembled dynamically (Foster and Tuecke, 2005). The applications are fully decoupled from the underlying hardware and neither hardware nor applications are dedicated to a specific business function.

With regard to IT Infrastructure Cost Allocation we derive two major implications from these trends:

1. Along with the predicted commodization of IT services, the importance of customer-oriented and usage-based cost allocation approaches will grow.

2. Traditional cost allocation methods, which are based on static mappings between hardware resources, applications and customers, are not applicable in future infrastructures.

The arising cost allocation problems concern mostly internal IT units. Outsourcing providers have a greater flexibility to adapt their accounting metrics to the needs of their customers. So, for instance, they must not necessarily consider resource consumption to determine fair cost shares. Their primary motivations are profit maximization and risk control. We identified no standardization efforts, which could create an overall technical solution. Internal IT units in particular require alternative cost allocation approaches to cope with the organizational and technological trends described above.

Chapter 3

Cost Allocation based on Resource Profiles

3.1 Scope

We illustrated in the previous chapter the difficulties of allocating IT infrastructure costs. These considerations motivated the development of an alternative approach, which is presented in the following sections. We thereby focus on a certain category of application systems.

Application systems built on databases can be divided into systems for *online transaction processing* (OLTP) and systems for *online analytical processing* (OLAP) (Kemper and Eickler, 2006, p. 495). OLTP systems typically automate clerical data processing tasks that are the day-to-day operations of companies (e.g., order entries, customer updates). The tasks are structured and repetitive. Database transactions are short, require detailed, up-to-date data and operate (read/write) on a small amount of records (Chaudhuri and Dayal, 1997). OLAP systems, in contrast, prepare decision support information for the management. They operate on large amounts of historical data, rather than on individual records. Database queries are complex and mostly created ad-hoc (Chaudhuri and Dayal, 1997). A typical example for OLAP application is the multidimensional analysis of sales or marketing data (e.g., sales volumes per product, district, time, salesperson). OLTP and OLAP systems have different performance requirements (e.g., transaction throughput vs. query runtimes) and workload profiles and thus usually operate on separate physical databases (Kemper and Eickler, 2006, p. 495).

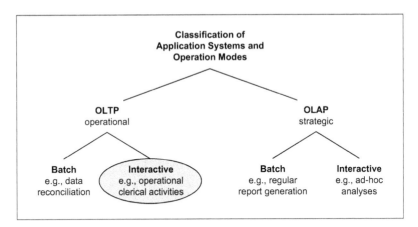

Figure 3.1: Classification of Application Systems and Operation Modes

Furthermore, we can distinguish between two different operation modes of application systems: *Interactive access* and *batch processing*. In the interactive operation mode the application prompts the users for input, while in batch mode the application typically processes large amounts of data without human interaction. For instance, in OLTP systems nightly batch jobs can be used to reconcile daily activities with master databases. In OLAP systems batch jobs could produce daily/weekly/monthly reports or import and consolidate data from various operational databases. The two types of application systems and the different operation modes are summarized in figure 3.1. We restrict our considerations in the following on **operational, interactive OLTP systems**. We claim that for these kinds of systems the determination of appropriate cost allocation keys is both particularly relevant and particularly difficult.

- Costs of **operational** IT systems can be considered as fixed or step costs of production and should be allocated accordingly. In contrast, costs for strategic management information systems are not directly related to cost objects such as products produced and can thus be treated as any other overhead.

- Batch processing, in contrast to **interactive** workload, can be centrally controlled, scheduled and monitored. This facilitates the measurement of resource consumption and thus the allocation of costs to the submitter of batch jobs.

- Compared to operational **OLTP systems**, OLAP systems are typically used by a small number of people with a management or a reporting function. Furthermore, the resource consumption per individual user in OLTP systems is far smaller than in OLAP systems. This causes higher efforts for measuring and allocating resource consumption, in particular if the users are distributed across business units.

The infrastructure of application systems can be realized with different technology bundles such as mainframe or client/server architectures (see section 2.1.5). We set the scope for the following considerations to **client/server architectures**, firstly, because they are predominant in today's data centers and, secondly, because their distributed and heterogeneous nature complicates the determination of usage-based cost shares (see section 2.4).

3.2 Concept

3.2.1 IT Services from a Customer Perspective

In section 2.1.5 a model of Information and Communication Technology was introduced (see figure 2.6). This model is technology-oriented and does not necessarily reflect a customer's perspective. For end users, the complexity of application systems, technology bundles and software and hardware infrastructure entities is typically not transparent. They perceive an application system largely as black-box, accessible through (graphical) user interfaces and providing a number of business-related *services*. In the context of the considered operational, interactive OLTP systems, possible kinds of services can be:

- **Execution of a business transaction** (e.g., "process order", "update stock", and "add customer")

- **Access to an Information System** (e.g., "retrieve order details", "browse catalog", and "check plant status")

The customer perspective and the notion of services lead to an adapted and simplified model of Information and Communication Technology (see figure 3.2). The users, grouped into business units, access the services of application systems through (graphical) user interfaces. An application system consists of at least one frontend and potentially several

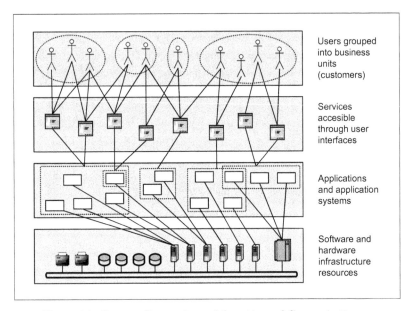

Figure 3.2: Customer Perspective on Information and Communication Technology

backend applications. An application either runs on a shared or dedicated computing resources and can be used in the context of one or more application systems. Furthermore, an application can access other infrastructure components (e.g., computing, storage, printing resources) over the communication networks.

The basic question, raised in the previous chapter (see section 2.1.4), is how costs for the provision of infrastructure resources can be allocated to the business customers. Common approaches based on measured usage or direct costs have flaws or are not applicable for shared infrastructure resources (see section 2.4). Taking into account customers' objectives, e.g., comprehensibility, reproducibility, predictability or controllability (see figure 2.11), services and their usage could be an appropriate basis for cost allocation. This is not a new idea. In the survey of literature (see section 2.2), we already presented two process costing approaches (see Fürer, 1994; Funke, 1999) and one IT Controlling framework (see Scheeg, 2005) which put forward this concept. However, there are two major difficulties; first, the definition of adequate services, and, second, the assignment of costs to services. Concerning the first difficulty, a process model for service engineering

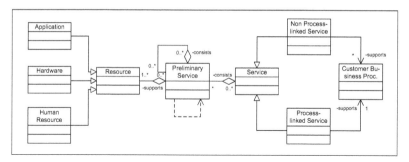

Figure 3.3: Meta-Model of IT Services (Source: Uebernickel et al., 2006b)

was recently proposed by Uebernickel et al. (2006a,b). The underlying meta model of IT services is depicted in figure 3.3. Concerning the second difficulty, comprehensive methodologies to relate business services with infrastructure costs are still missing. An equal or arbitrary allocation of costs to services would clash with the central objectives of IT Cost Accounting and Chargeback such as causer-based cost allocation or cost proportionality (see figure 2.11). This might lead to various acceptance problems:

- "Cost transparency is not achieved" (management)

- "Cost portions are arbitrary" (customers)

- "Usage forecasts are worthless for planning IT resources " (IT unit)

To overcome this difficulty, we focus below on the development of a methodology which bridges the gap between customer-oriented services and IT infrastructure resource consumption.

3.2.2 Determining Resource Profiles for Services

In shared infrastructures, the resource consumption of users, services or applications is a cost driver. It would be obvious to use metered consumption values as an objective basis for apportioning infrastructure costs. Unfortunately, in heterogeneous client/server environments metering and allocating resource consumption to users and applications is difficult, if not impossible (see section 2.4). For services, as defined in the last section, it is even worse as they have a business, but not necessarily a technical meaning. Hence, measuring at runtime is not a feasible solution. Against this background, we propose an alternative approach that is based on the assumption that the invocation of a service always results in the same resource consumption in the infrastructure. In other words:

The cumulated resource consumption of a service increases linearly with the number of concurrent or subsequent service invocations.

If estimates for the expected consumption of the different resources and the number of service invocations were known, this could constitute the basis of cost allocation keys. The elaborate process of measuring and consolidating log data from different components could be bypassed. Furthermore, these estimates would be valuable inputs for the alignment of business forecasting and IT Capacity Planning.

In the following, we propose a methodology to estimate for a service i a so-called resource profile, p, which is defined as a vector of n consumption values p_{ij} with $j = 1...n$ denoting the different resources[1]. The profile then multiplied by the number of service invocations of a certain customer should result in an estimator for the resource consumption of this customer. The number of service invocations per customer can be traced by the analysis of business records ("Execution of a business transaction") or by the authorization/authentication infrastructure ("Access to an Information System").

3.2.3 Resources in a Client/Server Environment

We propose categorizing resources according to the base functionalities of Information and Communication Technology: Communication, Computing and Storage (see figure 2.6). The resource profiles include estimates for resource consumption which is directly correlated with the actual service usage. They are not applicable to usage-independent resource consumption, such as permanently reserved network, server or disk capacities. Such resources are not shared, but dedicated to specific applications or business units.

For each resource in a resource profile an appropriate usage variable (measurement point) and a consumption metric (measurement unit) is required. They should represent the bottleneck of the resource, where increasing usage drives new investments. For the considered application systems (see section 3.1), we propose the following measurement points and units:

---

[1]   A list of symbols is provided in the appendix (see section A.1).

Communication: Amount of transferred data [bytes] The amount of transferred bytes reflects usage and is equally applicable to networking and communications equipment in Local Area Networks, Wide Area Networks and the Internet.

Computing: Processing time [seconds] For computing resources we propose including estimates of processing times at the different servers in the resource profiles. As measurements of processor times on different hardware are not directly comparable, they must be normalized, e.g., by using standard performance benchmarks (see SPEC, n.d.a). Memory is often also considered as a scarce resource. However, the maximum amount of physical memory a server can allocate on a machine is typically dedicated at startup (e.g., by setting a range for virtual memory) and it is possible to take this value as the basis for cost allocation.

Storage: Amount of transferred data [blocks] We exclude disk space from our considerations, as it is usually allocated a priori to a specific application or a database. Besides space constraints, the storage I/O of database servers is a typical bottleneck in OLTP systems. We propose using the amount of transferred data for the resource profiles, as the number of I/O operations may be dependent on the actual workload and factors like the disk fragmentation.

The proposed categories, resources, usage variables and consumption metrics are typical examples and can be adapted to the actual conditions. Fürer (1994) and Funke (1999) propose a similar categorization for their process costing approaches (see section 2.2.1.1). They group resources into activity centers and determine for each activity center a cost driver. While we are targeting distributed client/server environments, they focus on central mainframe architecture. They propose the category "Output" with printing and archiving resources, but do not explicitly consider "Communication".

3.2.4 Cost Allocation by Services and Resource Profiles

Although the categorization of resources is related to the activity centers of process costing approaches, the concept of allocating costs by resource profiles and services is not dependent on a specific costing system. It is applicable for traditional cost accounting (full and variable costing) as well as for process- or activity-based costing approaches. Based on

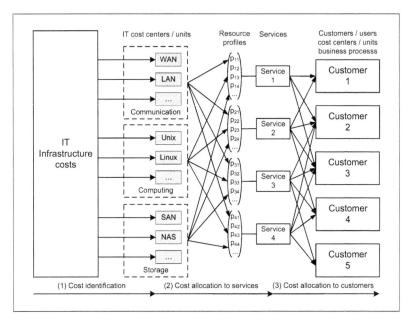

Figure 3.4: Cost Allocation by Services and Resource Profiles

the overall process structure of IT Cost Accounting and Chargeback (see section 2.1.3), we propose a three-stage approach for apportioning infrastructure costs:

1. **Cost identification.** Direct and indirect infrastructure costs are allocated to the accounts of the different resources (e.g., Unix server operations). These accounts may be organized as cost centers or as cost units (IT products). Each resource has a consumption metric (e.g., processor time). Based either on forecasted or on past consumption levels, the costs per consumption unit (e.g, processor second) are calculated.

2. **Cost allocation to services.** For each service, a resource profile which contains the estimated consumption at the different resources (e.g., processor time Unix, processor time Linux, number of SAN I/Os) is determined. By multiplication with the cost per consumption unit, the cost shares per service are calculated.

3. **Cost allocation to customers.** Depending on the costing approach, the infrastructure costs are finally allocated to cost centers (e.g., business units), to cost

units (e.g., products) or to business processes. Therefore, the measured, forecasted or estimated number of service invocations is multiplied by the cost shares of the services.

The concept is illustrated by figure 3.4. In the following we focus on the second stage ("Cost allocation to services") and, in particular, on the development of a methodology for the determination of the resource profiles.

3.3 Model Hypotheses

In section 3.2.2 we first introduced the concept of resource profiles: A resource profile p for a service i consists of n values p_{ij}, which are estimates of the expected resource consumption of service i at resource j. Our considerations were based on the following hypothesis:

1. The cumulated resource consumption of a service increases linearly with the number of concurrent or subsequent service invocations.

This hypothesis focuses on the increase of the resource consumption. To derive a model which describes the total observed resource consumption, we extend the first hypothesis as follows:

2. The total resource consumption is composed of the resource composition of background activities and of the resource consumption caused by service invocations.

3. The resource consumption caused by service invocations consists of a load-independent portion and a load-dependent portion.

Background activities, triggered for instance by operating systems, system management tools or performance monitors, cause a certain amount of resource consumption, even when there is no service workload on the resources. Consequently, this resource consumption should not be included in the resource profiles.

The resource consumption per service may depend to a certain degree on the actual load at the resources. Those effects are described for Communication, Computing and Storage resources. In the following, we illustrate such behavior with an example from each category.

- In Ethernet networks, the collision rate depends on the utilization of the network segment. If a packet collision occurs, the sender retries the transmission and thus raises the number of transferred bytes (Friedman and Pentakalos, 2002, p. 530). However, today's network technologies minimize this effect.

- A certain amount of the processor time triggered by service invocations is required for system activities, such as context switching or memory management. The effort for these overhead activities may depend on the actual system load. For instance, as the number of jobs in the memory increases, the work required by management routines also increases (Menascé et al., 2004, p. 151).

- Rising numbers of requests to hard disks may enable the scheduling mechanisms of the disk drives to reduce the average seek distance and thus increase the effective service rate (Padhye et al., 1995).

While it is unquestionable that those effects exists, it is unclear what their relative impact on the total resource consumption is.

We summarize the three hypotheses in the following model. The parameter y_{ij} describes the total consumption of resource j during the execution time t of x concurrent or subsequent invocations of service i. The parameter a_j indicates the resource consumption of the background activities, b_{ij} the load-independent and u_{ij} the load-dependent resource consumption caused by the service invocations. However, for the resource profile we require one estimate p_{ij} of the expected resource consumption, independent of the actual utilization of the resource j. We therefore define p_{ij} as sum of the baseline consumption b_{ij} and of $\overline{u_{ij}}$ as constant approximation of the load-dependent resource consumption u_{ij}:

$$p_{ij} = b_{ij} + \overline{u_{ij}} \tag{3.1}$$

Assuming that the utilization of the resources varies, the first and the third hypotheses are contradicting. We argue that the approximation and thus the determination of estimates for the resource consumption is justified if $b_{ij} >> u_{ij}$ or $u_{ij} \approx 0$, i.e. the resource consumption of a service invocation is not or is barely dependent on the actual workload. The total consumption y_{ij} can then be described as follows:

$$y_{ij}(x, t) = a_j(t) + x p_{ij} \tag{3.2}$$

The requirements from this model on a software tool supporting the estimation of resource profiles are twofold. First and foremost, it should enable the determination of the values p_{ij}. Secondly, it should enable a verification of the hypotheses required to construct the model, namely the composition of the total resource consumption and the constant approximation of the load-dependent resource consumption.

3.4 Requirements on Resource Profiles

Resource profiles for services are not readily available and the viability of the whole approach stands and falls with their determination. From the overall requirements and objectives for IT Cost Accounting and Chargeback (see section 2.3) and the model hypotheses (see section 3.3), we derived four requirements for resource profiles and the profiling process, which we consider as critical to the practical success of the concept.

Requirement 1: Accuracy   The resource profiles should be unbiased in the sense that on average it should not over- or underestimate the true resource consumption. If, from the perspective of the stakeholders, the resource profiles are not reliable, it might lead to various acceptance problems (see section 3.2.1) and questioning of the whole approach. This overall requirement has two major implications. On the one hand, instruments to validate the resource profiles should be available. On the other hand, potential sources of bias should be evaluated and, if possible, removed. We identified three major reasons for bias in resource profiles, formulated as sub-requirements in the following.

- **Requirement 1.1: Accurate measurement and analysis tools** Inaccuracies of the measurement and analysis tools may introduce a systematic error or also lead to high sample variance.

- **Requirement 1.2: Linear resource consumption** The model hypotheses formulated in section 3.3 must be fulfilled. If load-dependent behavior or other nonlinearities in the resource consumption affect a substantial share of the total consumption, the predictive accuracy may become insufficient for resource profiles.

- **Requirement 1.3: Correct assumptions about user behavior** If a service requires interaction or parameters entered by the users, wrong assumptions about the user behavior may lead to distorted resource profiles.

Requirement 2: Consistency The concept has been proposed for resolving the difficulties of usage-based cost allocation in heterogeneous and distributed client/server infrastructures. The estimation of resource profiles therefore should be in the same manner applicable to various kinds of hardware and software resources. Any dependencies on vendors or technologies should be avoided.

Requirement 3: Capacity Planning The idea behind resource profiles is to bridge the gap between the business and the IT units' requirements on a cost allocation approach. Hence, it should be possible to translate the forecasted service usage of the business units into IT resource requirements and thus support the IT Capacity Planning.

Requirement 4: Operating Efficiency The estimation should cause little extra work and integrate well with existing IT Service Management processes. If the determination of resource profiles is too costly, the advantages of a comprehensive consumption-based and customer-oriented cost allocation are outweighed by the existing approaches (see section 2.4).

These requirements are used below as a basis for the development and evaluation of an approach for the determination of resource profiles.

3.5 Software Support

In the previous section we specified a number of requirements on resource profiles and on the profiling process. We now focus on the development of a software toolkit realizing the concept. We start with a brief overview of existing tools and then describe the profiling process and the implementation of the *Service Profiler*.

3.5.1 Tool Categories

A broad range of tools for testing and profiling applications, simulating end-user behavior and metering performance and resource consumption is available on the software market. In the following, we briefly discuss three tool categories, which we consider as relevant in the context of resource profiles.

Profiling Tools   Profiling tools focus on the prevention or on the root cause analysis of performance problems. They typically provide a detailed breakdown of processor time and memory allocation. Overall, this kind of information is a valuable input for the estimation of expected resource consumption, but there are two practical restrictions which hamper the application of standard profiling tools for the determination of resource profiles. First, profiling tools are mostly technology- or vendor-dependent, e.g., Java/J2EE (see JavaPerformanceTuning, n.d.), .NET (see Schwichtenberg, n.d.) and different ERP/CRM systems (see Symantec, n.d.). In an heterogeneous environment, different tools and a consolidation of measurements would be required. Second, profiling tools mainly focus on information required for optimization or debugging. They analyze the resource consumption and behavior of technical procedures and entities such as objects, methods, requests, transactions or applications. Typically, this does not match with a customer's perception of services. Overall, profiling tools are not appropriate for the determination of the required kind of resource profiles, but recent developments point to an interesting direction.

"Application transaction profiling software tools prepare a profile for application transactions. This profile consists of resource use across all the IT components these transactions traverse through, which is then correlated with end-user response time, individual component response time and other parameters to improve root cause analysis, performance management and capacity planning. These tools can be used with custom and packaged applications, and they use business policies during transaction execution to modify execution behavior." (Gartner, 2006, p. 10)

The objective of such tools (see for instance Bristol, n.d.; OpTier, n.d.) is to enhance the capabilities of IT operations staff to maintain required service levels. The scope and functionalities goes far beyond cost allocation. According to the analysis of Gartner it is an emerging area, but it is still too early from a technology maturity perspective to successfully implement these tools (Gartner, 2006, p. 10).

Load Test Tools   In load tests the behavior and the performance of application systems under different workload levels is analyzed. A number of commercial (see Borland, n.d.; Mercury, n.d.a) and open-source (see Aberdour, n.d.) load test toolkits are available. Typically, such a toolkit consists of three components: A tool for recording real user behavior, a load generator which replays the user behavior and thus simulates tens, hundreds or even thousands of virtual users, and a tool for analyzing the results. Load test tools provide elaborate means to simulate real user behavior. However, the analysis focus lies on the performance experienced by the virtual users and on the utilization of the resources. It does not calculate the total resource consumption or the consumption per user or per request.

Performance Monitors   The resource consumption of server hardware components (e.g., processors, disks, memory, network interfaces) can be monitored either by custom hardware monitors (see for instance Intel, n.d.) or by using the monitoring facilities of the operating systems. They can be accessed via application interfaces by third-party monitors or by using standard operating systems tools such as perfmon (Windows), sar, iostat or vmstat (Unix/Linux). The information is used, for instance, for systems management, error detection, performance analysis, consumption metering and accounting (see for instance Krüll, 1997). The agents of the accounting and billing software introduced in section 2.4, as well as most of the profiling and load test tools presented above rely on these monitoring facilities. The advantage of Unix, Linux and Windows operating systems is that they offer a broad range of counters which provide comprehensive information about activities at the different hardware components. However, in contrast to the RMF, SMF and subsystem measurement tools available on MVS mainframes (see IBM, n.d.b and IBM, n.d.c), they are limited to this component-oriented view and lack transaction or request-oriented data (see Buzen and Shum, 1996, for a comparative analysis). They do not relate the observed resource consumption with user behavior or application activities and thus are not directly applicable to the determination of resource profiles.

3.5.2   Profiling Process

For the determination of resource profiles, we propose combining the strengths of a load test tool with local performance monitors. The basic idea is to use a load generator for systematic service invocations and to meter at the same time the resource consumption at the different components. However, as neither the load test tool nor the performance monitors explicitly determines the resource consumption per service invocation, an additional analysis toolkit is required, which correlates the data and calculates the resource profiles.

Overall, the profiling process can be broken down into the following steps:

1. The application system is deployed in a dedicated test environment. Such environments with minimal or no differences to the production environments are typically

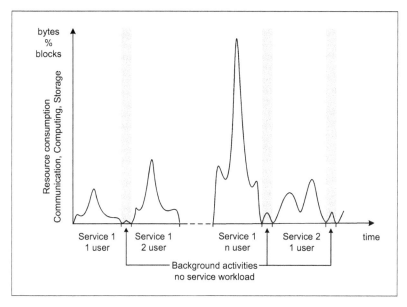

Figure 3.5: Profiling Process

used in larger organizations for approval tests[2] prior to the roll-out of a new software release. It is important to isolate the resources in a test environment as far as possible from the influence of other application systems in the network. Their activities could distort the measurements.

2. The service invocations are recorded in load test scripts. The different services have to be defined in cooperation with the customers and, if possible, based on historical usage data. If a service requires multiple user interactions and no information about the expected user behavior is available, different user profiles can be recorded to determine not an exact value, but an interval for the expected resource consumption.

3. The load generator replays the script and thereby successively raises the number of concurrent service invocations, until the first component reaches its bottleneck. The process is depicted in figure 3.5. A *measurement interval* starts with the first of a set of concurrent service invocations and ends when all these service invocations are

---

[2] also known as acceptance tests (Office of Government Commerce, 2002a, ch. 5.3.4)

completed. The time between two measurement intervals is represented by grayed-out periods. During the whole time, performance monitors at the involved servers meter the incurred resource consumption. As at any one moment only one kind of service is active, resource consumption that is hardly traceable during regular operations (e.g., network traffic) can also be allocated. In figure 3.5 the load test starts with the first service and one virtual user (x-axis). After the service invocation has been completed, the load generator waits a certain time to make sure that the resources have finished the work associated with the initial service invocation. It then starts an additional virtual user and initiates two concurrent service invocations. The incurred resource consumption (y-axis) during the measurement interval rises accordingly. The process is continued until for n concurrent users the first resource reaches its bottleneck. Then it is restarted with the second service.

4. After the load test the log data of the performance monitors and of the load tests tools are correlated. For the data analysis it is assumed, first, that the measured resource consumption is composed according to the model introduced in section 3.3 and, second, that the length of the measurement interval t remains constant for each service i during the load test. Thus, the function 3.2 can be simplified as follows:

$$y_{ij}(x) = a_{ij} + x p_{ij} \qquad (3.3)$$

The analysis component calculates the values p_{ij} in two major steps. First, it determines from the log data the total resource consumption values y_{ij} for each measurement interval. Second, it applies linear regressions to the results and derives the values p_{ij} as slopes of the regression lines. They reflect the average resource consumption per additional user. As the measurements were obtained from the full load spectrum ("until the first component reaches its bottleneck"), possible load-dependent effects are factored in. We thus consider these values to be estimates for the expected resource consumption of a service invocation.

To validate the process and the underlying hypotheses, we combined a number of off-the-self and custom software components. An overview of the software and detailed descriptions are presented in the following sections.

3.5.3   Software Overview

Three kinds of tool are required for the process: A load test tool to simulate user behavior, performance monitors to meter the resource consumption at the involved components, and an analysis component to calculate the resource profiles. For the first and second purpose, we chose commercial off-the-shelf tools; for the data analysis we developed a custom software package.

3.5.3.1   Load Test Tool

As the load test tool, we chose Mercury LoadRunner (see Mercury, n.d.a). The choice was based on the following considerations.

- The Mercury LoadRunner is the leading product with an estimated market share of 77 % in the load testing market worldwide (Hamilton, 2005 cited by Mercury, n.d.b).

- It supports around 30 protocols for different front- and backend interfaces, including HTTP, J2EE, .NET as well as protocols for major ERP/CRM systems (see Mercury, n.d.c). Thus, we obtain a broad coverage of existing application systems.

- The tool has been used for load tests at our industrial partner, the BMW Group. We could therefore directly use the software solution for experiments with real-word applications (see section 3.6.3).

We describe the structure and the application of the different LoadRunner components in section 3.5.4. The process can be realized in the same manner with other load tests tools, as long as they are able to group multiple client interactions to services and support simultaneous invocations of such user-defined services.

3.5.3.2   Performance Monitors

For metering the resource consumption, we decided to rely on standard operating system tools. For Unix and Linux servers we chose the *System Activity Reporter* (sar) (see Godard, n.d.; Hewlett-Packard, n.d.b) and for Microsoft Windows servers the *Performance Monitor* (perfmon) (see Microsoft, n.d.b). The usage of such standard tools has the following advantages:

- Support for performance monitors of the Windows, Unix and Linux operating systems results in an almost complete coverage of client/server architectures.

- Each tool provides counters for all relevant system resources: Network, processors and disks (see section 3.2.3).

- As there is no additional software installation required, new resources can be easily integrated.

- The measurements are non-intrusive and impose no requirements on applications and server software.

The operation principles of the three tools are similar. First, the user selects on the command line (sar) or by using a graphical user interface (perfmon) the relevant counters and determines the measurement interval and log runtime. According to these specifications the tools then record the system behavior in log files. The Unix and Linux tool sar creates binary files which can be read out and transformed to space separated text files. The Windows tool perfmon directly creates comma-separated text files. Against the background of resource profiles, the tools have the following drawbacks:

- The minimal measurement interval is one value per second. This might not be sufficient for short-running services.

- The measurement points and units of the different tools are not standardized. Data normalization is required for a comparative analysis.

- As the performance monitors are totally decoupled from the load generator, the local system times must be exactly synchronized.

Whether these kinds of performance monitors are appropriate for the determination of resource profiles is validated by a set of experiments (see section 3.6).

3.5.3.3 Service Profiler

For data analysis and calculation of resource profiles we developed a custom software toolkit, the *Service Profiler*. It consists of three separate components: *Import, Analyze* and *Visualize* (see figure 3.6). The software is implemented in Java 1.5. Database management systems Oracle, MySQL and Microsoft Access are supported. In the following, we first provide an overview of the toolkit and then, in section 3.5.5, detail the determination of the resource profiles.

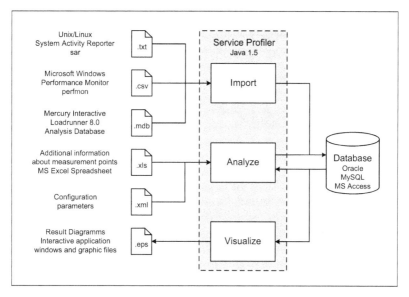

Figure 3.6: Overview of the Service Profiler

Import   The Import component parses the different kinds of log files (see figure 3.6) and consolidates the measurements in the database. In doing so it standardizes the different time formats and resolves data inconsistencies caused by recording errors. Sometimes two subsequent measurements carry for instance the same timestamp or string values such as "nan" (not a number) or "inf" (infinity) are recorded instead of numerical values.

Analyze   The Analyze component first enriches the measurement points in the database with additional context information which could not be retrieved from the log files. It then normalizes the data, for example by converting values measured in milliseconds to seconds. Following these preparatory activities, the tool groups concurrent service invocations to measurement intervals and determines for each measurement interval the total resource consumptions. By means of a linear regression, the Analyze component finally calculates the values p_{ij}. The whole process is detailed in section 3.5.5.

Visualize   The Visualize component supports three major activities: Report generation, consistency checking and performance analysis. Therefore it offers different kinds of parameterizable analysis queries. The results are depicted in charts, generated by means of the open source library JFreeChart (see Object Refinery, n.d.). The charts are either written to graphic files or displayed in interactive applications windows. Overall, the following types are available:

- **Report Generation** The final resource profile is presented in bar charts sorted either per service or per resource.

- **Consistency Checking** Besides the resource profiles, major intermediate results can also be visualized. This facilitates the root cause analysis of non-linearities and inconsistencies. The tool supports, for instance, the analysis of autocorrelations by x/y-line charts comparing the total resource consumption with the regression lines.

- **Performance Analysis** The raw measurements of the performance monitors and the LoadRunner can be combined in one time series chart (similar to figure 3.5). Thus, the user and the system behavior can be reconstructed and analyzed at each point in time.

The charts, used in the following chapters to illustrate experimental results, are encapsulated postscript files, generated by the Visualize component.

3.5.4 Mercury LoadRunner

The Mercury LoadRunner consists of three major components: *Virtual User Generator* to record and edit the test scripts, *Controller* to manage the load tests and *Analysis* to examine the test results. In the following, we describe how these applications are instrumented for the determination of resource profiles.

3.5.4.1 LoadRunner Virtual User Generator

In load tests, the behavior of human users is emulated by virtual users (Vusers). The actions a Vuser performs are specified in a Vuser script. The LoadRunner tool for creating and editing scripts for server-based application systems is the Virtual User Generator (VuGen). Overall, the LoadRunner toolkit supports more than 30 different frontend and backend protocols (Mercury, n.d.c), or, in other words, more than 30 types of Vusers. The structure and the content of the scripts vary accordingly. While database scripts contain SQL calls and resemble C, Java-Corba scripts are written in a Java-based language. The

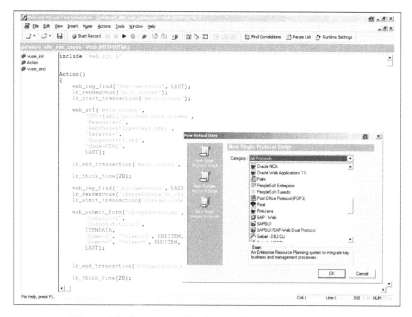

Figure 3.7: Screenshot: LoadRunner Virtual User Generator

screenshot in figure 3.7 shows a HTTP/HTML script in the edit mode and a secondary window with a list of alternative protocols. For all types of Vusers, the script development process is similar. It can be outlined as follows (Mercury, 2004, p. 6):

1. **Record a basic Vuser script.** VuGen automatically creates a basic script by recording the interactions of a real user with the application system.

2. **Enhance/edit the Vuser script.** Typically, a basic script must be revised, for instance to integrate functions which guarantee a proper handling of dynamically created data (e.g., session cookies), to generate arbitrary form inputs or to adapt the think times between two activities.

3. **Configure runtime settings.** In the runtime settings further parameters, such as the simulated network speed, the browser behavior or the run logic of the script, can be adjusted.

4. **Run the Vuser script in stand-alone mode.** Once the configuration is completed the script can be readily tested within the VuGen application.

5. **Integrate the Vuser script.** If the test was successful, the script can be transferred to the Controller and integrated into a load test scenario (see next section).

The scripts for the determination of resource profiles are generated in the same manner. First, VuGen records the service invocations of a human user in a basic script. During the following revision of the script, the following LoadRunner functions are inserted:

- `lr_start_transaction()` ... `lr_end_transaction()`
  The LoadRunner concept of transactions is used to mark the beginning and the end of service invocations. Thus, services can comprise single requests as well as complex user interactions. The start and the execution time of each transaction is written to the LoadRunner result file. This information is afterward analyzed by the Service Profiler (see section 3.5.5).

- `lr_rendezvous()`
  Rendezvous points enable a runtime synchronization of concurrent active Vusers. When a Vuser arrives at a rendezvous point, it waits until all the other Vusers currently executing the same script arrive. When complete, they simultaneously perform the next task in the script. Typically, rendezvous points are used to simulate heavy user loads and load peaks. We insert rendezvous points before each transaction and thus realize simultaneous service invocations.

The concept of transactions and rendezvous points is applicable to all protocols supported by the LoadRunner. We illustrate it below with a section of a HTTP/HTML script. Thus, we consider as service "search" a single request to a search engine of an example application.

```
1    (...)
2    lr_think_time( 7 );
3    lr_rendezvous("search");
4    lr_start_transaction("search");
5
6    web_submit_data("search.screen",
7            "Action={url}/exampleApplication/search.screen",
```

```
 8        "Method=GET",
 9        "EncType=",
10        "RecContentType=text/html",
11        "Referer={url}/exampleApplication/main.screen",
12        "Snapshot=t60.inf",
13        "Mode=HTTP",
14        ITEMDATA,
15        "Name=keywords",
16        "Value={random_string_value}",
17        ENDITEM,
18        LAST);
19
20   lr_end_transaction("search", LR_AUTO);
21
22   lr_think_time( 7 );
23   (...)
24
```

During the profiling process, subsequent service invocations are framed by think times with no Vuser actions. Thus, potential impact from precedent service invocations on the resource consumption in the measurement interval should be excluded (see section 3.5.2). In the above script, these think times are 7 seconds (lines 2 and 22). After the think time, the concurrent active users meet at a rendezvous point (line 3), and, when complete, simultaneously start the transaction (line 4). In the example script, the transaction (service) consists only of a single HTTP request (lines 6 to 18). The strings in braces are manually inserted parameters, which are set at runtime. The url (line 11 and 7) is read from a configuration file, to enhance script portability. The search string is generated randomly (line 16), to avoid unrealistic cache effects.

Once the scripts are created and tested, they can be integrated into load test scenarios, managed and executed by the LoadRunner Controller.

3.5.4.2 LoadRunner Controller

The LoadRunner organizes load test configurations into *scenarios*. The scenarios are created and executed by the Controller. Each scenario contains a list of computers used for load generation, references to the integrated Vuser scripts, Vuser schedules and runtime settings. During the execution of a scenario, the Controller manages the load generators and provides an online console for performance monitoring. The scenario design depends on the load test objectives. Typical objectives are the identification of bottlenecks, determining the system capacity, checking system reliability and error handling or analyzing

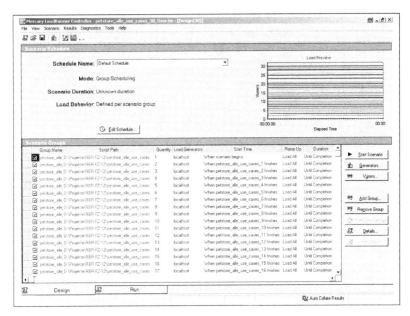

Figure 3.8: Screenshot: LoadRunner Controller

the system behavior in overload situations. For the determination of resource profiles, the following aspects must be considered:

1. For an unambiguous allocation of incurred resource consumption, only one kind of active service is allowed at each moment during the load test.

2. As the average resource consumption is calculated by a linear regression over measurements at different workload levels, the Controller must successively raise the number of concurrent service invocations, until the first component reaches its bottleneck.

3. Interactive services include think times of users. The length of these think times can be generated randomly. This might be reasonable in situations where load peaks should be avoided. However, the parameters of the random generator must be adjusted in a way that the total length of the measurement intervals remains approximately constant (see section 3.5.2).

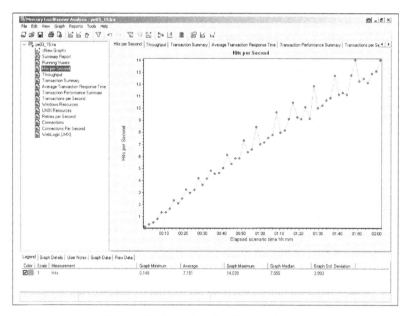

Figure 3.9: Screenshot: LoadRunner Analysis

The screenshot in figure 3.8 shows an example Vuser schedule. During the load test the Controller successively raises the number of Vusers from 1 to 30. A group of Vusers is executed as soon as the previous group has finished the execution. The synchronization within a group of Vusers is performed by the rendezvous points.

The Controller also manages the execution of the scenarios. During a load test various kinds of online monitors are available to control performance counters of Vusers and involved resources. As soon as the test has finished, the data can be transferred to the LoadRunner Analysis tool.

3.5.4.3 LoadRunner Analysis

The LoadRunner Analysis enables a detailed examination of load test results. The primary focus lies on Vuser performance metrics (e.g., transaction response times, number of failed transactions) and measurements of the load generators (e.g., number of open connections, data throughput). Additionally, the performance of the involved computing and network resources can be analyzed. The data is obtained either manually by file imports or automatically from the measurements of online monitors activated during the

Resources	Normalized data of the Service Profiler		Raw measurements of the performance monitors		
	points	units	Linux sar	Unix sar	Windows perfmon
Network	Transferred Bytes	bytes	rxbyt/s + txbyt/s	n/a	Bytes Total/sec
Disk	Disk Time	percent	%util	%busy	% Disk Time
	Average Queue Length	number	avgqu-sz	avque	Avg. Disk Queue Length
	Average Transfer Time	seconds	await / 1000	(avserv + avwait) / 1000	Average Disk sec/Transfer
	Read/write Blocks	bytes	rd_sec/s + wr_sec/s	blks/s	Disk Bytes/sec / 512
Processor	Processor Time	percent	%user + %system	%usr + %sys	% Processor Time
	User Time	percent	%user	%usr	% User Time
	System Time	percent	%system	%sys	% Privileged Time
	Processor Queue Length	number	runq-sz	runq-sz	Processor Queue Length

Table 3.1: Rules for Raw Data Normalization

load test (see previous section). However, as the remote monitoring intervals cannot be set lower than 3 s (Windows) and 6 s (Unix, Linux), these resource consumption counters cannot substitute the local performance monitors. The Analysis tool displays the information in interactive graphs (see figure 3.9 for an example) and generates reports in the form of HTML or Microsoft Word documents. Furthermore, the raw data can be copied to spreadsheet applications for custom analysis. Beyond this manual solution, the Load-Runner provides no documented interface which would enable third-party applications to access the raw data. Fortunately, the Analysis tool internally uses the Microsoft Access database format for data storage. The Service Profiler connects to this database and can thus read out the timestamps of the transactions for the determination of resource profiles.

3.5.5   Resource Profile Determination

In section 3.5.3.3 we presented an overview of the Service Profiler. In the following, we focus on the Analyze component and detail the process for the determination of the resource profiles. We assume that the Import component has successfully transferred the raw data into the database. The Analyze component then conducts the following steps:

1. **Addition of context information** The measurement points are first enriched with additional context information which could not be retrieved from the log files.

For instance, the Import component might have extracted from a sar-log file the *server name* (machine) and a data column with the title %usr. The measurement point is now completed with the information that %usr stands for the *percentage of time* (unit) a *processor* (object) spent in *user mode* (counter) and with information about the server configuration such as the *number of processors* (instances) and a *performance index*. The context information is kept and administered in a Microsoft Excel spreadsheet. It also contains the information for which measurement points consumption estimates should be calculated and which are intended for performance analysis only.

2. **Normalization of measurements** Neither measurement points nor measurement units provided by the different performance monitors are standardized. For a comparative performance analysis and the determination of resource profiles, normalized values are required. A normalization is not always trivial. Table 3.1 illustrates how the Service Profiler normalizes the raw data by example of some major measurement points[3]. The data conversion rules are specified in the spreadsheet introduced above.

3. **Determination of measurements intervals** The raw data read out from the LoadRunner database contains for each transaction an entry with the transaction name, as specified in the script (see section 3.5.4.1), the transaction start time and its execution time. The Service Profiler consolidates this data and determines the measurement intervals together with the corresponding numbers of concurrent service invocations. The major difficulty thereby is the identification of outliers. During the load test it might happen that transactions fail, require extraordinary long execution times or that virtual users miss one or more rendezvous points. During normal load tests sporadic errors of this kind are typically negligible. However, in the present case they can lead to distorted or overlapping measurement intervals and thus reduce the quality of the resource profiles. The Service Profiler implements several analysis functions which try to identify such outliers and exclude ambiguous measurement intervals from the subsequent resource profile calculations. The required threshold values are specified in the configuration files.

---

[3]   For a detailed description of the counters in table 3.1, the interested reader is referred to the manual pages of the performance monitors (Linux sar: Godard, n.d., Unix sar: Hewlett-Packard, n.d.b, Windows perfmon: Microsoft, n.d.b).

4. **Correlation of transactions and resource consumption** The measurement
   intervals, as determined from the raw transaction data, are then correlated with
   the measurements of the performance monitors. Each measurement value in the
   database is supplemented by the transaction and the number of virtual users, which
   were active at the moment the measurement was taken. The different time granu-
   larities of the measurements must thereby be considered. Start and response times
   of transactions are measured in milliseconds. The performance monitors report average values of the resource consumption during the last second. Furthermore, the
   sar tools (Unix, Linux) round the timestamps. Hence, a value measured at the point
   in time *1* could include the resource consumption between *0.0* and *1.0* as well as
   between *0.9* and *1.9*. The Service Profiler uses by default the following formulas for
   determining the measurement interval for the resource consumption.

$$[\lfloor t_{start} + 0.5 \rfloor; \lfloor t_{end} + 0.5 \rfloor] \tag{3.4}$$

The parameter t_{start} represents the exact start time of the first and t_{end} the end
time of the last transaction of the measurement cycle. The values are measured
in milliseconds. The conversion to seconds intervals described above has been well
tried and tested in several experiments. Whether it was successful, i.e., whether the
determined intervals cover the incurred resource consumption, can be controlled by
time series charts provided by the Visualize component (see section 3.5.3.3).

We illustrate the correlation of transactions and resource consumption measurements with two examples[4]. Figure 3.10 depicts a 30 second excerpt of a load test in
a time series chart. In the lower diagram the raw data of the LoadRunner database
is displayed. Each arrow indicates the start (black arrows) or stop (gray arrows)
of a transaction. The horizontal line shows the number of concurrent active Vusers
(lower y-Axis). In the upper diagram, measurements of the performance monitors
are displayed (here: the utilization of an application server). The white areas in both
diagrams indicate the different measurement intervals. The gray areas in-between
represent the think times the load generator waits to make sure that the resources
have finished the work associated with the previous service invocation (here: 7 seconds). In figure 3.10 the LoadRunner transactions include only single client re-

---

[4] The experimental setup and the example applications are detailed in section 4.1. The LoadRunner
     scripts are provided in the appendix (see section A.5).

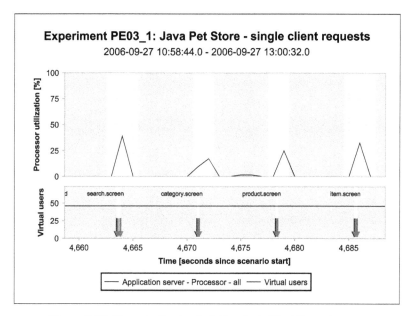

Figure 3.10: Example: Services including single Client Requests

quests ("search.screen", "category.screen", "product.screen", "item.screen"). In the depicted time period the transactions are simultaneously started by 46 Vusers. The application system always requires less than one second to process all 46 requests (lower diagram). However, due to the inaccuracies of the performance monitors described above, the Service Profiler allocates the incurred resource consumption within a 2 or 3 second interval to the transactions.

In the second example the whole application is considered as single service and resource profiles are now determined for different kinds of user behavior (user profiles). Figure 3.11 shows a 4 minute excerpt of a load test and three measurement cycles. During the depicted time period 40, 50 and 60 concurrent Vusers simulate a "power_shopper" behavior. The corresponding LoadRunner transaction includes multiple requests to the application system. To avoid load peaks the Vusers wait a random time between 0.5 and 1.5 seconds between two subsequent requests. Again the transactions start synchronously (black arrows), but the random think times result in different execution times (gray arrows). The transaction measurement

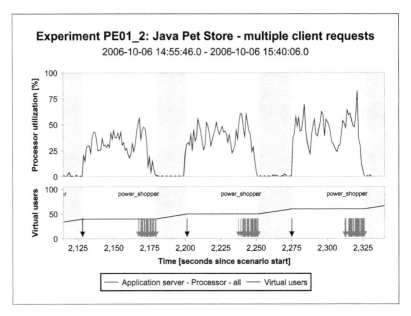

Figure 3.11: Example: Services including multiple Client Requests

interval begins with the start of the first transaction and ends when the last trans-action of a measurement cycle finishes. The measurement interval for the resource consumption is calculated as in the previous example. In the upper diagram an increase of the resource consumption along with the number of concurrent transactions is visible. During the periods with no Vuser activities (here: 20 seconds) the resource consumption of background activities can be observed.

5. **Calculation of resource consumption** The calculation of the resource consumption per service invocation is implemented according to the process description in section 3.5.2 (step 4).

First, for all services i and resources j the values $y_{ij}(x)$ are calculated. Therefore, the consumption values during the measurement intervals are summed up. We illustrate this step with the example in figure 3.10. During the first measurement

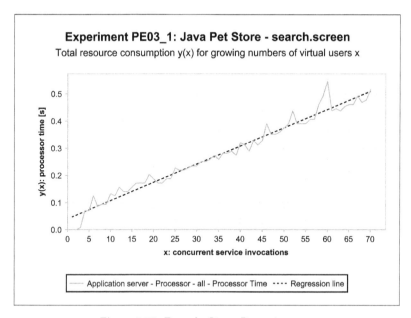

Figure 3.12: Example: Linear Regression

interval the consumption values 0%, 39% and 0% were observed[5]. Hence, the Service Profiler calculates for the service "search.screen" and the resource "Application server - Processor - all" the value $y(46) = 0 + 0.39 + 0 = 0.39$.

In a second step, a linear regression is applied to the results. Thus, the slopes of the regression lines p_{ij}, considered as average resource consumption values per service invocation, and the correlation coefficients r_{ij}, considered as quality measures, are determined. The example introduced above is supplemented in figure 3.12 by the remaining values $y(x)$ for $x = 1, 2, ..., 70$ and the regression line as determined by the Service Profiler ($p = 0.007$, $r = 0.984$).

6. **Preparation of results** Finally, the resource profiles are prepared for their further usage (e.g., cost accounting, capacity planning). This includes, first, a normalization of the processor times of different servers by the number of processors and perfor-

---

[5] 39% average processor utilization during an interval of 1 second is equal to 0.39 seconds processor time.

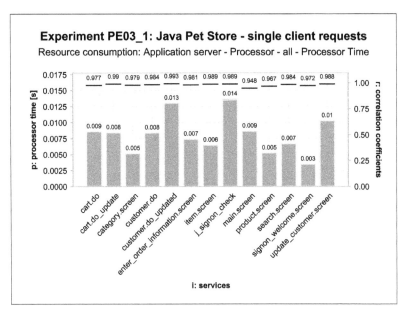

Figure 3.13: Example: Consumption Estimates per Service

mance indexes, retrieved for instance from public processor benchmark databases
(see SPEC, n.d.a). The Service Profiler then exports the resource profiles either to
spreadsheets or visualizes them in charts. Figure 3.13 continues the above example
and shows an overview of the resource consumption and the correlation coefficients
of all services. A table with the complete resource profiles can be found in the
appendix (see table A.5 in section A.3.1).

3.6   Overview of Validation Approaches

In section 3.2 we presented a cost allocation methodology based on customer-oriented
services and resource profiles. For the determination of these resource profiles we then
introduced a model describing the composition of resource consumption (section 3.3), a
number of practical requirements (section 3.4), a profiling methodology and a software
toolkit (section 3.5). In the subsequent chapters we focus on the validation of these

concepts. We therefore propose three different approaches, which are briefly summarized below.

3.6.1 Experiments: Resource Profiles

For an initial assessment of the model hypotheses and the software tools we conduct a set of experiments with two different application systems and services consisting of single and of multiple client requests (chapter 4). We therefore define the following seven test scenarios:

- **Background Activities** Experiments with no service workload to analyze the background resource consumption caused for instance by the performance monitors (section 4.3.1).

- **Resource profiles** Experiments to analyze correlation coefficients and scale and range of the determined resource consumption (section 4.3.2).

- **Repeatability** Experiments under equal conditions to verify the repeatability of results (section 4.3.3).

- **Load-dependent Behavior** Experiments with different profiling workloads to analyze total and per-user resource consumptions (section 4.3.4).

- **Linear Regression** Experiments with rising user think times and thus rising impact of background activities on total resource consumption; the linear regression should eliminate any influence on the resource profiles (section 4.3.5).

- **Linear Regression – cross check** Experiments with rising think times and no linear regression; the increasing impact of background activities should be now measurable (section 4.3.6).

- **Database Sizes** Experiments with full and empty databases (section 4.3.7).

Aims and purposes are threefold. First, we verify if our model describing the total resource consumption holds in principle. Second, we test the measurement and analysis tools and control the accuracy and consistency of the results. Third, we analyze how a change of parameters, namely workload, user think time and database size, affects the resource profiles. These experiments should enable an initial validation; they are not intended to be repeated during the regular profiling process.

3.6.2 Experiments: Analytical Models

The resource profiles should bridge the gap between customer-oriented services and IT resources. In other words, they should support the translation of business forecasts into hardware requirements. We therefore propose the use of a well-known instrument from Analytical Capacity Planning, namely Queuing Network (QN) Theory. The basic idea is to take the processor times from the resource profiles as input parameters for a QN Model of the infrastructure. By means of the respective algorithms for a given user behavior (i.e., service usage) and a given workload scenario (i.e., number of active users and think times between two activities) the expected server utilizations can be calculated. We validate the concept with a set of experiments (chapter 5). Thus, we replay the user behavior and the workload scenario in a load test, measure the actual server utilizations and analyze the deviation from the predicted values. This approach has several advantages:

1. In the load tests required for the estimation of the resource profiles, the infrastructure is at any time exclusively used by a single service (see section 3.5.2). In contrast, in the load tests for QN validation, real world scenarios with multiple concurrently active services are replayed. It can therefore be verified whether the estimated resource consumption and the underlying hypotheses also hold in these scenarios.

2. If the load test simulates different workload levels, for instance by successively increasing the number of active users, nonlinearities in the resource consumption and load-dependent behavior can be discovered.

3. For the estimation of resource profiles, the cumulated processor times during the completion time of concurrent service invocations are analyzed. In contrast, for the validation of the QN Models the average utilizations over longer time intervals are determined. The two analysis and measurement approaches enable a mutual validation of the accuracy and consistency of the results.

4. If the load test has verified the QN Model and its input parameters, it can readily be used for capacity planning. The model enables capacity planners to conduct "what-if" analyses and thus anticipate the effects of changes in the workload composition or the hardware configuration.

In chapter 5 we first provide a short introduction to QN Theory and describe the software tools required for solving and verifying QN Models. We then present the results of experiments conducted with services consisting of single and of multiple client requests. Besides a validation of the resource profiles, the support for capacity planning is a major added value of the approach. Thus, it might be reasonable to conduct the load tests for QN Model validation on a regular basis.

3.6.3 Proof of Concept: BMW Group

Finally, we present in chapter 6 the results of a proof of concept, conducted in cooperation with our industrial partner, the BMW Group. It is organized in three stages:

1. Analysis of objectives, requirements and practices of IT Cost Accounting and Charge-back at the BMW Group.

2. Development of a proposal how the determination of resource profiles could be integrated into the existing IT Service Management processes.

3. Application of the software in a data center of the BMW Group.

The objectives are twofold. First, we intend to underpin the overall considerations on IT Cost Accounting and Chargeback of chapter 2 with a real-world case. Second, we want to test the viability of the concept and the software in an industrial environment and evaluate an integration into existing IT Service Management Processes.

3.6.4 Summary

The three different validation approaches are summarized below by means of the requirements presented in section 3.4. Therefore, we list the requirements again and describe whether and how they are addressed by the Service Profiler and the validation approaches.

Requirement 1: Accuracy The Service Profiler implements no kind of auto-correction mechanisms for the resource profiles which would guarantee a certain level of accuracy. However, the visualizing components and the correlation coefficients facilitate the identification of bias and inconsistencies in the resource profiles (see section 3.5.5).

Requirement 1.1: Accurate measurement and analysis tools This is the basic condition for accurate resource profiles. With regard to the software toolkit it is unclear whether the accuracy of standard performance monitors is sufficient for the determination of resource profiles (see section 3.5.3.2). We address these questions in our experiments in chapter 4 and demonstrate in chapter 5 how QN Models can be used to cross-check the accuracy of the processor time estimates.

Requirement 1.2: Linear resource consumption   In the experiments in chapter 4 we analyze whether the model hypotheses on the composition of resource consumption holds in the test environment. However, these results cannot be generalized. During the estimation of resource profiles the visualizing components and the correlation coefficients facilitate the identification of nonlinearities in the resource consumption (see section 3.5.5). The processor time estimates can be further cross-verified by the results of load tests for the validation of QN Models (see chapter 5).

Requirement 1.3: Correct assumptions about user behavior   Generally, a full validation of the assumptions on user behavior is only ex-post and by measurements at the productive system possible. If historical usage data is available, this can be used to derive respective user behavior models. Particularly for web-based applications a variety of different tools (see Ideal Observer, n.d.) and modeling approaches (see Menascé and Almeida, 2000, p. 41-64) exist. In the experiments in chapter 4 we analyze the more difficult case of highly interactive applications and no historical usage data. We present two strategies. First, the definition of very fine-grain services and, second, the profiling of different user behaviors to determine not an exact value, but an interval for the expected resource consumption.

Requirement 2: Consistency   We combined a professional load generator with the standard performance monitors of Unix, Linux and Windows operating systems to maximize the applicability of the analysis software. The viability of the concept and the accuracy of the results is the subject of the experiments in chapter 4 and the proof-of-concept at the BMW Group (chapter 6).

Requirement 3: Capacity Planning   We evaluate in a set of experiments whether processor time estimates from the resource profiles can be used as input parameters for Analytical Capacity Planning based on QN Models (see chapter 5).

Requirement 4: Operating Efficiency   The experiments presented in chapter 4 and 5 were conducted in a data center of our industrial partner. Thus, we could analyze the efforts required for the determination of resource profiles and evaluate on-site the integration into the existing IT Service Management processes. The results are summarized in chapter 6.

3.7 Related Work

We structure the discussion of related work into two parts. First, we refer to concepts, which also propose the usage of customer-oriented services for IT Cost Allocation and, second, we compare the profiling methodology and the software toolkit (see section 3.5) to a related approach.

3.7.1 Cost Allocation by Services

The allocation of IT costs based on customer-oriented services such as business transactions is already practiced (see section 2.4). It has a number of advantages for business units in particular (see section 2.3). We picked up the concept and propose the use of predetermined resource profiles to relate the customer-oriented services of application systems with IT resource requirements. In the survey of literature, we presented two process costing approaches (section 2.2.1.1: Fürer, 1994; Funke, 1999) and one IT Controlling framework (section 2.2.1.2: Scheeg, 2005) that are based on similar ideas. The concepts differ in the way they translate the services into IT resource requirements and infrastructure cost shares. Fürer proposes the analysis of historical data to determine the average resource consumption for each transaction (Fürer, 1994, p. 137 et seqq.). Funke mentions conversion tables (which are seemingly similar to resource profiles) and, furthermore, additional requirements (e.g., throughput, response time) as valuation standard for services (Funke, 1999, p. 201). Fürer and Funke formulated their concepts against the background of centralized mainframe architectures. In contrast, Scheeg (2005) explicitly addresses the characteristics of client/server environments. He proposes the use of Application Benchmarks such as TPC-C (see TPPC, n.d.b) or SAPS (see SAP, n.d.b) to compare hardware capacity and the resource requirements of services (Scheeg, 2005, p. 178).

The focus of studies mentioned above lies on Cost Accounting (Fürer, Funke) and IT Controlling (Scheeg). Although the authors describe why and how the resource requirements for services should be determined, they neither provide any technical details nor illustrate their concepts with real-world examples or experimental results. The present work aims to fill this gap.

	Nagaprabhanjan and Apte (2005)	Concept presented in section 3.5
Services	A service is defined by an URI (i.e. a single client request)	A service can comprise multiple client requests
Load generation	Custom load generator (master), which sequentially generates HTTP requests	Mercury LoadRunner (various protocols)
Performance monitoring	Agents (slaves) on the different components collect data from OS tools and an in-process java profiler	OS tools record system behavior in log files
Coordination between load generation and performance monitoring	The master coordinates the load generation with the monitoring processes at the slaves (start/stop)	No direct coordination – exact time synchronization is required
Supported Platforms	Linux / (Java)	Linux/Unix/Windows
Data analysis	The slaves transfer the performance data to the master, which immediately analyzes the data	The data from the log files and the load generator are separately consolidated and analyzed
Duration (measurement and analysis)	~minutes	~hours

Table 3.2: Comparison of Method and Software Toolkit with Nagaprabhanjan and Apte (2005)

3.7.2 Determination of Resource Profiles

The problem of determining resource profiles in client/server environments has also been addressed by Nagaprabhanjan and Apte, who recently presented a tool (see Nagaprabhanjan and Apte, 2005) for automated profiling of distributed transactions. Their focus is not the allocation of infrastructure costs, but the determination of input parameters for performance analysis and capacity planning. The differences to our approach are pointed out in table 3.2.

Nagaprabhanjan and Apt also combine load generation with performance monitors for the determination of resource consumption. They use a custom load generator which requires measurement agents installed on the different servers. This enables more precise measurements. Accordingly, they require fewer measurement cycles and generate less data for the analysis. However, the use of custom agents limits the flexibility of the implementation (currently to Linux servers and Web applications, see Nagaprabhanjan and Apte, 2005). In contrast, we use a commercial off-the-shelf load generator and require no additional software installations on the servers. Thus, we gain three major advantages. First, we can simulate complex interactive user behavior. Second, the approach is not restricted to application systems with web interfaces. The load generator supports more than 30 different frontend and backend protocols. Third, as we solely use standard performance monitors of operating systems, additional resources can be easily integrated.

Chapter 4

Experiments: Resource profiles

4.1 Experimental Setup

We tested the model hypotheses on resource consumption (see section 3.3) and the software tools implementing the profiling methodology (see section 3.5) in a set of experiments. As example application platform we chose the widely used *Java 2 Platform, Enterprise Edition* (J2EE) of Sun Microystems (see Sun Microsystems, n.d.c). J2EE is a platform specification and a branding initiative that provides a unifying umbrella for enterprise-oriented Java technologies[1]. We conducted the experiments in close cooperation with our industrial partner, the BMW Group. They provided the data center infrastructure as well as an example application system. We could therefore analyze the viability of concept and software under realistic conditions and evaluate the integration into existing IT Service Management processes (see chapter 6).

4.1.1 Test Infrastructure

In the experiments we used a multi-tier client/server architecture as typical for J2EE application scenarios (Singh et al., 2002, p. 14). The setup of the infrastructure is oriented toward standards of the BMW Group (see section 6.3.1). Figure 4.1 provides a schematic overview. A detailed specification is given in the appendix (see section A.2).

The test environment reflects the heterogeneity of client/server architectures mentioned above (see section 2.1.4). Three operating systems (Linux/Windows/Unix) are combined

---

[1] We do not go into details of the J2EE platform here. The interested reader is referred to Singh et al. (2002) for a comprehensive technology overview.

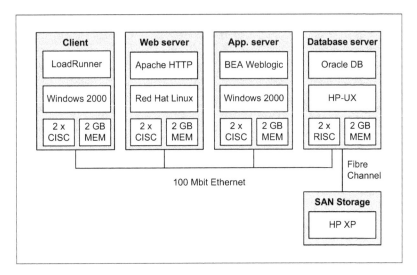

Figure 4.1: Overview of the Test Infrastructure

with three different kinds of server software. Core element is a Java application server
from the Weblogic product family of Bea Systems (see BEA, n.d.b). It provides a web
container as runtime environment for Java Server Pages (JSPs) and Servlets and an EJB
container as runtime environment for Enterprise Java Beans (EJBs). An Apache web
server acts as a proxy between client and application server. Static web content, such
as html or image files, is directly delivered to the client from the web server. Dynamic
content is generated by the web container of the application server. The business logic
can be located either in the web container or in the EJB container. Combining business
and presentation logic in the web container can enable a quick start for small applications
with few transactional needs. In contrast, the EJB-centric concept is better for building
a large-scale enterprise application where code and performance scalability are prime
factors (Singh et al., 2002, p. 356). As database management system (DBMS) we use
Oracle Database. Due to performance and security reasons, the data files are located in a
Storage Area Network (SAN) connected via fibre channel with the database server. The
clients are simulated by a Mercury LoadRunner Controller (see section 3.5.4).

4.1.2   Example Applications

We conducted experiments with two very different kinds of application systems to enhance
the significance of the results:

- **PASTA**, a custom application system of the BMW Group, to analyze the viability
  of the concept with a real-world example (see section 4.1.2.1). PASTA only uses
  the web container of the application server. It is designed for a small number of
  concurrent users. Hardware bottleneck of the system is the database server.

- **Java Pet Store**, a well-known reference application system of Sun Microsystems,
  which is freely available and well documented (see section 4.1.2.2). We provide all
  information that an interested reader requires to redo the experiments and compare
  the results. The Java Pet Store uses both, web and EJB container of the application
  server. The software architecture is highly scalable and can handle hundreds of
  concurrent users. Hardware bottleneck of the system is the application server.

Both application systems are highly interactive. This complicates the determination
of resource profiles. Wrong assumptions about the expected user behavior may lead
to distorted consumption estimates (see section 3.4). For the experiments we assumed
furthermore that no historical usage data is available. In the previous chapter (see sections 3.5.5 and 3.6.4), we presented two strategies to cope with this problem. First, the
definition of very fine-grain services and, second, the profiling of different user behaviors
to determine, instead of an exact value, an interval of the expected resource consumption.
In the experiments we evaluated both strategies and prepared load test scripts with services including single client requests and load test scripts with services including multiple
client requests, which represent different user profiles.

4.1.2.1   PASTA

PASTA ("**P**rojekt **A**ktivitäten und **ST**atus **A**nzeige") is a custom application system of
the BMW Group. It was chosen for the experiments because it can be considered as a typical representative of a large number of similar non-critical systems at the BMW Group.
PASTA is used as a central project management dashboard for IT projects in the production department. It implements the BMW-specific IT Project Management processes,
ranging from the initial business proposal to the system roll-out (see figure 4.2). The
different project teams use PASTA to communicate the current project status, activities,

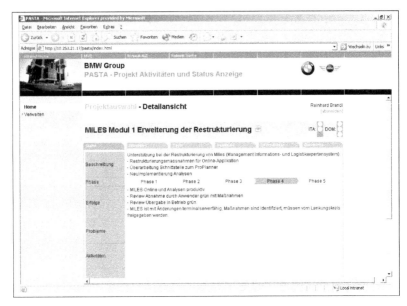

Figure 4.2: Screenshot: PASTA

team members, gateway documents and so forth. The business logic, required for the administration and visualization of project information, is not complex. Both business and presentation logic reside in the web container of the application server. Servlets are used to process client requests and to generate dynamic responses in the form of web pages. Static web content such as image files or stylesheets are located at a separate web server (see section 4.1.1). The data is stored in an Oracle database. PASTA accesses the database using preconfigured connection pools of the application server. In the experiments we worked on a copy of the real database content. Furthermore, PASTA has an interface to the group directory to automatically update the contact information of project team members (e.g., telephone and department numbers). User access and read/write permissions are controlled by a central authentication/authorization service. Web servers, application servers and database servers are shared with certain numbers of different application systems. For each system a single business owner is defined, to whom hardware and server operations costs are allocated on a flat rate basis. The resource consumption is not considered in the cost allocation keys.

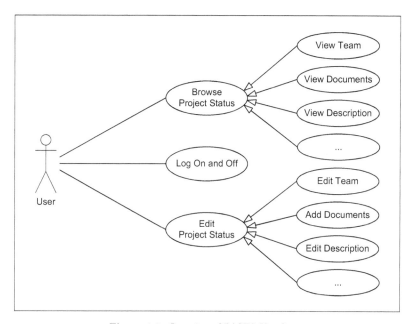

Figure 4.3: Overview of PASTA Use Cases

Basically, two different kinds of PASTA user exists. The majority are *read users*, who solely browse through the projects. *Edit users*, in contrast, also change project information (see figure 4.3). For estimating an interval of the expected resource consumption of a PASTA user, we created load test scripts with the following user behavior:

- **read_user** The user logs in, checks the status of a single project and logs out (11 user interactions).

- **edit_user** The user logs in, fully updates a project, verifies the changes and logs out (21 user interactions).

We assumed that the read_user and edit_user profiles reflect minimum and maximum bounds of PASTA usage. Additionally, we created a script in which all possible kinds of read and edit requests are considered as separate services. Thus, we tried to obtain in the experiments, even without any historical data on user behavior, as much information on the expected resource consumption as possible.

Figure 4.4: Screenshot: Java Pet Store

4.1.2.2   Java Pet Store

The Java Pet Store is a sample application of the Java BluePrints program at Sun Microsystems (see Sun Microsystems, n.d.a). The software architecture is used as a showcase in the book of Singh et al. (2002). Additionally, Sun Microsystems provides on its web site a supplement to the book, containing detailed information on design and implementation of the application (see Sun Microsystems, n.d.b). We chose Pet Store over commercial benchmarks such as TPC-App (see TPPC, n.d.a) for three reasons. First, it is readily available and the experiments are easy to repeat. Second, it covers most J2EE technologies and, third, the software architecture, with several interacting applications in the frontend and backend, is an appropriate representation of the structure of modern enterprise systems. The Java Pet Store is frequently used for performance studies (see for instance Juse et al., 2003). Microsoft and Macromedia have even reimplemented the functionalities of the Java Pet Store to compare the capabilities of .NET and Flash with the J2EE platform (see Adobe, n.d.; Microsoft, n.d.a).

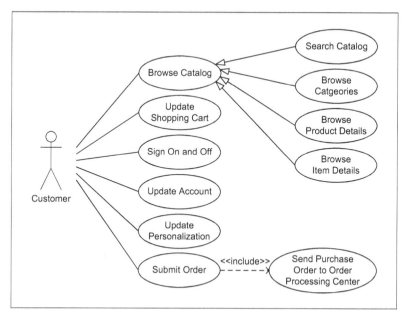

Figure 4.5: Overview of Java Pet Store Use Cases (adapted from Singh et al., 2002, p. 362)

The Java Pet Store is as a typical e-commerce application: An online shop that sells products (animals) to customers. It has a web site through which it presents an interface to customers (see figure 4.4). Administrators and external businesses such as suppliers use other application interfaces to maintain inventory and perform managerial tasks (Singh et al., 2002, p. 352). We focus in the experiments on the interactions between customer and web site (see figure 4.5). The customer can select items from a catalog, place them in a shopping cart and, when ready, purchase the shopping cart contents. The shopping cart content can be displayed and revised. To complete the purchase, the customer must provide a shipping address and a credit card number. Returning customers can reuse the contact and payment information of their last order (Singh et al., 2002, p. 353).

Two separate applications are involved in the scenario. First, a web application that provides the *online shop* (petstore.ear) including all functionalities customers require to purchase merchandise through a web browser. As soon as a customer has completed the purchase, the online shop sends the order in form of an XML document and via Java Mes-

sage Service (JMS) to the *order processing center* (opc.ear). This second, process-oriented
application manages the order fulfillment in the backend. It provides the following services
(Sun Microsystems, n.d.b, p. 2):

- Receive and process XML documents, via JMS, containing orders from the online
  shop

- Provide order data via XML messaging over HTTP to the shop administrator

- Send email to customers acknowledging orders using JavaMail

- Send XML order documents to suppliers via JMS

- Maintain purchase order database

The Java Pet Store uses both web and EJB container of the application server. For the
experiments, we used a configuration template provided by Bea Systems which supports
the deployment of the Java Pet Store files on Bea Weblogic application servers and Oracle
databases (see BEA, n.d.a). We populated the database with the default content provided
by Sun Microsystems.
Compared to PASTA (see section 4.1.2.1), the Java Pet Store is far more complex and
user profiles are not so clear-cut. Hence, we created load test scripts for four different
kinds of user behavior to estimate an interval of the expected resource consumption of a
Pet Store customer.

- **curious_visitor** The customer browses to four different item descriptions and then
  leaves the online store without having used the shopping cart, registering or purchasing functionalities (12 user interactions).

- **first_time_shopper** Like the curious_visitor, the customer browses first to four
  different product descriptions, then registers with the store and buys two different
  products (32 user interactions).

- **determined_shopper** The customer directly uses the search engine to find the
  first product, adds it to the shopping cart, then browses on the shortest path to two
  further products, adds them also, checks out and purchases the cart contents (17
  user interactions).

- **power_shopper** The customer browses through the store, uses the search engine, performs multiple updates of the shopping cart and finally buys 6 different products (41 user interactions).

We assumed that the determined_shopper and the power_shopper are returning customers, who are already registered with the store. As for PASTA, we also created a load test script, in which all possible kinds of customer requests are considered as separate services. However, services including single client requests require a synchronous fulfillment of the requests. Those kinds of services are not applicable to asynchronous backend applications such as the order processing center.

LoadRunner scripts for the Java Pet Store and services including single requests and multiple requests (power_shopper) are given in the appendix (see sections A.5.1 and A.5.2).

4.2   Overview of Experiments

In the previous chapter we presented a methodology and a software toolkit for the determination of resource profiles. The concept is based on the hypotheses that the resource consumption evolves according to the following function (see sections 3.3 and 3.5.2):

$$y_{ij}(x,t) = a_j(t) + xp_{ij} \qquad (4.1)$$

We evaluated the hypotheses and the software implementing the concept in a set of experiments. Aims and purposes were threefold. First, we tried to verify if the model describing the total resource consumption holds in the example environment. Second, we tested the precision of the measurement and analysis tools introduced in section 3.5. Third, we analyzed the effects of parameter changes during the profiling process and compared the experimental results with the model predictions.

The experiments were organized into seven test scenarios with different analysis objectives and parameters:

- **Background Activities** $- a_j$: The resource consumption of background activities was measured during tests with no service workload. To analyze the impact of performance monitoring thereon, we conducted three experiments with local and remote monitors and different logging configurations (see section 4.3.1).

- **Resource profiles** $- p_{ij}, r_{ij}$: Resource profiles were regularly determined for services including single and multiple client requests. We first analyzed the correlation coefficients of the linear regression and then, for services including multiple client requests, the influence of varying user behavior on the mean resource consumption (see section 4.3.2).

- **Repeatability** – p_{ij} : The process for the determination of resource profiles was repeated five times under equal conditions. We compared the resulting resource profiles and analyzed the repeatability of the results (see section 4.3.3).

- **Load-dependent Behavior** – $\frac{y_{ij}(x)}{x}$: The total resource consumption $y_{ij}(x)$ was measured at five different workload levels x. By comparing the normalized values, we could analyze the influence of the workload on the average resource consumption per service (see section 4.3.4).

- **Linear Regression** – p_{ij} : The process for the determination of resource profiles was repeated five times. After each test the average think time between two user activities was doubled. By comparing the results we verified whether the linear regression eliminates the influence of the increasing measurement interval lengths on the resource profiles. This kind of experiment is only suitable for services including multiple client requests (see section 4.3.5).

- **Linear Regression – cross check** – $\frac{y_{ij}(t)}{x}$: These experiments with increasing think times were repeated with a constant number of concurrent service invocations x. No linear regression was applicable. We cross checked the model hypotheses by verifying whether the normalized total resource consumption rises with the length of the measurement interval t (see section 4.3.6).

- **Database Sizes** – p_{ij} : In this experiment we analyzed how the number of entries in a database can influence the mean resource consumption. Those effects are not considered in the model describing the total resource consumption. However, as database sizes may significantly change during the lifecycle of application systems, they are highly relevant for the practicability of the concept (see section 4.3.7).

All experiments were conducted on the infrastructure described above and with the example application systems PASTA and Java Pet Store (see section 4.1). After each load test the servers were restarted, the initial system configuration restored and the system clocks synchronized.

	PASTA		Java Pet Store	
Service type	multiple req.	single requests	multiple req.	single requests
Example user profile/service	edit_user	actitemsave.do	power_shopper	cart.do
Background activities	BA01_1-3			
Resource profiles	PA01_1	PA03_1	PE01_1	PE03_1
Repeatability	PA01_0-5	PA03_0-5	PE01_0-5	PE03_0-5
Load-dependent behavior	PA02_1-5	PA04_1-5	PE04_1-5	PE02_1-5
Linear regression	PA05_1-5		PE05_1-5	
Linear regression (cross check)	PA06_1-5			
Database size			PE07_1	

Table 4.1: Overview of Experiments on Resource Profiles

For each application system we analyzed services including single client requests and services including multiple client requests (user profiles). We focus in the following considerations on representative examples of one service and one user profile per application system. The user profiles *edit_user* (PASTA) and *power_shopper* (Java Pet Store) were described in sections 4.1.2.1 and 4.1.2.2. The PASTA service *actitemsave.do* updates the list of current project activities (see figure 4.2). The Java Pet Store service *cart.do* adds a product to the shopping cart of the online shop.

Overall, the experiments described above comprise 59 separate load tests. For purposes of clarity, we introduce a notation for experiments and load tests (see table 4.1). The identifier PA01_1 denotes, for instance, the first load test of experiment PA01 (PASTA: Resource profiles and Repeatability). PA01_0 describes the consolidated analysis of all measurements of experiment PA01 (load tests PA01_1-5). The different resources are described and categorized according to the following scheme: *Server type - object - instance - counter* (see section 3.5.5).

In the experiments we determined consumption estimates for the following resources:

- Application server - Network - all - Bytes total

- Application server - Processor - all - Processor time

- Client - Network - all - Bytes total

- Database server - Processor - all - Processor time

- Database server - Disk - SAN - Read/Write blocks

- Web server - Processor - all - Processor time

	Application server			Database server		Web server
	perfmon (local)	perfmon (remote)	Bea JMX (remote)	sar (local)	rstatd (remote)	sar (local)
BA01	41 counters	2 counters	2 counters	all measure-ments	9 counters	all measure-ments
BA02	41 counters	–	–	CPU / Disk	–	CPU / Net / Disk
BA03	2 counters	–	–	CPU / Disk	–	CPU / Net

Table 4.2: Experiments on Background Activities: Configuration of Performance Monitors

The list is adopted from the above considerations on typical resources in client/server environments (see section 3.2.3). Network traffic is measured at the client and the application server, to differentiate between the traffic between client and data center and traffic within the data center. We illustrate the following result descriptions with processor time examples and provide result tables including data from all resources in the appendix.

4.3   Experimental Results

4.3.1   Background Activities

Background activities, triggered for instance by operating systems, system management tools or performance monitors, cause a certain amount of resource consumption, which should not be included in the resource profiles. However, the performance monitors used during the profiling process (see section 3.5.3.2) do not enable a distinct separation of resource consumption caused by services and resource consumption caused by background activities. Hence, we monitored the environment for 1 hour without any service workload ($t = 1\,h, x = 0$) to analyze form and impact of background activities. The test was repeated three times with different performance monitor configurations, to gain an understanding of the resource consumption caused by the monitors. Table 4.2 provides an overview of experiments and settings.

The resource consumption at the application server (Windows 2000) is locally logged by *perfmon*. Additionally, the LoadRunner Controller (see section 3.5.4.2) can retrieve remote measurements from perfmon and can monitor the Bea Weblogic application server via Java Management Extensions (JMX). At the database server the tool *sar* is used.

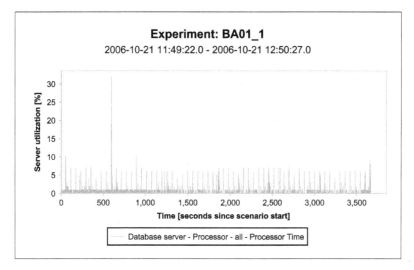

Figure 4.6: Background Processor Utilization at the Database Server
(HP-UX 11.11)

The version of sar shipped with the operating system (HP-UX 11.11) does not provide counters for network activities. However, the LoadRunner Controller can connect to the kernel statistics server (rstatd) and read out the missing information (see Hewlett-Packard, n.d.a). In contrast, the sar version available on the web server (Red Hat Linux) provides all necessary counters. No further local or remote tools are required. The experiments should clarify how these different performance monitoring possibilities affect the background resource consumption.

Figure 4.6 shows the processor utilization at the database server during a measurement interval of one hour with no service workload (Experiment BA01_01). The measured utilization is not constant, but fluctuates between discrete values. We observed a similar behavior at the other servers, each with a different set of discrete measurements:

- **perfmon** (Windows 2000): 0, 0.78125, 1.5625, 2.34375, ...

- **sar** (HP-UX 11.11): 0, 1, 2, 3, ...

- **sar** (Linux RH AS 2.1): 0.25, 0.5, 0.75, 1, ...

We conclude that the performance monitors only record rounded values and that the underlying rounding rules are different at each server. The rounding has a higher rela-

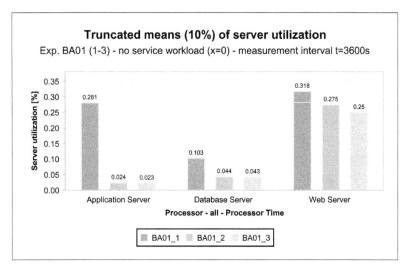

Figure 4.7: Truncated Means (10 %) of Background Processor Utilizations

tive impact on small utilization values. Consumption estimates derived from this may be imprecise and comparisons of consumption or utilization values between different servers may be biased. Additionally, the measurement intervals are very coarsely-grained. The minimum interval length configurable at the local monitors is 1 second. The remote monitors record measurements at intervals of 3 seconds (perfmon, BEA JMX) or 6 seconds (rstatd).

Figure 4.6 also illustrates that even when there is no service workload on the system, sudden load peaks may appear. During a regular profiling process such peaks may distort the resource consumption allocated to the currently active service. In the experiments with no service workload, such outliers determined for the most part the total observed resource consumption. Hence, we base the comparative analysis on the truncated mean (10 %) of the measured utilization values[2] (see figure 4.7).

Overall, the mean processor utilization was in all tests and on all servers very small ($< 0.35 \%$). The remote monitoring of Windows server and Unix server during experiment BA01_01 significantly raised the measured background resource consumption. At the Windows server no difference between the local monitoring of 41 counters (BA01_02)

---

[2]   The lowest 5 % and the highest 5 % of the sample values are discarded.

and of 2 counters (BA01_03) was measurable. Due to the different measurement granu-
larities, the absolute server utilizations are barely comparable. For instance, the lowest
value measured at the Linux server is 0.25, while at the Windows and Unix server most
measurements are (rounded to) 0.0. Accordingly, the calculated mean utilization of the
Linux server is significantly higher (see figure 4.7).

In the appendix, time series graphs depicting the number of read/write blocks at the SAN
(see figure A.1) and of the transferred bytes in the network (see figure A.2) are included.
At the SAN no regular background activity was measurable. However, we also recorded
sudden load peaks which could possibly distort resource profile measurements. At the
application server we observed a constant baseline network traffic of approximately 400
bytes/sec. The remote monitoring caused regular peaks of approximately 6,000 bytes/sec
every three seconds (load test BA01_01).

In the experiments described below, we used the monitoring configuration of BA01_01
load test (see table 4.2). We omitted the remote monitoring of the database server. According to the above considerations, we can expect most influence of background activities
on the processor time at the application server (Windows).

4.3.2 Resource Profiles

The experiments with the example application systems PASTA and Java Pet Store started
with the determination of resource profiles for the services described above (see sections 4.1.2.1 and sections 4.1.2.2). The profiling process is detailed in section 3.5.2. We
specified there that during the load test the number of concurrent service invocations
rises until the first component reaches its bottleneck. The maximum capacities of the
considered application systems were different. PASTA was able to process 20 concurrent
service invocations, while the Java Pet Store could handle 70 concurrent invocations of
services including single requests and even 100 invocations of services including multiple
requests and random think times between 0.5 s and 1.5 s. In the load tests, we raised the
number of concurrent virtual users in steps of one, or ten for Java Pet Store and services
including multiple requests. The analysis objectives were twofold. First, we verified if the
correlation coefficients r support the assumptions of linearly increasing resource consumption. Second, we analyzed for services including multiple client requests the impact of the
user behavior on the resource profiles. Table 4.1 provides an overview of the experiments.
The complete resource profiles, the correlation coefficients and additional information on
the load tests are given in the appendix (see A.3.1). In all four experiments the vast

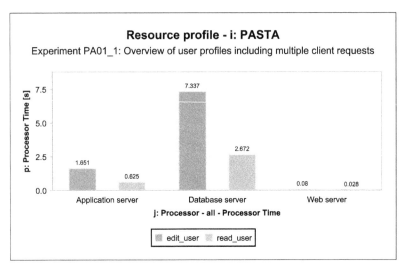

Figure 4.8: Resource Profile: PASTA – Services including multiple Client Requests

majority of correlation coefficients was greater than 0.9. Two types of exceptions could be identified; first, very small processor time values ($< 0.01\,s$) and, second, resource consumption at the SAN (read/write blocks). While the first category can be explained by the lacking precision of the performance monitors and the impact of background activities (see section 4.3.1), the resource consumption at the SAN seems not to be fully in line with the model hypotheses. These exceptions aside, the correlation coefficients support the assumptions on a linear increase of resource consumption.

The impact of the user behavior on resource profiles is illustrated in figure 4.8 (PASTA) and figure 4.9 (Java Pet Store). Most interesting is a comparison between the application systems. The by far more complex Java Pet Store caused only a small fraction of the resource consumption of the custom application system PASTA. Certainly, a direct comparison is not fair. Java Pet Store was developed by specialists to demonstrate Java capabilities and performance. Nevertheless, the example underlines the impact and the resource-saving potential of system and software design. For instance, a user activity in PASTA mostly triggers one or more SQL queries which are directly executed on the database server. Java Pet Store deliberately avoids "expensive" database and disk accesses by using caching mechanisms of the application server. Summing up, the user

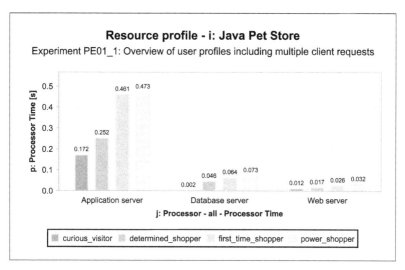

Figure 4.9: Resource Profile: Java Pet Store – Services including multiple Client Requests

behavior influences the range of the resource consumption values, but the overall scale is predetermined by the design of the application system.

4.3.3 Repeatability

The repeatability of the profiling process is a major precondition for the practical applicability of concept and software. Under *repeatability* we understand in this context that the variation of resource profiles determined under equal conditions is minimal. *Equal conditions* comprises the configuration of application systems, services and infrastructure as well as parameter settings during the profiling process (e.g., workload, measurement intervals). We tested the repeatability by means of the example application systems PASTA and Java Pet Store and services including single and multiple requests (see section 4.1.2). Starting points were the load tests and resource profiles described in the previous section. For each combination of application system and service type we conducted four additional load tests under equal conditions. We analyzed the variation of the consumption estimates from the different load tests by the coefficient of variation (cv). This statistical measure is defined as ratio of standard deviation to arithmetic mean. Table 4.1 provides an overview of the experiments.

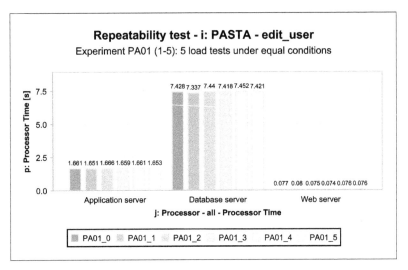

Figure 4.10: Repeatability: PASTA – Services including multiple Client Requests

The processor time results are shown in figures 4.10 and 4.11 (PASTA) and figures 4.12 and figures 4.13 (Java Pet Store). In experiment PE01 one load test failed. For comparison we additionally calculated the mean consumption values from all load tests (labeled as xxxx_0). The result tables including all resources and statistical information on the distributions of the mean consumption values (minimum, maximum, standard deviation, coefficient of variation) are given in the appendix (see section A.3.3).

Overall, for most resources and experiments the variation of mean consumption values is minimal (cv < 5 %). As in the previous section, two kind of exceptions could be identified. First, at the SAN (read/write blocks) the coefficients of variation of the resource consumption range up to 25.8 % (PA01). We explain this by caching effects, which are not reproducible in this kind of load test. However, those effects must be considered if the mean number of read/write blocks determined in a single load test is used as a basis for cost allocation. Second, for very small processor times sporadically higher variations occurred. We refer this to the higher relative impact of background activities and the lacking precision of the performance monitors. For cost allocation, we consider these variations as negligible. Apart from these exceptions, the experiments confirmed the repeatability and the precision of measurement tools and software. In the experiments described below, we went one step further and deliberately changed workload (section 4.3.4), client

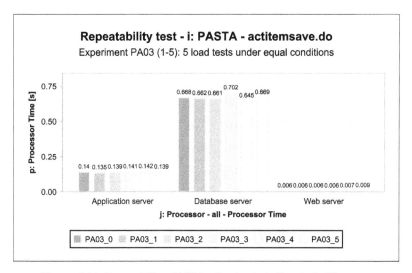

Figure 4.11: Repeatability: PASTA – Services including single Client Requests

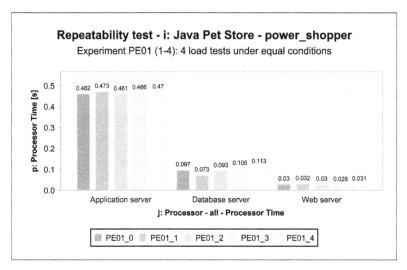

Figure 4.12: Repeatability: Java Pet Store – Services including multiple Client Requests

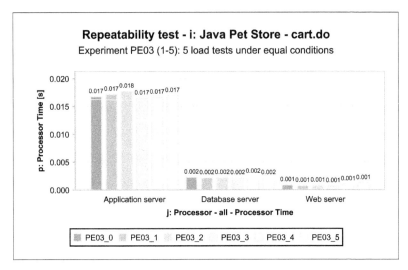

Figure 4.13: Repeatability: Java Pet Store – Services including single Client Requests

think times (section 4.3.5 and 4.3.6) and database size (section 4.3.7). In doing so, we evaluated the robustness of resource profiles and the consistency of explanatory model and experimental results.

4.3.4 Load-dependent Behavior

The concept of resource profiles is based on some fundamental hypotheses on the structure of resource consumption (see section 3.3). In particular, we suppose that the resource consumption p_{ij} is not or is barely dependent on the system workload. The following experiments aim to verify if this precondition is fulfilled in the test environment described above.

Basically, we considered two possible kinds of experiments to identify load-dependent behavior. First, an autocorrelation analysis of linear regression residuals and, second, a comparison of the total resource consumption at different workload levels. We focus in the following on the second test, because it is less sensitive to outliers – short periods with sudden load peaks caused by background activities may already bias residuals. It also enables an estimation of the background resource consumption a_{ij}.

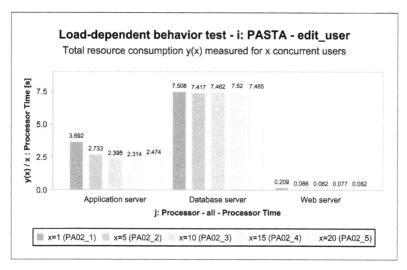

Figure 4.14: Load-dependent Behavior: PASTA – Services including multiple Client Requests

Again, we used the example applications PASTA and Java Pet Store and services including single and multiple client requests. In the PASTA experiments PA02 and PA04 we conducted load tests with 1, 5, 10, 15 and 20 virtual users and in the Java Pet Store experiments PE02 and PE04 load tests with 1, 10, 30, 50 and 70 virtual users. During each load test the number of virtual users x remained constant over 20 repeated measurement intervals. No linear regression was applicable. Instead, the Service Profiler divided the total resource consumption during each measurement interval by the number of virtual users and then calculated mean results. So, we could analyze for PASTA and Java Pet Store and five values x the behavior of the following function:

$$\frac{y_{ij}(x)}{x} = \frac{a_{ij}}{x} + p_{ij} \qquad (4.2)$$

According to the model hypotheses, the value $\frac{y_{ij}(x)}{x}$ should be maximal for $x = 1$: $a_{ij} + p_{ij}$ and then converge for growing x toward p_{ij}. The processor time results are shown in figures 4.14 and 4.15 (PASTA) and figures 4.16 and figures 4.17 (Java Pet Store). The results are compared with the values p_{ij} from the experiments on repeatability (see section 4.3.3).

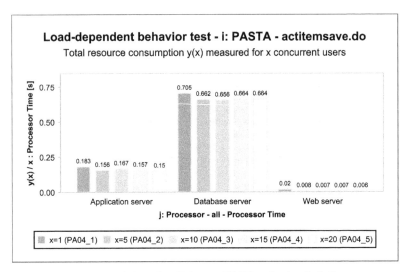

Figure 4.15: Load-dependent Behavior: PASTA – Services including single Client Requests

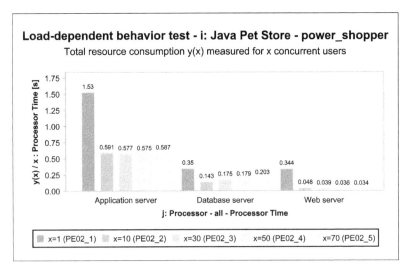

Figure 4.16: Load-dependent Behavior: Java Pet Store – Services including multiple Client Requests

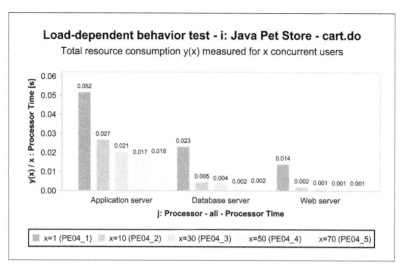

Figure 4.17: Load-dependent Behavior: Java Pet Store – Services including single Client Requests

Concerning processor times, the basic model hypotheses could be validated in all four experiments. However, the impact of background consumption is seemingly different. First, it is far higher for the application server (Windows) than for the database server (Unix) or the web server (Linux). Second, it is higher for services including multiple requests than for services including single requests. The latter aspect confirms the evident dependency of background resource consumption on the length of the measurement interval t. Although load test configuration and data analysis during the experiments on repeatability were completely different (rising load and linear regression vs. constant load and arithmetic means), the convergence of the results is surprisingly exact. We observed significant deviations only for the processor time at the application server and services including multiple client requests (experiment PA01 compared to PA02 and experiment PE01 compared to PE02).

The results for storage and network resources are given in the appendix (see section A.3.4). The number of read/write operations at the SAN show a similar variation as in the repeatability experiments (see section 4.3.3). Regarding load-dependent behavior, no further information could be derived from the results. In contrast, the measured mean network traffic was fully in line with the processor time results. No significant nonlinearities in the resource consumption at different workload levels could be identified.

Experiment	tt=1s	tt=2s	tt=4s	tt=8s	tt=16s
PA05	1h 11min	1h 39min	2h 36min	4h 37min	8h 57min
PE05	failed	1h 23min	2h 40min	5h 15min	10h 23min
PA06	1h 14min	1h 38min	2h 35min	4h 46min	9h 9min

Table 4.3: Average Client Think Times and Load Test Runtimes

These experiments strongly confirm our model hypotheses. However, the results are not necessarily generalizable. So, for instance, neither network nor the storage resources were substantially utilized during the experiments. Furthermore, the infrastructure was at all times exclusively used by a single kind of service. The latter aspect is addressed in chapter 5. There we verify if the assumption of load-independent behavior also holds in scenarios with multiple types of concurrent active services.

4.3.5 Linear Regression

The absolute amount of the background resource consumption $a_j(t)$ grows with the length of the measurement interval t (see section 4.3.4). In services consisting of multiple client requests, the length of the measurement interval is mostly determined by client think times between the requests. With regard to the required accuracy of resource profiles (see section 3.4), it is evident that consumption estimates for services should be independent of background activities and think times. However, this requirement also has major implications for the operating efficiency of the concept. If the resource profiles are independent of the think times, they can be minimized during the profiling load test and thus the whole process significantly accelerated. This property is given in the model describing the total resource consumption. We assume that if the length of the measurement interval t is kept approximately constant for each service i, the time-dependent background resource consumption $a_j(t)$ can be considered as constant term a_{ij}. In the linear function $y_{ij}(x)$ this term then represents the intercept of the regression line.

We tested the independence of resource profiles and think times in experiments with the example applications PASTA and Java Pet Store and services including multiple client requests. The clients waited a random think time between two requests. The average think time length and the random range (here: 50 % to 150 %) are configured in the load test scenario. During each experiment we conducted five load tests and after each load test we doubled the average client think times. In experiment PE05 one load test failed. Table 4.3 provides an overview of average client think times and test runtimes.

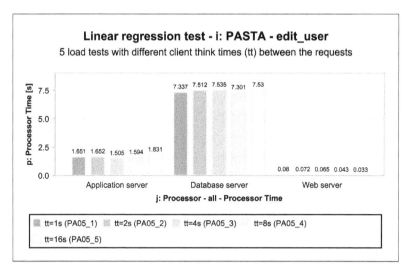

Figure 4.18: Linear Regression: PASTA – Services including multiple Client Requests

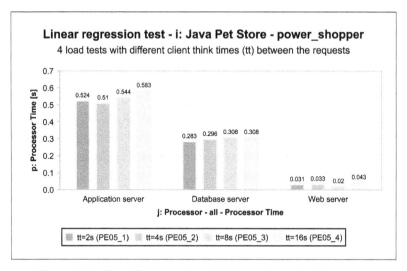

Figure 4.19: Linear Regression: Java Pet Store – Services including multiple Client Requests

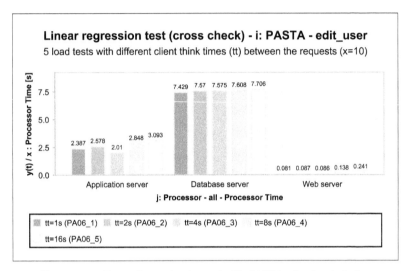

Figure 4.20: Linear Regression (cross check): PASTA – Services including multiple Client Requests

The processor time results are shown in figure 4.18 (PASTA) and figure 4.19 (Java Pet Store). Despite the very different lengths of measurement intervals, the determined consumption estimates show only small variations. Tables including data from storage and network resources are given in the appendix (see section A.3.5). As in the previous experiments, the fluctuating number of read/write blocks at the SAN complicates the identification of clear trends. The resource consumption at the network interfaces is in line with the processor time results.

Both experiments confirmed the model assumptions and the robustness of resource profiles against varying think times. For a cross check of these results, we conducted a supplemental experiment with PASTA.

4.3.6 Linear Regression (cross check)

The experiments in the previous section demonstrated that resource profiles are barely influenced by client think times. According to the model hypotheses, this is achieved by the linear regression. To verify this assumption, we performed a supplemental experiment with PASTA (PA06). Again, we conducted five load tests and after each load test doubled the average client think times (see table 4.3). In the previous experiments the number of active virtual users x successively rose during each load test, so that a linear regression was applicable. In contrast, in this experiment the number of virtual users remained constant ($x = 10$) during each load test and over all five load tests. The measurements were processed by the Service Profiler as in the experiments on load-dependent behavior (see section 4.3.4). We could therefore analyze for constant x and five values t the behavior of the following function:

$$\frac{y_{ij}(t)}{x} = \frac{a_{ij}(t)}{x} + p_{ij} \tag{4.3}$$

According to the model hypotheses, the value $\frac{y_{ij}(t)}{x}$ should be minimal if the length of the measurement interval, determined by the average think time length tt, is minimal. The value should grow with rising average think times. Overall, $\frac{y_{ij}(t)}{x}$ should be higher than the values determined for p_{ij} during the experiments PA01 (see figure 4.10) and PA05 (see figure 4.18).

The processor time results are shown in figure 4.20. With the exception of PA06_3 (processor time, application server), the results confirm the above assumptions. However, although the impact of background activities at the database server (Unix) and the web server (Linux) is clearly measurable, the absolute amount is negligible. A results table with data from network and storage resources is provided in the appendix (see section A.3.6). As in the previous experiments, the network resource consumption confirmed the processor time results. The number of read/write blocks at the SAN again showed high variations. No information on the appropriateness of the linear regression concept can be derived from this.

4.3.7 Database Size

Resource profiles, determined according to the concept described above, are associated with a certain infrastructure configuration. While changes to hardware or software configurations typical require a manual intervention, content and size of databases change dynamically during regular operations. Obviously, the resource consumption of a service including database requests may depend to a a certain degree on the number of entries in the queried tables. If the database size i.e. the number of entries changes, the accuracy of the consumption estimates may be affected. The actual impact depends strongly on database and query design. Overall, we recommend the use of realistic database sizes

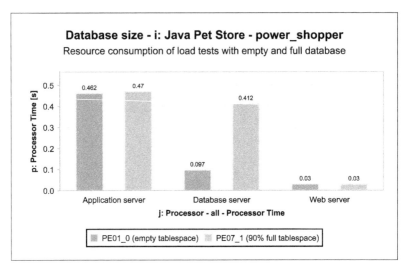

Figure 4.21: Database Size: Java Pet Store – Services including multiple Client Requests

during the profiling process, and the estimation (and if required testing) of the impact of potential changes.

In the PASTA case the responsible persons at the BMW Group expect no significant changes in the database size. In contrast, application systems such as the Java Pet Store store information on business transactions (e.g., order details) and in a real world scenario a constant database growth would be expected. The resource profiles, determined during the experiments on repeatability (see section 4.3.3), are based on the default database content as provided by Sun Microsystems. To assess the impact of the database size on the resource profiles, we conducted a further experiment (PE07). For this, we added more than 400,000 order entries to the database, so that the available tablespace (200 MB) was about 90 % utilized. We then conducted a new load test and determined mean consumption values.

In figure 4.21 the processor time results of experiment PE07 are compared with the results of experiment PE01. A significant growth in the processor time at the database server can be observed. The complete resource profile, including all user profiles, is given in the appendix (see section A.3.7). Although this result is not generalizable, it supports the idea of considering an interval rather than exact consumption estimates for cost allocation. Those effects could thus be, at least partially, anticipated. Nevertheless, it is still required that software architects and load test engineers are aware of the consequences of changes at the application system or the infrastructure on resource consumption and performance.

4.4 Summary

The aims and purposes of the experiments were threefold. First, we tried to verify if the model describing the total resource consumption holds in the example environment. Second, we tested the precision of the measurement and analysis tools introduced in section 3.5. Third, we analyzed the effects of parameter changes during the profiling process and compared the experimental results with the model predictions. The results can be summarized as follows:

1. The model hypotheses could be confirmed for the computing resources (processor time) and the communication resources (transferred bytes). At the storage resource (read/write blocks) we observed high variations of the consumption values. Mean consumption values determined during a single load test can be considered only as very rough estimates for the expected resource consumption during regular operations.

2. Although the performance monitors record only coarsely-grained consumption data, we achieved through multiple measurements very precise and repeatable results.

3. We analyzed the robustness and consistency of the results by changing client think times and workload during the profiling process. The experimental results were in line with the explanatory model. No load-dependent behavior could be observed.

4. In particular we could demonstrate that the resource profiles are independent of the client think times during the profiling process. Thus, the think times could be minimized during the load tests. This accelerated the whole process significantly. In the Java Pet Store example a load test with four different user profiles required less than 45 minutes (see section 4.3.2).

5. Resource profiles are always tied to a certain infrastructure configuration. Through experiments with an empty and a full database, we showed how the mean resource

consumption could change during regular operations. Software architects and load test engineers determining resource profiles must be aware of those effects.

Based on these experiences, we recommend considering an interval rather than exact consumption estimates for cost allocation. Uncertainties about the exact user behavior and variations as observed for the storage resource and due to changing database sizes could thus be anticipated. In the experiments we demonstrated how these factors can affect the mean resource consumption values. However, at least in the examples, they had no significant influence on the overall dimension of the resource consumption. Instead, it was predefined by the software design of the application system.

Chapter 5

Experiments: Analytical Models

5.1 Motivation

In the previous chapters we presented a method, a software toolkit and experimental results on the determination of resource profiles for customer-oriented services. We will now analyze whether the determined consumption estimates are appropriate input parameters for analytical performance models. The basic approach is to set up a performance model according to the respective guidelines in the literature and calculate model predictions of system performance in different workload scenarios. We then validate model and input parameters by comparing the results, i.e., processor utilizations, response times, throughput with measurements from load tests. The motivation therefore stems from the overall requirements on resource profiles (see section 3.4):

1. **Accuracy** The resource profiles should be unbiased even if the workload at the respective resources varies. We have already addressed this central requirement in the experiments presented in section 4.3.4. However, during those load tests the resources were at all times exclusively used by a single service. Furthermore, the profiling workload consisting of x concurrent services invocations is not comparable to the workload during regular operations. In contrast, in load tests for the validation of performance models realistic scenarios with multiple concurrently active services and varying workload can be simulated. We claim that if performance models parameterized with consumption estimates from the resource profiles accurately predict system performance (utilization, response time, throughput) during those load tests, the accuracy of the resource profiles is also sufficient for cost allocation.

2. **Capacity Planning** In contrast to arbitrarily chosen cost allocation keys, the resource profiles should bridge the gap between business forecasts and IT resource
   requirements. The major advantage of an analytical performance model is that
   once has it has been validated it can be readily used for capacity planning. It
   enables capacity planners to conduct "what-if" analyses and thus anticipate the
   effects of changes in the workload composition, hardware configuration or system
   architecture.

In the following sections we first provide a general overview of IT Capacity Planning
methods (section 5.2). We then introduce basic concepts of Queueing Network Theory
(section 5.3) and describe the software tools developed to solve and validate respective
performance models (sections 5.4). To evaluate the approach we continued the experiments presented in chapter 4 (see section 5.5 and 5.6). We conclude this chapter with a
comparison to related experimental results (section 5.7) and a summary of the findings
(section 5.8).

5.2   IT Capacity Planning Methods

Capacity Management is a central task of IT Service Management. It is responsible
to ensure that the capacity of the IT infrastructure matches the evolving demands of
the business in a cost-effective and timely manner (see Office of Government Commerce,
2001, ch. 6.1). The term "cost-effective" implies that capacity managers must balance
two objectives. On the one hand, they must optimize resource utilization and avoid over-
investments. On the other hand, they must ensure that the IT infrastructure is able to
deliver agreed Service Level Targets. System breakdowns or poor performance of business-
critical applications can cause severe economic damage to a company.

Capacity Planning is an activity within Capacity Management (see Office of Government
Commerce, 2001, ch. 6.3). Capacity planners develop and maintain forecasts of system
performance and future resource requirements. Input factors are more or less precise information on the expected workload, hardware performance and system architectures. We
distinguish *experience-based*, *model-based* and *load test-based* approaches to IT Capacity
Planning (see figure 5.1).

Rules-of-thumb estimates are typically based on experiences of system experts and ven-
dor guidelines. They require little effort and are usually the quickest and cheapest way

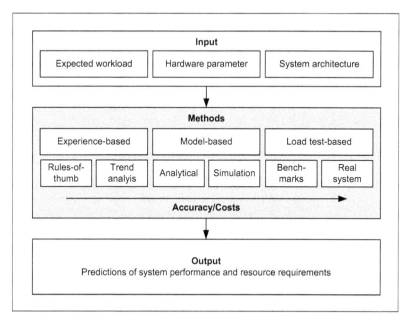

Figure 5.1: Overview of IT Capacity Planning Methods (adapted from Müller-Clostermann, 2001, p. I-78; Scheeg, 2005, p. 155)

to a rough, but possibly biased, capacity planning. In contrast, *trend analysis* derives forecasts from historical data on workload and system performance. It requires long-term measurements and thus causes more effort than the rules-of-thumb. Approaches based on linear extrapolation cannot anticipate changes in the workload composition or predict non-linear behavior of systems close to saturation points. So, particularly for highly-utilized systems, such forecasts are questionable (Müller-Clostermann, 2001, p. I-79).

Model-based approaches[1] use abstractions of real systems (models) to study their expected behavior under different conditions. The level of abstraction depends on the analysis purpose. Generally, models should not be made more complex than necessary. Two major types of model can be distinguished. *Simulation* models are based on computer programs that emulate different dynamic aspects as well as the static structure of IT systems (see MacDougall, 1987, for an overview of simulation techniques). *Analytical* models are

---

[1]   The considerations on model-based approaches are mainly based on Menascé et al. (2004, pp. 36-38).

composed of a set of formulas and/or computational algorithms that provide desired performance measures as a function of the set of input workload parameters. Compared to simulation models, analytical models are less expensive to construct and tend to be computationally more efficient. Furthermore, due to their higher level of abstraction it is easier to obtain the necessary input parameters. Simulation models, in contrast, can be made as detailed as needed, thus delivering more accurate results. They are also less restrictive, regarding for instance distributions of arrival rates or prioritization strategies, and can emulate system behavior that cannot be captured (or only approximated) in analytical models. Both kind of models, however, require a validation, if possible against real systems, to verify that the chosen abstraction is an appropriate representation of reality. Once validated, capacity planners can use the model to conduct "what-if" analyses. So, they can study how changes in the workload composition, hardware configuration or system architecture affect the expected system behavior. Due to their flexibility and efficiency, analytical models are generally preferable for capacity planning purposes (Menascé et al., 2004, p. 38). Simulation models, in contrast, are particularly useful for detailed analyses of important details (Müller-Clostermann, 2001, p. I-85).

Nevertheless, the highest planning accuracy can be achieved in *load tests* with the *real system*. If the real application system is not available, custom or standardized *benchmarks* (e.g., TPC-App: TPPC, n.d.a or SAPS: SAP, n.d.b) can be used to simulate comparable workloads and to assess the overall capacity of the infrastructure. Load test tools typically provide elaborate means to simulate real user behavior (see section 3.5.1). Thus, they enable detailed analyses of system behavior in different workload scenarios. In contrast, "what-if" changes to hardware parameters or system architectures usually require time-consuming and costly system reconfigurations. Against this background, load test-based methods are typically applied for the basic validation of performance models or rules-of-thumb estimates and for the final approval of a system configuration prior to the roll-out of a new software release (Office of Government Commerce, 2002a, ch. 5.3.4).

Despite the numerous advantages of model-based approaches (e.g., flexibility, efficiency, costs), they are rarely used in practice. A major reason for this is that necessary input parameters such as service demands are mostly not readily available. Consumption estimates, as determined for resource profiles, could fill this gap. In the following, we evaluate their appropriateness for Capacity Planning by means of analytical Queueing Network Models. We use load tests to validate respective models (see chapter 5). Alternative analytical modeling approaches are based for instance on Stochastic Petri Nets

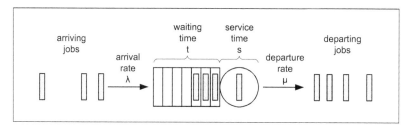

Figure 5.2: Elementary Queueing System with a single Service Station

(see Marsan et al., 1984) or on extensions of Queueing Network Theory (see Rolia and Sevcik, 1995; Woodside et al., 1995). We chose standard Queueing Network Models over those approaches because a broad range of modeling guidelines (see for instance Menascé et al., 2004) and comparable experimental results are available (see section 5.7).

5.3 Queueing Network Theory

Queueing Network Theory (QN Theory) is a well-studied methodology for the mathematical analysis of systems with waiting lines and service stations. It was first introduced by Erlang (1909) for the study of traffic in telephone networks. Today, QN Theory is used in various domains, ranging from manufacturing system planning via transportation and logistics to telecommunication and computer performance modeling (see Bolch et al., 2006, pp .703-806, for several case-studies on real-world applications).

The study objects of QN Theory are queueing systems. Figure 5.2 shows an example of an elementary queueing system consisting of a service station and a waiting room. Jobs (customers) arrive at the back of the queue with an arrival rate λ and are served at the front of the queue in an average time s. Arrival rate as well as service time may be deterministic or stochastic variables. If the service station is occupied, jobs have to line up. QN Theory provides mathematical means to analyze such and related processes. Thus, central performance measures such as mean utilization, waiting time, throughput or queue lengths can be determined. Several kinds of elementary queueing systems (see section 5.3.1) and workloads (see section 5.3.2) as well as networks of interconnected queueing systems (see section 5.3.3) are supported. Approximate and exact analysis techniques exist (see section 5.3.4).

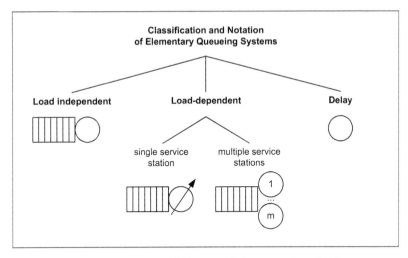

Figure 5.3: Classification and Notation of Elementary Queueing Systems

5.3.1 Elementary Queueing Systems

Three general categories of elementary queueing systems can be distinguished: Load independent, load-dependent and delay systems (Menascé et al., 2004, p. 46). Figure 5.3 provides an overview of this classification and the corresponding graphical notations. The three categories can be described as follows:

- **Load independent**: The service rate is not dependent on the current workload, i.e., the number of jobs in the queue.

- **Load-dependent** The service rate is a function of the number of jobs in the queue. Typical examples are queueing systems with multiple service stations (e.g., models of multi-processor machines). The effective service rate increases as the number of current jobs grows from 1 to m (number of service stations). Load-dependent queueing systems with single service stations are marked with an arrow (see figure 5.3). In the context of computer systems, various forms of load-dependent behavior exist (see section 3.3).

- **Delay** Each job that arrives at a delay system is served immediately. A delay system has an (assumed) infinite capacity and thus requires (and has) no waiting line. In computer performance models, delay systems are typically used to represent human users, resources dedicated to certain jobs or third party components.

Beyond this rough classification, the so-called Kendall notation (see Kendall, 1953) is widely used to describe elementary queueing systems. Its basic form takes into account stochastic characteristics of the arrival process and of the service times, the number of parallel service stations and the queueing discipline:

$$arrival\ process\ |\ service\ time\ |\ no.\ of\ service\ stations\ -\ queueing\ discipline$$

The basic Kendall notation is occasionally extended by the number of places in the queue or the total number of jobs (both assumed as infinite by default). The placeholders *arrival process* and *service time* may take very different values. In the context of computer performance models, the following symbols and distributions are mostly used:

- **M**: Exponential distribution (memoryless property)

- **G**: General distribution

- **GI**: General distribution with independent interarrival rates.

- **D**: Deterministic distribution (i.e., arrival rate and/or service time is constant)

The *queueing discipline* determines which job is selected next from the queue, when a service station becomes available. Commonly used queueing strategies are:

- **FCFS** (First-Come-First-Served): The jobs are served in the order of their arrival. If no queueing discipline is given, FCFS is considered default.

- **LCFS** (Last-Come-First-Served): The job that arrived last is served next.

- **LCFS PR** (Last-Come-First-Served Preemptive Resume): A newly arriving job is served immediately. The service of the current job is therefore interrupted and the job is queued. The waiting line is served according to LCFS.

- **RR** (Round Robin): Each job is served for a fixed period of time (timeslice). If a job could not be finished during that time, it has to queue for one of the subsequent timeslices. The waiting line is served according to FCFS. The process is repeated until the job is completed.

- **PS** (Processor Sharing): This queueing discipline corresponds to RR with infinitesimal small timeslices.

- **IS** (Infinite Server): There is an ample number of service stations. IS queues correspond to the delay queues described above.

The expression M|M|1 describes for example a single server queueing system with exponentially distributed interarrival rates and service times. The queueing discipline is FCFS (default). The exponential distribution is of paramount importance in QN Theory because it has some pleasant mathematical properties and because it is an appropriate mathematical representation of many real-world processes. The exponential distribution is the only continuous distribution with the memoryless property. This implies for the arrival process that if the time between two consecutive arrivals is exponentially distributed with parameter λ, then the distribution of the residual time until the next arrival is also exponential with the same parameter λ. For service times it implies that the expected time remaining to complete a job is independent of the service already provided (see Menascé et al., 2004, p. 294, for further characteristics of the exponential distribution). The above M|M|1 example specifies the simplest kind of an elementary queueing system. Examples of mathematically more difficult, but well-studied, elementary queueing systems include the M|G|1, the G|M|m or the G|G|1 queueing system (see Kleinrock, 1975, chapters 3,5,6 and 8).

5.3.2 Workload Parameter

The queueing systems introduced in the previous section require two kinds of workload input parameter: *Service demand* and *workload intensity* (Menascé et al., 2004, p. 109). The service demand specifies the total average amount of time an elementary queueing system requires to serve a certain class of jobs. The workload intensity provides measures of the load placed on the system. At load-dependent queueing systems the service demand depends on the workload intensity. With regard to computer performance models, system workload and workload intensity parameters can be further classified into *interactive*[2], *transaction* and *batch* workload (see Menascé et al., 2004, p. 54).

- **Interactive workload** A fixed number of users (terminals, clients) interact with the system in a request/reply fashion. The time which has elapsed since a reply to

---

[2]   In earlier works mostly referred to as *terminal workload* (see for instance Allen, 1990, p. 378).

a request has been received before the next request (job) is submitted by the same user is defined as *think time*. The workload intensity is specified by the number of users and their think times.

- **Transaction workload** Jobs from outside arrive at the system and leave the system after their service is completed. In contrast to interactive workload, the job arrivals are independent of the internal system state (e.g., queue length). The workload intensity is specified by the arrival rate.

- **Batch workload** The system has to serve a fixed number of batch jobs. The workload intensity is defined by that number of jobs.

QN Theory furthermore supports workloads consisting of *single* or *multiple job classes*. For computer performance models a differentiation of job classes may be reasonable in the following situations (Menascé et al., 2004, p. 41):

- **Heterogeneous service demands** The jobs that form the workload can be clustered into groups that exhibit significantly different average service demands.

- **Different types of workload** The jobs are different in nature (e.g., batch and interactive jobs).

- **Different service level objectives** For jobs with different service level objectives, a differentiated analysis, for instance of response times, may be necessary.

The analytical determination of the desired performance measures requires that the workload and the queueing system are completely characterized. In the context of computer performance modeling, not all input parameters are readily available. The static configuration of queueing systems can mostly be derived from the system architecture and from appropriate modeling guidelines (see section 5.5.2 for an overview of literature). Workload intensity parameters can be estimated by means of the expected number/behavior of users (see Menascé and Almeida, 2000, pp. 41-64) or by the analysis of data from similar systems. Service demands, however, should be determined from measurements on real systems. This can be costly and time consuming or even impossible, if the system is not (yet) available[3].

---

[3] For an overview of parameterization techniques for models of existing, evolving and proposed systems, we refer the interested reader to Lazowska (1984, pp. 273 et seqq.).

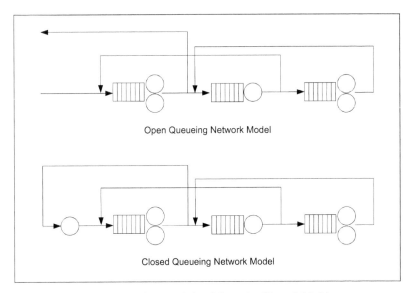

Figure 5.4: Open and closed Queueing Network Models

5.3.3 Queueing Network Models

QN Theory provides analysis techniques for elementary queueing systems (see section 5.3.1) as well as for networks of interconnected queueing systems. Such Queueing Network Models (QN Models) are typically more appropriate for modeling real-world systems with multiple resources rather than single queueing systems. In a queueing network the job input stream of one queueing system can be formed by the superposition of the output streams of one or more other systems. Apart from this relationship, the individual systems are independent of one another (Haverkort, 1998, p. 200). According to the workload characteristics (see section 5.3.2), queueing networks can be classified into open, closed or mixed networks[4].

A queueing network is called *open* when jobs can enter or leave the network. The total number of jobs is assumed to be infinite. The workload intensity is specified by a job arrival rate. In equilibrium, the flow into the network (i.e., the arrival rate) is equal to the flow out of the network (i.e., the throughput). Thus, throughput is an input parameter.

---

[4]   The considerations on open, closed and mixed queueing networks are mainly based on Menascé et al. (2004, pp. 42-45).

Transaction workload (see section 5.3.2) is an example of workload requiring an open QN Model.

A queueing network is referred to as *closed* if the number of jobs in the network remains constant, either because jobs cannot enter or leave the network or, whenever a job leaves, a new one enters. The total number of jobs is known and determines as model input parameter the workload intensity. In contrast, the throughput of the network is an output parameter of the model. Interactive or batch workloads (see section 5.3.2) are examples of workload requiring a closed QN Model.

Mixed queueing networks represent workloads consisting of open and closed job classes. Such models are required, for instance, when the real-world system executes batch jobs and online transactions at the same time.

Figure 5.4 shows an example of an open and a closed QN Model. In the open model the jobs arrive from outside and leave the network after completion. In the closed model, the jobs circulate indefinitely among the queueing systems. So, for instance, the request/reply interaction between human users (represented by the delay systems in figure 5.4) and IT resources could be modeled.

5.3.4 Analysis Techniques

IT systems, as considered in the present context, consist of multiple resources (e.g., servers, processors, disks). We therefore require queueing networks rather than single queueing systems for creating adequate performance models. Unfortunately, very little can be done, analytically, with general queueing networks (Allen, 1990, p. 378). Numerical analysis techniques are only applicable to small numbers of jobs and queueing systems, otherwise the number of equations becomes unreasonably large (see Bolch et al., 2006, pp. 332-335). However, if all queueing systems in the network fulfill certain assumptions concerning the distribution of interarrival rates and service times and the queueing discipline, each single queueing system can be examined on its own, in isolation from the rest of the network. Networks fulfilling these conditions are referred to as *separable* or *product-form* networks. Efficient analysis techniques exist for product-form networks. Jackson (1957, 1963) and Gordon and Newell (1967) found first product-form solutions for open and closed queueing networks with exponentially distributed interarrival and service times and FCFS as queueing discipline. Baskett, Chandy, Muntz, and Palacios (1975) extended these results to open, closed and mixed queueing networks with multiple job classes and queueing systems belonging to one of the following categories (see Bolch et al., 2006, p. 340 and p. 358):

- **M|M|m – FCFS** : The service rates for different job classes must be equal. Examples of such queueing systems are disks or other I/O devices.

- **M|G|1 – PS** : Processors can very often be modeled as such a queueing system.

- **M|G|∞ – IS** : User think times can be modeled as such delay systems.

- **M|M|m – LCFS PR** : There is no practical example of an application in computer system models.

These networks are referred to as *BCMP* networks (after the four authors).

Product-form solutions can be expressed very easily as formulas. For closed queueing networks, however, the determination of the desired performance measures requires the computation of state probabilities and of a normalization constant (Gordon and Newell, 1967). Due to the large number of states the solution causes a high computational effort, even for moderately sized networks. The breakthrough came with the development of the *Mean Value Analysis* (MVA) algorithm by Reiser and Lavenberg (1980) and Reiser (1981). The MVA is an iterative analysis technique for closed product-form networks. It enables an efficient determination of mean values for central performance measures such as queue lengths, response times, throughputs and utilizations. As the name implies, the MVA calculates only mean values and not the associated distributions. It is therefore not helpful for questions such as "probability of more than three jobs in queue xy?". However, for most performance models, mean values are sufficient.

A drawback of the MVA and other exact solution algorithms for closed networks is that memory and storage requirements grow exponentially with the number of classes. MVA-based approximation techniques, based on the MVA, overcome this problem and yet give very accurate results (Bolch et al., 2006, p. 421). An often used approximation technique was suggested by Bard (1979) and Schweitzer (1979) for queueing systems with single service stations. The *Self-Correcting Approximation Technique* (SCAT) extended the Bard-Schweitzer approximation to queueing systems with multiple service stations and improved its accuracy (see Neuse and Chandy, 1981). An alternative to MVA-based approximation techniques is the *Summation* Method (SUM). It is easier to implement and to understand, but less accurate than SCAT (Bolch et al., 2006, p. 460). Bounds analysis techniques, such as *Asymptotic Bounds Analysis* (ABA) or *Balanced Job Bound Analysis* (BJB), provide only upper and lower bounds for the performance measures. Such an approximation might be sufficient for bottleneck analysis or to obtain a rough prediction of system performance already during the design phase. ABA and BJB are applicable to open and closed queueing networks. Generally, exact analysis techniques for open queueing networks do not suffer from the state space explosion problem of closed networks. Thus, approximations are usually not required. For mixed networks Bolch et al. (1992) proposed the *closing method*. The basic idea is to extend the network by a queueing system that represents the external world of the open classes so that the network can be analyzed with the same exact and approximate techniques as closed networks (see also Bolch et al., 2006, pp. 507-512).

For the mathematical analysis of non-product-form queueing networks, three basic approaches exist (Bolch and Riedel, 1997, p. 171):

1. **Approximation by a product-form network** The model can then be analyzed with one of the techniques introduced above.

2. **Numerical Analysis** Due to high computing and memory requirements, this approach is only applicable for very small networks.

3. **Approximation technique for non-product form networks** Depending on which product-form condition is not satisfied, different approximation techniques exist.

Several approximation techniques for non-product-form networks exist. The most important strategy is *Decomposition* (Bolch and Riedel, 1997, p. 172). The queueing network is first decomposed into several sub-networks, which are separately analyzed. The results are then combined to a result for the complete model. This approach leads to exact solutions for product-form networks and approximate solutions for non-product-form networks. A multitude of decomposition approaches for open and closed networks are available (see for instance Bolch and Riedel, 1997, pp. 172-211). Furthermore, several extensions to the MVA, SCAT and Summation methods exists for analyzing closed queueing networks including non-product-form queueing systems (e.g., due to non-exponentially distributed service times or asymmetric service stations). Closed queueing networks, however, are quite robust, in particular toward variations of the service time distributions. *Robustness* in this context means that a major change in system parameters generates

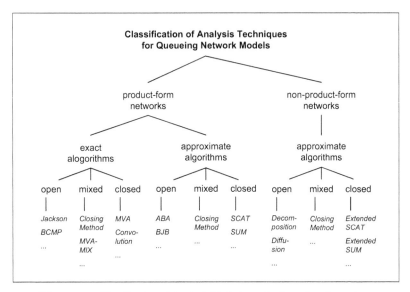

Figure 5.5: Classification of Analysis Techniques for Queueing Network Models (adapted from Bolch et al., 2006, p. 370 and p. 462)

only minor changes in the calculated performance measures (Bolch et al., 2006, p. 488). Thus, they can often be very good approximated by product-form networks (approach 1). Open networks in contrast do not have that robustness property and it is recommended to use an approximation technique for non-product-form networks (approach 3) instead (see Bolch et al., 2006, p. 489).

Figure 5.5 provides an overview of analysis techniques for QN Models. Further details on the algorithms can be found in various textbooks on QN Theory. In particular, we refer the interested reader to Bolch et al. (2006); Gross and Harris (1998); Tjims (1995) (general aspects of QN Theory and comprehensive sets of algorithms), Kleinrock (1976); Lazowska (1984); Menascé et al. (2004) (special focus on computer system applications) and Bolch and Riedel (1997) (German textbook including major algorithms).

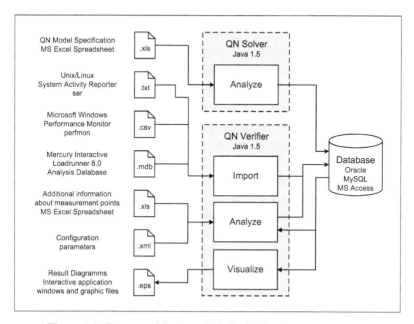

Figure 5.6: Overview of Software Tools for QN Analysis and Validation

5.4 Software Support

5.4.1 Software Overview

We could not identify appropriate off-the-shelf tools that enable an integrated analysis and validation of Queueing Network Models. We therefore propose a software toolkit which combines a commercial load generator and standard performance monitors with two custom software tools, the *QN Solver* and the *QN Verifier* (see figure 5.6).

QN Solver The QN Solver implements several algorithms for the analysis of open and closed QN Models. It consists of a single software component (*Analyze*). Model and workload parameters are specified in a Microsoft Excel spreadsheet. The Analyze component reads out the input parameters, applies the selected algorithm and writes the results (e.g., response time, throughput, utilization) to a central database. These values can then be compared to measurements obtained during load tests with the real system. The QN Solver is introduced in section 5.4.2.

QN Verifier The QN Verifier processes measurement data from load tests for the validation of analytical performance models. It consists of three components: *Import*, *Analyze* and *Visualize*. Analogous to the determination of resource profiles, we use Mercury LoadRunner as load generator (see section 3.5.4) and standard operating system tools as performance monitors (see section 3.5.3.2). We could therefore directly reuse the Import and the Visualize component from the Service Profiler (see section 3.5.3.3). The Analysis component and the load test process are detailed in section 5.4.3.

The Service Profiler, the QN Solver and the QN Verifier operate on the same data model. This allows for a direct transfer of data from resource profiles into QN Models and for an automated analysis of the model accuracy. The interplay of the software tools is further described in section 5.4.4.

5.4.2 Analysis of Queueing Network Models

The QN Solver is implemented for the mathematical analysis of QN Models. It calculates, on the basis of a queueing network specification and given workload parameters, the following performance measures: Utilization, throughput, response time and queue length. We opted for the development of a custom software component because we aimed to achieve a seamless integration with the Service Profiler and the QN Verifier. Alternatively, we could have used an existing tool such as TeamQuest Model (commercial, see TeamQuest, n.d.) or Java Modelling Tools (academic/open-source, see Bertoli et al., 2006; SourceForge, n.d.)[5].

The input parameters for the QN Solver originate from different sources: The QN Model is specified manually. The service demands are taken from resource profiles. The workload intensity (i.e., the arrival rates respectively the number of users and their think times, see section 5.3.2) is also specified manually. However, if the results are validated against a load test, the modeled workload intensity must be in line with the load test configuration. The QN Solver reads out all input parameters from a Microsoft Excel spreadsheet (see figure 5.6). We chose this data format because, on the one hand, Java can interact with spreadsheets as if they were databases. Especially, the support for SQL statements enables a convenient read/write access to the parameters. On the other hand, Microsoft Excel provides an appropriate user interface for the manual entry of parameter values.

---

[5]   Hlynka (n.d.) provides a comprehensive list of tools for QN Analysis.

The QN Solver supports open and closed product-form networks, workloads consisting of single or multiple job classes, and queueing systems with one or more service stations. The following algorithms are used (references to the textbooks that served as the basis for the implementation are given in brackets):

- Open QN: Exact formulas based on Jackson (1957, 1963) (see Menascé et al., 2004, p. 400)

- Closed QN: Mean Value Analysis (MVA) – exact algorithm based on Reiser (1981); Reiser and Lavenberg (1980) (Menascé et al., 2004, p. 389)

- Closed QN: Mean Value Analysis (MVA) – approximation based on Bard (1979); Schweitzer (1979) (Menascé et al., 2004, p. 395)

- Closed QN: Self-Correcting Approximation Technique (SCAT) – approximation based on Neuse and Chandy (1981) (Bolch and Riedel, 1997, p. 152-153)

Due to the robustness property (see section 5.3.4), closed non-product-form networks can mostly be approximated by product-form networks and analyzed with one of the techniques listed above (see section 5.3.4, approach 1). Open non-product-form networks are not supported by the QN Solver. The exact MVA algorithm for closed networks, however, suffers from state space explosion problems and is not applicable to networks with multiple job classes. The QN Solver implements two different approximation techniques for such networks, so the user can cross-check the results.

The algorithm that should be applied to the input parameters is determined in the spreadsheet. The results are then written to a central database (see figure 5.6). By means of the QN Verifier, they can be visualized and compared to measurements obtained during load tests with the real system.

5.4.3   Validation of Queueing Network Models

The predictive accuracy of the analytical performance models is validated in load tests with real systems. As for the determination of resource profiles, we use Mercury Load-Runner for the emulation of user behavior (see section 3.5.4) and operating system performance monitors to record the resource consumption at the components involved (see section 3.5.3.2). A custom software tool, the QN Verifier, then analyzes the measurement data and prepares it for comparison with the analytical results. The software architecture of the QN Verifier is the same as for the Service Profiler (see figures 5.6 and 3.6). The Import component parses the different log files and consolidates the measurements in the database. The Analyze component then processes the data according to the parameter settings specified in the configuration files. The Visualize component finally displays the results in interactive application windows or writes them to graphic files. The Import and the Visualize component could be directly reused from the Service Profiler (see section 3.5.3 for further descriptions).

The load tests for the determination of resource profiles are characterized by synchronous service invocations of a continuously increasing number of virtual users (Vusers). The infrastructure is at all times exclusively used by a single service (see section 3.5.2). In contrast, in load tests for the validation of QN Models, we put the Vusers in endless loops, insert random think times and omit all rendezvous points in the script. The infrastructure is therefore used by a constant number of Vusers with unsynchronized service invocations. The number of users and the mean think times are configured in the load test scenario (see section 3.5.4.2). These values equal the workload intensity parameters in the analytical model (see section 5.4.2). During a load test, the workload intensity can be varied by changing the number of concurrently active Vusers.

We illustrate the approach with an example. Figure 5.7 shows a time series chart of a 90-minute load test. The horizontal line in the lower diagram indicates the number of concurrent active Vusers (lower y-axis). In the upper diagram, measurements of the performance monitors are displayed (here: processor utilization of an application server). The load test starts with ten Vusers in an endless loop. Every five minutes, ten more users are added until the load test stops after 90 minutes and with 180 concurrently active Vusers. The upper diagram shows how the utilization of the application server evolves with the increasing workload.

The Import component transfers the log files of the performance monitors and of the load generator into the database. The Analyze component then conducts the following steps[6]:

1. Addition of context information

2. Normalization of measurements

3. **Determination of measurements intervals** An entry in the LoadRunner transaction log file contains, besides the transaction name and a timestamp, a unique

---

[6]   Steps 1 and 2 were taken over without any modifications from the determination of resource profiles (see section 3.5.5 for a description).

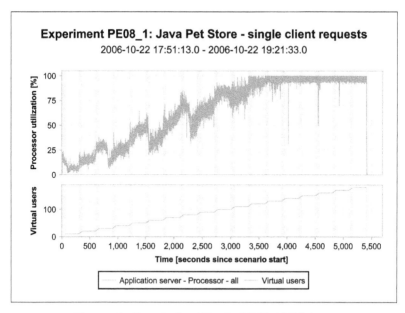

Figure 5.7: Example: Load Test for QN Model Validation

identifier of the Vuser that executed the transaction. The Analyze component processes this data and derives measurement intervals with constant workload from it. As the start or stop of virtual users may lead to a non-steady transient behavior in the system, the Analyze component can exclude a configurable time period after a change in the workload from the further analysis. In the example of figure 5.7, the white areas indicate the measurement intervals and the gray areas represent the time periods excluded from the analysis (here: 1 minute after a change in the number of concurrently active users).

4. **Calculation of mean performance values** The measurement points of interest for a comparison with analytical values are specified in the configuration files. The Analyze component reads out this list and calculates for each measurement interval the arithmetic mean of the values recorded by the performance monitors. This step is illustrated by figure 5.8. The graph shows the mean processor utilization of the application server during the 18 measurement intervals depicted in figure 5.7. Besides the performance of the involved components, the tool also analyzes the

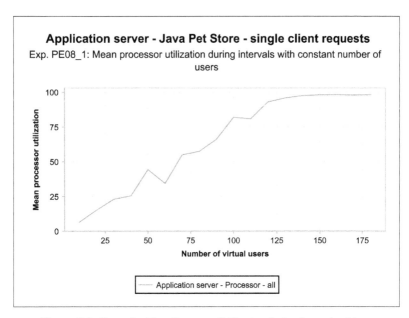

Figure 5.8: Example: Mean Processor Utilization during Intervals with constant Numbers of Users

LoadRunner transactions and determines mean values for transaction throughput and execution times.

5. **Preparation of results** Finally, the Analyze component prepares the data for comparison with analytical values and consolidates the results in database tables that can be read out by the Visualize component or exported to other applications later.

After the analysis of the load test measurements, the results can be compared to performance values calculated by the QN Solver or other third-party tools. The QN Verifier therefore provides the custom Visualize component and a database interface for external applications such as Microsoft Excel.

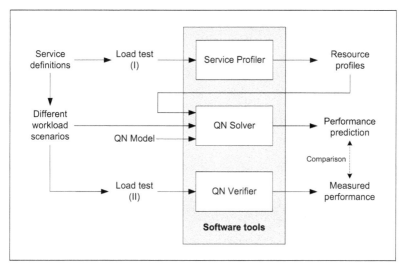

Figure 5.9: Interplay of the different Software Tools

5.4.4   Interplay of Software Tools

The motivation for the development of the software toolkit introduced above was to verify, on the one hand, whether the consumption estimates determined for resource profiles are also unbiased in scenarios with multiple concurrently active services and varying workloads, and on the other hand, whether the estimates are appropriate input parameters for analytical performance models (see section 5.1). Figure 5.9 therefore illustrates the interplay of the different software tools.

Starting point is a set of services that adequately reflects the usage of the considered application system. These services can include single or multiple client requests. By means of a first load test and the Service Profiler, resource consumption estimates for the different services are determined. This process is detailed in chapter 3. The model-based validation approach described above requires a QN Model of the test infrastructure. This model must be constructed manually. Consumption estimates of the resource profiles serve as the model input parameter (service demands). For given workload scenarios, i.e., number of users and think times (workload intensity), the QN Solver then calculates performance predictions (utilization, response time, throughput). The same workload scenarios are then replayed in a second load test. The QN Verifier analyzes the performance measurements obtained during the load test and prepares them for comparison with the analytical results. We claim that if the analytical results accurately predict the measured system performance, the accuracy of the consumption estimates is also sufficient for cost allocation. Furthermore, the QN Model and the input parameters from the resource profiles can then be readily used for "what-if" analyses and Capacity Planning.

In chapter 4 we already presented results of experiments with the Service Profiler. In the following sections, we focus on experiments with the QN Solver and the QN Verifier and thus complete the experimental validation of the approach.

5.5 Experimental Setup

5.5.1 Overview of Experiments

We applied the model-based validation approach to resource profiles determined during the experiments presented in chapter 4. Therefore, we conducted a number of additional experiments on the test infrastructure and with Java Pet Store as example application system (see section 4.1 for a detailed description of the setup). We chose Java Pet Store over PASTA because it is far more scalable and thus enables a more differentiated model validation. As in the experiments with resource profiles, we separately analyzed services including single client requests and services including multiple requests:

- **Experiment PE08**: 13 services including single client requests (see section 5.6.1)

- **Experiment PE09**: 1 service (user profile) including multiple client requests (see section 5.6.2)

In both experiments, we conducted load tests according to the process described in section 5.4.3. The corresponding LoadRunner scripts are given in the appendix (see section A.5). The measurements were analyzed with the QN Verifier and compared to analytical results determined by the QN Solver. The underlying QN Model of the test infrastructure is detailed below.

5.5.2 Queueing Network Model

The model-based validation approach requires the manual specification of a QN Model of the test infrastructure. In general, the development of an analytical model that appropriately represents a real system is not trivial. However, particularly for models of computer systems, a broad range of guidelines exists. We therefore refer practice-oriented readers to the textbooks of Menascé et al. (Menascé and Almeida, 2000, 2002; Menascé et al., 2004). Readers interested in literature with an emphasis on algorithms and on mathematical fundamentals of QN Theory are referred to Allen (1990); Bolch et al. (2006); Bolch and Riedel (1997); Kleinrock (1976) and Lazowska (1984).

In the following, we detail the modeling decisions that led to the QN Model of the test infrastructure that was used during the experiments. A technical description and an exact specification of the infrastructure is given in sections 4.1.1 and A.2.

- In load tests as described in section 5.4.3, the number of concurrently active Vusers is constant during each measurement interval. The Vusers interact with the system in endless loops. This kind of workload requires a closed QN Model (see section 5.3.3).

- We modeled solely the processors, since the disk times and the network delay were negligible. Hard disks would be typically modeled as M|M|n – FCFS queueing system (see Bolch et al., 2006, p. 340). Load-independent network delay could be represented as M|G|∞ queueing system (delay system).

- A processor can very often be modeled as M|G|1 – PS queueing system (see Bolch et al., 2006, p. 340). In our test infrastructure we use dual-processor machines, which would be modeled accordingly as M|G|2 – PS queueing systems. Unfortunately, product-form solutions for queueing systems with multiple service stations exist only for M|M|m – FCFS systems. With regard to the robustness of closed networks (see Bolch et al., 2006, pp. 488-489), we opted for an approximation based on M|M|2 – FCFS queueing systems. Alternatively, we could have used two separate M|G|1 – PS systems (see section 5.7 for an example).

- The think time of the users is represented by a M|G|∞ queueing system (delay system). The infinite number of service stations indicates that independent from the actual load no queueing effects occur. This reflects reality as the think time of a user is not dependent on the number of concurrently active users.

The structure of the resulting QN Model is depicted in figure 5.10. The model conforms to the product-form conditions (see section 5.3.4) and can be analyzed by the QN Solver either with the exact MVA algorithm or with one of the implemented approximation techniques. We validated the QN Model and the input parameters taken from resource

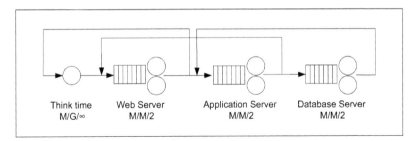

Figure 5.10: QN Model of the Test Infrastructure

profiles by load tests with the real system and services including single and multiple client requests.

5.6 Experimental Results

5.6.1 Services including single Client Requests

In the experiments on analytical models we tried to predict system performance (utilization, response time, throughput) in a multi-tier client/server environment. As an example scenario, we considered the interactions of an online customer with the Java Pet Store shop application (see section 4.1).

In the first experiment (PE08) we used 13 different types of requests (job classes) to specify the workload of a Java Pet Store customer. These were the same requests, as considered during the experiments on resource profiles as services including single client requests (e.g., search.screen or cart.do). During those experiments, the disk times and the network delay were negligible. Hence, we included solely the processors in the QN Model (see section 5.5.2). As service demands, we used processor time estimates determined during the experiment PE03 (analysis PE03_0, see section 4.3.3).

In the LoadRunner script for experiment PE08, we specified that each Vuser subsequently submits one request of each kind (see section A.5.1). During the load test, the Vusers ran in endless loops (see section 5.4.3). We therefore assumed in the model that the time between the submission of two requests of the same kind by a certain user is composed of the total user think time plus the execution time of the other 12 requests.

We analyzed the predictive accuracy of the analytical model in 18 different workload scenarios. The load test started with ten Vusers in an endless loop. Every five minutes, we added ten more users until the load test stopped after 90 minutes and with 180 concurrently active Vusers. The mean think time between two subsequent requests was 1 second (random range: 50 % to 150 %) for all Vusers and at all workloads. A times series graph of the load test is depicted in figure 5.7. The load test measurements were analyzed by the QN Verifier according to the process description in section 5.4.3. The load test configuration (numbers of users and mean think times) served as input parameter (workload intensity) for the QN Model. The QN Solver calculated on this basis for each workload scenario an individual performance prediction. Due to state space explosion problems, the exact MVA algorithm is not applicable to QN Models with multiple job classes (here: 13). Hence, we used the SCAT approximation to analyze the model and the Bard-Schweitzer/Menascé algorithm to cross check the results (see section 5.4.2). A summary of all input parameters as well as full result tables are provided in the appendix (see section A.4.1).

Regarding the accuracy of the processor time estimates and their appropriateness for Capacity Planning, most interesting is how well the performance model predicts the processor utilizations. In figures 5.11, 5.12 and 5.13 the mean processor utilization of the application server, the database server and the web server during each measurement interval is compared to the analytically determined values. Basically, the processor utilizations evolved with increasing load, as we had expected in our theoretical considerations. No significant non-linearities in the resource consumption could be observed. Mean absolute deviations of the analytically determined values were 3.6 % (application server), 0.9 % (web server) and 0.9 % (database server). Relative values are given in the appendix (see table A.19). In the test scenario the application server emerged as the bottleneck of the system. At workloads beyond 120 concurrently active users its mean processor utilization was above 90 %. From that point on, the measured response times showed high variations that could not be explained by the performance model (see figure 5.14). Database server and web server were far less utilized during the whole load test.

The highest predictive accuracy, however, could be achieved for the throughput values (see figure 5.15 for an example). As long as the system is not close to its capacity limit the throughput grows approximately linearly with the number of concurrently active users. Therefore, the throughput graph is a valuable cross check whether the modeled workload intensity equals the workload intensity emulated by the load generator. In experiment PE08 the analytically determined and the measured throughput values are nearly congruent for all workloads. This confirms the accuracy of workload intensity parameters (i.e.,

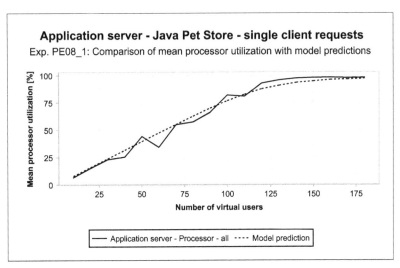

Figure 5.11: QN Model Validation: Application Server Processor
Utilization – Services including single Client Requests

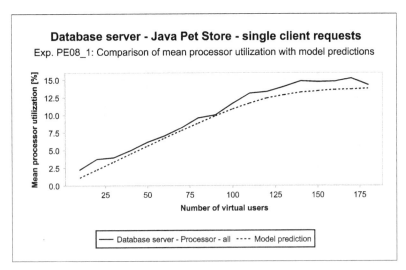

Figure 5.12: QN Model Validation: Database Server Processor Utilization
– Services including single Client Requests

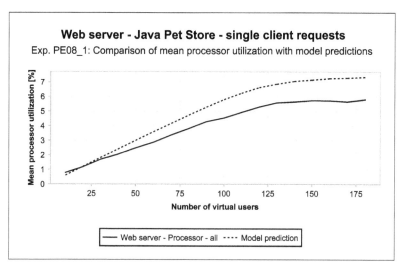

Figure 5.13: QN Model Validation: Web Server Processor Utilization –
Services including single Client Requests

the calculated arrival rate of requests), as well as of model results (predicted capacity
limit).

Overall, and despite the required approximations (e.g., processor models or SCAT algorithm, see section 5.5.2), the predictive accuracy of the analytical model was quite high
in this experiment (see section 5.7 for a comparison with related results). The observations underpin our approach in three different ways. First, during the load tests we
could not identify major non-linearities in the resource consumption (see requirement 1.2
in section 3.4). Second, the processor estimates emerged as largely unbiased at different
workloads and with multiple concurrently active services. Third, the predictive accuracy of the results indicated the appropriateness of consumption estimates from resource
profiles as input parameters for analytical performance models (see section 5.1).

5.6.2   Services including multiple Client Requests

In experiment PE09, we analyzed whether the model-based validation approach is also
applicable to services including multiple client requests (and hence user think times). This
was unclear, as we could not identify any related experimental results with QN Models
and such kind of job classes.

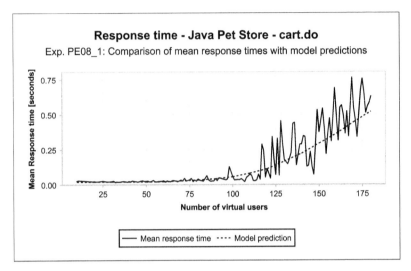

Figure 5.14: QN Model Validation: Response Time – Services including single Client Requests

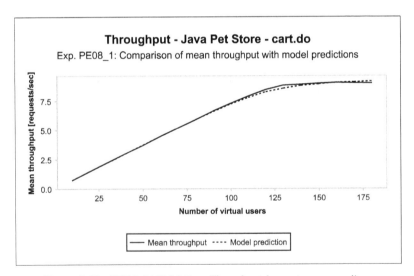

Figure 5.15: QN Model Validation: Throughput (requests per second) – Services including single Client Requests

As an example scenario, we considered again the interactions of an online customer with the Java Pet Store shop application. In the experiment described in the previous section, we specified the workload through 13 different kinds of requests (job classes). Now, we abstract from the level of single requests and consider the entirety of interactions of a certain kind of user as job class. In the experiments on resource profiles, we introduced an analogous abstraction and determined consumption estimates for different user profiles (i.e., services including multiple client requests).

For experiment PE09, we considered the power_shopper user profile, introduced in section 4.1.2.2, as the example job class. We slightly adapted the LoadRunner script to enable a comparison with the results of experiment PE08. The script and the modifications are documented in the appendix (see section A.5). In total, it contains 40 customer requests to the shop application.

The configuration of the load test PE09_1 is similar to the configuration of load test PE08_1 presented in the previous section. Due to a less resource-intensive workload composition, we could analyze the predictive accuracy of the analytical model in 20 instead of 18 different workload scenarios. The load test started again with ten Vusers in an endless loop. Every five minutes, we added ten more users until the load test stopped after 100 minutes and with 200 concurrently active Vusers. The mean think time between two subsequent requests was 1 second (random range: 50 % to 150 %) for all Vusers and at all workloads. Thus, the mean total think time was 40 seconds. In the QN Model, we considered this value as service demand of the power_shopper at the delay queue (see figure 5.10). The service demands at the other queueing systems were extracted from the corresponding resource profile (see table A.20). Again, we used the QN Verifier and the QN Solver to analyze the load test measurements and the QN Model.

Overall, the performance model was far less complex than the model used for experiment PE08. Instead of 39 (13 job classes x 3 queueing systems) we required only 3 service demand input parameters. As we considered only one job class, the QN Model could be analyzed with the exact MVA algorithm. Approximations due to state space explosion problems were not required. A summary of all input parameters as well as full result tables are provided in the appendix (see section A.4.2).

In figures 5.16, 5.17 and 5.18 the analytically determined values are compared to the mean processor utilization of the application server, the database server and the web servers. Overall, the mean utilizations evolve with increasing workload as expected and similar to the observations in experiment PE08. Mean absolute deviations of analytical values

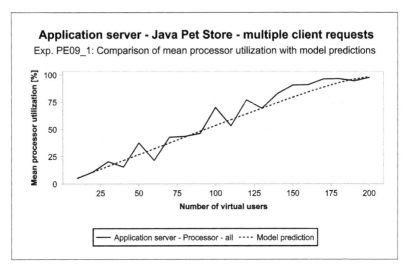

Figure 5.16: QN Model Validation: Application Server Processor
Utilization – Services including multiple Client Requests

to load test measurements were 5.7 % (application server), 0.3 % (web server) and 0.3 %
(database server). Relative values are given in the appendix (see table A.21). Although
the predicted capacity limit is slightly too high (see figures 5.16 and 5.19), the model
accuracy is directly comparable to the results of experiment PE08. This is particularly
interesting, as the service demand input parameters are far more coarse-grained (total
resource consumption of 40 requests). This reduces the complexity not only for the QN
Solver, but also for the people responsible for modeling and Capacity Planning.

The experimental results basically confirm the conclusions drawn in the previous section.
The analysis of load test measurements provided no indications of major non-linearities
in the resource consumption. The processor time estimates seemed to be largely unbiased
at different workloads and with multiple concurrently active services, and emerged as
appropriate input parameters for analytical performance models.

5.7   Related Experimental Results

We chose Java Pet Store for the above experiments because we consider it an appropriate example of modern multi-tier client/server systems. This architectural concept is

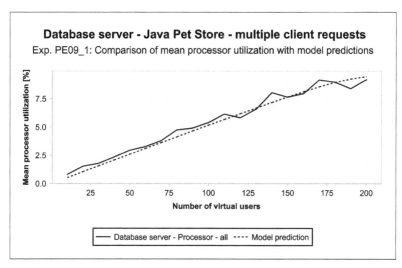

Figure 5.17: QN Model Validation: Database Server Processor Utilization – Services including multiple Client Requests

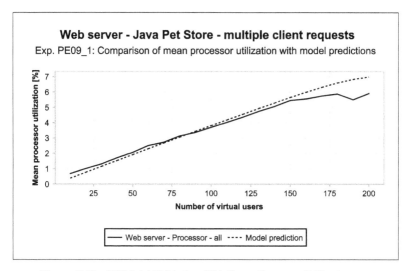

Figure 5.18: QN Model Validation: Web Server Processor Utilization – Services including multiple Client Requests

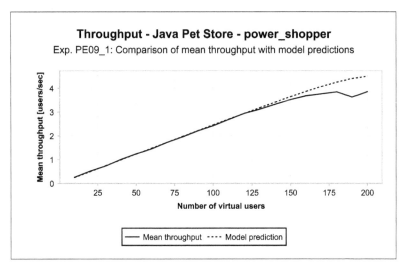

Figure 5.19: QN Model Validation: Throughput (users per second) –
Services including multiple Client Requests

widely used in today's data centers and analytical models of respective systems can support various tasks. Closed Queueing Network Models have been proposed for multi-tier client/server architectures in the context of Dynamic Resource Allocation (see for instance Bennani and Menascé, 2005; Urgaonkar et al., 2007), Service Level Management (see for instance Cherkasova et al., 2007; Liu et al., 2005) and Capacity Planning (see for instance Kounev and Buchmann, 2003; Zhang et al., 2007).

From these related works we chose Kounev and Buchmann (2003) for a closer analysis because their experimental results are well documented and the test scenario is directly comparable to the one presented above (see section 5.5.1). A shortened version of their paper is included as an example case study in the textbook of Bolch et al. (2006, pp. 733-745).

Kounev and Buchmann (2003) analyzed the applicability of Queueing Network Models for performance prediction and capacity planning in a distributed multi-tier Java/J2EE environment. They chose the *SPECjAppServer2002* benchmark (see SPEC, n.d.b) as an example application system. Similar to Java Pet Store, it represents a distributed e-business environment. It includes components supporting manufacturing, supply-chain management and order/inventory processes. The business logic of both application systems is implemented using the J2EE EJB technologies (J2EE server version 1.3). The test infrastructure of Kounev and Buchmann consisted of a Bea Weblogic Server cluster (single processor machines) and a Oracle database server (dual processor machine). The QN Model of Kounev and Buchmann is slightly different to the model presented in section 5.5.2:

- CPU Application Server: $-|M|1 - PS$

- CPU Database Server: $-|M|1 - PS$

- Disk Database Server: $-|M|1 - FCFS$

- Client: $-|M|\infty - FCFS$

- Production Line Stations: $-|M|\infty - FCFS$

In the Java Pet Store example, the time consumed by the SAN was negligible, so we omitted it in the model. Production Line Stations representing a "manufacturing think time" are a specific characteristic of the SPECjAppServer2002 example. The model above does not conform to the product-form conditions (see section 5.3.4). While we opted for an approximation by a product-form network (see section 5.3.4, approach 1), Kounev and Buchmann used an extension of the summation method (see Bolch et al., 2006, pp. 505-507), i.e., an approximation technique for non-product-form networks (approach 3). However, many efficient analysis techniques for non-product networks do not support $-|M|m - PS$ queueing systems. Therefore, they approximated the dual-processor machine with two single processor machines. We opted instead for a product-form approximation using $M|M|2 - FCFS$ queueing systems (see section 5.5.2). This enabled us to apply the MVA and the SCAT algorithms, which are more accurate than the summation method (Bolch et al., 2006, p. 460).

Kounev and Buchmann solely analyzed their model for services (job classes) including single client requests (analogous to experiment PE08, see section 5.6.1). They distinguished five request classes:

- *NewOrder* places a new order in the system

- *ChangeOrder* modifies an existing order

- *OrderStatus* retrieves the status of a given order

Metric	1 Application Server			2 Application Servers		
	Model	Measured	Error	Model	Measured	Error
NewOrder Throughput	14.59	14.37	1.5 %	14.72	14.49	1.6 %
ChangeOrder Throughput	4.85	4.76	1.9 %	4.90	4.82	1.7 %
OrderStatus Throughput	24.84	24.76	0.3 %	24.89	24.88	0.0 %
CustStatus Throughput	19.89	19.85	0.2 %	19.92	19.99	0.4 %
WorkOrder Throughput	12.11	12.19	0.7 %	12.20	12.02	1.5 %
NewOrder Response Time	56 ms	68 ms	17.6 %	37 ms	47 ms	21.3 %
ChangeOrder Response Time	58 ms	67 ms	13.4 %	38 ms	46 ms	17.4 %
OrderStatus Response Time	12 ms	16 ms	25.0 %	8 ms	10 ms	20.0 %
CustStatus Response Time	11 ms	17 ms	35.2 %	7 ms	10 ms	30.0 %
WorkOrder Response Time	1127 ms	1141 ms	1.2 %	1092 ms	1103 ms	1.0 %
WebLogic Server CPU Utilization	66 %	70 %	5.7 %	33 %	37 %	10.8 %
Database Server CPU Utilization	36 %	40 %	10 %	36 %	38 %	5.2 %

Table 5.1: Experimental Results of Kounev and Buchmann (2003)

- *CustStatus* lists all orders of a given customer

- *WorkOrder* controls the order production

The service demands were retrieved manually by analysis of the server utilization (application server) and of data monitored by an Oracle agent (database server). As in the Java Pet Store example, most of the service time was consumed by the processors. The disk time was minimal.

During the experiments, Kounev and Buchmann applied a certain workload to different numbers of parallel application servers. They could therefore evaluate the predictive accuracy of the model in scenarios with varying capacities. Mean results of experiments with 1 and 2 application servers are given in table 5.1. Additional experiments with three different workloads and 3, 4, 6 and 9 parallel application servers led to comparable results (see full result tables in Kounev and Buchmann, 2003). The experiments presented in the previous sections are complementary to that approach. In contrast to Kounev and Buchmann, we analyzed the predictive accuracy of the model in scenarios with a fixed capacity but varying workloads.

Both types of experiments led to a similar result accuracy (see table 5.1 and table A.19, and figures in section 5.6.1). Overall, the best predictions could be achieved for throughput values, whereas in both cases the measured response times showed relatively high variations. Regarding the accuracy of utilization values, Kounev and Buchmann determined in their experiments with a single application server a relative deviation of 5.7 %

at the application server and 10 % at the database server (see table 5.1). At a comparable workload level we measured relative deviations of 5.8 % and 1.3 % respectively (see table A.19: 90 concurrent users and 66.1 % utilization of the application server).

5.8 Summary

The motivation for the development of the software tools, QN Solver and QN Verifier, and for the experiments described in the previous sections was twofold (see section 5.1). First, we wanted to analyze whether the consumption estimates determined for resource profiles are also unbiased in scenarios with multiple concurrently active services and varying workloads (Requirement 1: Accuracy, see section 3.4). Second, we aimed to evaluate the appropriateness of consumption estimates as input parameters for analytical performance models (Requirement 3: Capacity Planning, see section 3.4).

During the load tests described in the previous sections, we could not observe any significant load-dependent behavior in the consumed processor time. This confirmed the basic model hypothesis on the linear increase of resource consumption (see section 3.3). Furthermore, in both experiments, the QN Model emerged as a viable representation of the real system. The predictive accuracy was surprisingly high and directly comparable to related results. Thus, we concluded that the processor time estimates were largely unbiased in the considered workload scenarios and appropriate input parameters for the analytical model.

Basically, such results cannot be directly transferred to other environments. Analytical models always require a validation, if possible against the real system (see section 5.2). Although model-based approaches have been proposed for various tasks within IT Service Management (see section 5.7 for some examples), the need for validation and often not readily available input parameters hamper their application in practice. We claim that there resource profiles and the validation methodology presented in the previous sections could fill a gap.

Chapter 6

Proof of Concept: BMW Group

6.1 Motivation

The initial objective of the work presented in this thesis was to contribute a viable alternative to existing cost allocation methodologies (see section 1.2). To evaluate the "viability" of the approach presented in the previous chapters we conducted a proof of concept in cooperation with our industrial partner, the BMW Group. The project was organized into three stages. First, we analyzed the cost allocation practices for IT infrastructure services and verified whether the situation is in accord with our general assumptions on IT Cost Accounting and Chargeback (see chapter 2). Second, by example of Java/J2EE-based application systems we examined how the determination of resource profiles could be integrated into the existing IT Service Management processes. Finally, we applied method and software to two different application systems in a data center of the BMW Group. Results from experiments on that infrastructure were already presented in chapters 4 and 5. During the proof of concept, we put a particular analysis focus on the following two requirements (see section 3.4):

1. **Consistency** This requirement means that the estimation should be applicable to various IT infrastructures, without a need to change the respective systems. We deliberately chose Java/J2EE technologies for the proof of concept, as the respective guidelines at the BMW Group facilitate the design of distributed and heterogeneous software and hardware architectures. So, we combined in the test infrastructure three different operating systems (Linux, Windows, Unix) with server software from Apache, Bea and Oracle. All hardware and software components were typical enterprise products. By means of this rather heterogeneous, but realistic, infrastructure,

we tried to gather significant results on the consistency of the estimation process and the determined resource profiles.

2. **Operating Efficiency** The determination of resource profiles should integrate well with existing IT Service Management processes and cause little extra work. We addressed this requirement with a feasibility study with Java/J2EE-based application systems. We first developed an integration into existing processes and then conducted a number of test series with two example application systems. Thereby, we tried to adhere to all relevant process and architectural guidelines to get sound estimates for the expected efforts and the operating efficiency of the approach for the determination of resource profiles.

In the following, we first introduce the case of the BMW Group and discuss the current cost allocation practices of the Central IT unit (section 6.2). In section 6.3 we then present the results of the feasibility study with Java/J2EE-based application systems. As experimental results were already provided in chapters 4 and 5, we focus in this section on the integration into existing IT Service Management processes and our experiences regarding the operating efficiency and the efforts required for the determination of resource profiles. Section 6.4 summarizes the findings from the proof of concept and describes some potential benefits of resource profiles beyond Cost Accounting.

6.2 Organizational Context

The *BMW AG* is an independent automobile and motorcycle company, headquartered in Munich (Germany). It develops and sells cars and motorcycles manufactured by itself and by foreign subsidiaries. The vehicles are sold through the company's own branches, independent dealers, subsidiaries and importers (BMW Group, 2006, p. 52). The BMW AG is the parent company of the *BMW Group*, which comprises all German and foreign subsidiaries as well as the car brands MINI and Rolls-Royce Motor Cars. As of 31 December 2005 the BMW Group had 105,798 employees, of which 76,536 were in the BMW AG (BMW Group, 2006, p. 3).

6.2.1 Overview of IT Organization

The IT organization of the BMW Group is structured into two levels (see figure 6.1 and Gammel, 2005). Each of the business departments "Development and Purchasing",

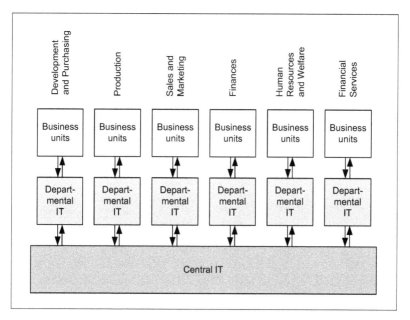

Figure 6.1: Organizational Structure (adapted from internal documentation)

"Production", "Sales and Marketing", "Finances", "Human Resources and Welfare" and "Financial Services" has a *Departmental IT*, which coordinates all IT resources in the department. The Departmental IT units are focused on supporting and designing business processes in their departments. General IT topics such as IT strategy and infrastructure operations are steered by the *Central IT*. Departmental IT units and Central IT have the world-wide responsibility for controlling and planning IT resources and providing IT services. The necessary tasks are distributed between the two levels (see figure 6.2).

The need for IT support arises from the business processes and from the business units. Their primary contractor is the corresponding Departmental IT. This IT unit is responsible for development, maintenance, support and operations of all business applications in the department. Additionally, it optimizes, in cooperation with the business units, the business processes and enforces the department-wide standardization of processes as well as of application and data architectures. In contrast, Central IT is responsible for cross-departmental processes and services. This includes, on the one hand, the provision of a

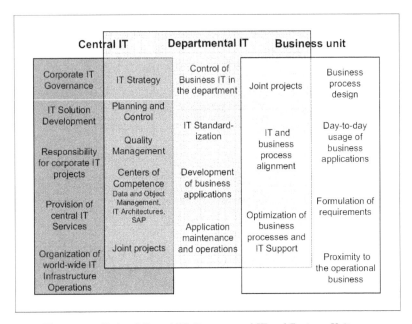

Figure 6.2: Tasks of Central IT, Departmental IT and Business Units
(adapted from internal documentation)

common data center infrastructure (communication, computing, storage) and of central
IT services (e.g., help desks, desktop computers, office applications, telephony services).
On the other hand, it has a lead function for overall IT processes and projects. For
instance, the IT strategy is cooperatively created and implemented by all IT functions.
Central IT is responsible for the process and the coherence of the content. It has also the
leadership of the cross-departmental Centers of Competence. They were established for
standardizing and consolidating the usage of standard software, of IT architectures and of
data and object models. The Centers of Competence develop mandatory standards and
guidelines for the whole group.

6.2.2 IT Service Management Processes

The overall objective of the BMW Group IT is to provide services which meet the business
requirements in an effective and an efficient manner. IT Service Management processes are
therefore standardized across the organizational levels introduced above. The IT Process

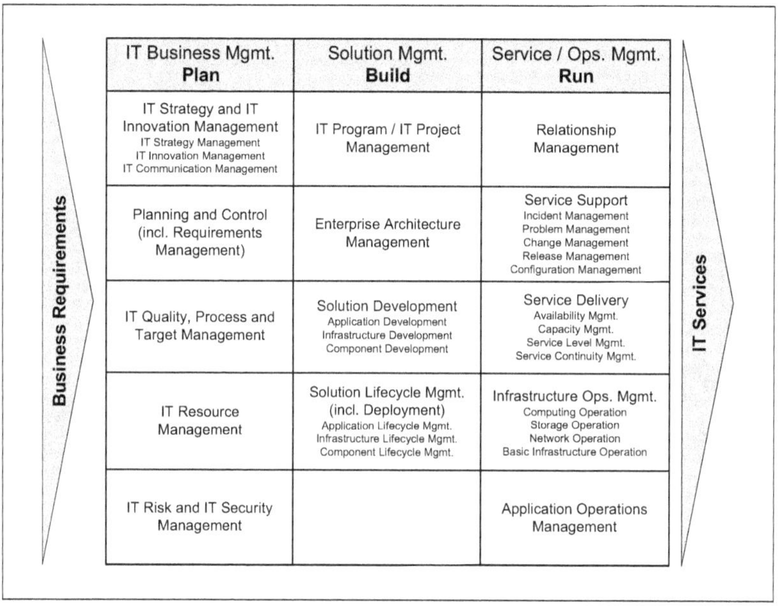

IT Business Mgmt. Plan	Solution Mgmt. Build	Service / Ops. Mgmt. Run
IT Strategy and IT Innovation Management IT Strategy Management IT Innovation Management IT Communication Management	IT Program / IT Project Management	Relationship Management
Planning and Control (incl. Requirements Management)	Enterprise Architecture Management	Service Support Incident Management Problem Management Change Management Release Management Configuration Management
IT Quality, Process and Target Management	Solution Development Application Development Infrastructure Development Component Development	Service Delivery Availability Mgmt. Capacity Mgmt. Service Level Mgmt. Service Continuity Mgmt.
IT Resource Management	Solution Lifecycle Mgmt. (incl. Deployment) Application Lifecycle Mgmt. Infrastructure Lifecycle Mgmt. Component Lifecycle Mgmt.	Infrastructure Ops. Mgmt. Computing Operation Storage Operation Network Operation Basic Infrastructure Operation
IT Risk and IT Security Management		Application Operations Management

(Business Requirements — left vertical label; IT Services — right vertical label)

Figure 6.3: IT Service Management Process Map (adapted from internal documentation)

Map in figure 6.3 shows the underlying structural framework. The categories *Plan*, *Build* and *Run* follow the lifecycle of application systems. The different processes are oriented toward external standards such as ITIL and CobiT (see section 2.2.3 for a brief overview). For each process a responsible manager, process maturity metrics, performance indicators and targets are defined. A Performance Measurement System reports the current state of the IT processes to the stakeholders. The motivation for the standardization of IT Process Management is to create a uniform and comprehensive management information basis. This transparency should enable an optimal control of employment and utilization of the IT resources.

6.2.3 IT Cost Accounting and Chargeback

A major instrument to control supply and demand for internal IT services and thus ensure an optimal allocation of scarce resources is IT Cost Accounting and Chargeback (see section 2.1). At the BMW Group cost allocation was historically used to control the

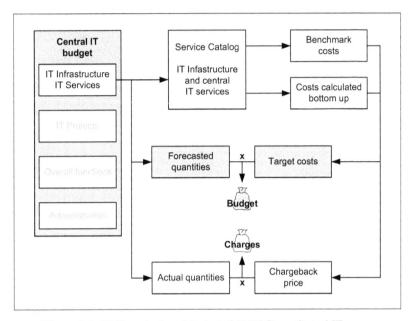

Figure 6.4: IT Chargeback and Budget of BMW Group Central IT
(adapted from internal documentation)

considerably increasing IT budgets. The controlling aspect, in the sense of encouraging
desired behavior, was less important. This has changed over recent years. Besides *transparency* and *operating efficiency*, the *controlling and planning function* (see section 2.3)
has become the major objective of IT Cost Accounting and Chargeback. We illustrate
BMW's approach by means of the data center infrastructure and central IT services (see
figure 6.4). Service provider is Central IT. Contractors for end-user services are business
units. Contractors for data center services are Departmental IT units. The different IT
services are described in a Service Catalog. The services are composed in a way that
external benchmark costs can be determined. Examples of such services include:

- Mainframe processor time (MIPS/hour)

- Network Attached Storage (GB/month)

- Database (instance/month)

- Java/J2EE Server Environment (instance/month)

- Windows/Unix/Linux Server Operations (server/month)

- Desktop computer (computer/month)

- Support Center (ticket)

- Internet Connectivity (user/month)

Once a year benchmark costs for the services are determined. They constitute, in combination with internal bottom-up calculations, the basis for the derivation of target costs. The target costs are determined by the IT Controlling units and confirmed by the IT committee of the management board. The primary budget for the provision of IT services results from the demand forecasts of the contractors multiplied by the target costs. The budgets are adapted during the year if demand quantities vary from forecasts. While the budgeting process is used to control the supply side, IT Chargeback is used to control the demand for IT services. The concepts are decoupled in the sense that chargeback does not affect the size of the budgets. The chargeback revenues are deposited into an account of Central Controlling and the Departmental IT and/or the business units are only charged for their use of IT services if one of the following conditions is fulfilled:

1. Charges are appropriate to encourage desired behavior (e.g., cost consciousness, use of certain technologies).

2. Legal authorities prescribe monetary transparency between service provider and service receiver. This situation arises if the provider and receiver are organized in different legal entities (e.g., the BMW AG and a foreign subsidy).

Consequently, business units are not charged for services such as e-mail or calendaring. As every office worker requires one (and only one) mailbox and calendar account, there is only a limited potential for demand control. If the service provider/receiver relationship is not subject to legal restrictions, IT Controlling even has the possibility to set "political prices" to enhance the desired incentives.

6.2.4   Analysis of the current Situation

In the following, the IT Cost Accounting and Chargeback approach of the BMW Group is analyzed with regard to general objectives (see section 2.3). The concept focuses, as illustrated, on *transparency* for IT Controlling, *operating efficiency* and the *controlling and planning function* of charges. However, it also harbors some principal conflicts, which partially outweigh the benefits. The desired operating efficiency requires the overhead caused by measuring and apportioning resource consumption to be small. At Central IT no charges or charges based on flat rates are collected for resource consumption, which is hardly measurable or allocatable. Instead of controlling interests, technical aspects determine the way customers are charged for their resource usage. This concerns particular services based on shared data center infrastructures (e.g., network traffic or processor usage in distributed environments). The resulting chargeback heterogeneity causes free-rider problems and partially undermines the objectives of the stakeholders.

- **Transparency** The approach creates transparency for the IT Controlling functions. Demand and cost variations are clearly distinguishable. The efficiency of the service provision can be controlled by external benchmarks. However, the chargeback policy is not always transparent to customers and is partially considered as arbitrary.

- **Incentives for cost consciousness** The unequal treatment of resources creates incentives for developers and architects to shift consumption from chargeable to non-chargeable resources. For instance, turning off compression mechanisms shifts resource consumption from processors to networks and storage devices. If Departmental IT are not charged for the incurred network traffic such a measure might reduce their charges, even if it incurs additional costs for the company.

- **Capacity Planning, Planning and cost calculation instrument** The primary budget for the provision of IT services relies on the forecasted demand of the customers. The customers have incentives for precise forecasts of the resource consumption they are charged for. In contrast, they cannot forecast resource consumption which is not allocated to them. The process is further complicated as the customers usually forecast business operations which must be converted to technical IT resource consumption.

Furthermore, chargeback heterogeneity is at odds with overall objectives such as *comprehensibility, consistency, cost proportionality, causer-based cost allocation* and *precision*.

At the BMW Group, two major problems arise from the shortcomings of the approach. First, the chargeback system suffers from a lack of acceptance and trust by the customers. Second, it does not achieve an alignment of business and IT planning. The correlation between actual and future costs for the provision of IT services and business operations figures is not transparent. So, on the one hand, customers are mostly not aware of the consequences of their decisions on IT costs. On the other hand, IT Capacity Planning, which determines to a large extent future resource costs, is often imprecise.

6.2.5 Customer-oriented Services and Resource Profiles

The basic question to answer, prior to any feasibility considerations, is whether customer-oriented services and resource profiles improve the situation described above. We approach this question by examining the objectives for the IT planning and control processes (see figure 6.3):

> "Overall IT planning and control is responsible for the business-relevant op-
> timal employment of existing IT resources by comprehensive planning and
> controlling of the BMW Group IT. It takes place in close coordination with
> the company's financial planning and controlling." (cited from an internal
> process documentation)

"Optimal employment" comprises effectiveness as well as efficiency of IT service provision. Concerning the data center infrastructure, controlling and planning is predominantly resource-oriented (see section 6.2.3). Measures such as operational costs, provisioning times or achieved service levels of data center resources are used to control the efficiency of the service provision. The resource-orientation thereby facilitates the identification of external benchmarks and the management of internal targets. In contrast, controlling and planning based on business- or customer-oriented services focuses on the effectiveness of IT resource employment. At the BMW Group, service-orientation and resource profiles could address central conflicts of IT Cost Accounting and Chargeback (see section 6.2.4):

- **Transparency** Services and costs associated with business processes can create a new form of transparency for customers and service provider. As not every business process is of equal importance, IT costs per process are valuable information for controlling IT effectiveness and prioritizing scarce resources.

- **Incentives for cost consciousness** Resource profiles for services can include all relevant data center resources. They can thus prevent free-rider problems caused by exploiting the unequal treatment of resources. Furthermore, end-users can better control cost allocations based on service invocations than on technical resource consumption (e.g., processor time).

- **Capacity Planning, Planning and cost calculation instrument** Services and resource profiles support the translation of business forecasts into IT resource requirements. The approach can thus provide a solid analytical basis for Capacity Planning and infrastructure cost estimates.

Focusing on business- or customer-oriented services, at least as a complement to the existing IT Controlling perspectives, seems promising. The management has recognized this and forces process-costing initiatives. As service-orientation has been widely discussed in literature (see sections 2.2 and 3.7), we focus in the following on the determination of resource profiles. By means of the Java/J2EE infrastructure at the BMW Group, we analyze whether this second building block of the concept (see section 3.2) is applicable in an industrial environment and how it integrates into the existing IT Service Management processes.

6.3 Feasibility Study: Java/J2EE Application Systems

At the BMW Group, Java/J2EE is the predominant platform technology for custom software development. The Center of Competence IT Architectures has therefore published two master solution guidelines (see section 6.3.1). They are mainly based on open standards and provide comprehensive means for backend integration. The guidelines enable "best-of-breed" strategies and facilitate the design of distributed and heterogeneous software and hardware architectures. The majority of the application systems are hosted on shared resources (October 2006). We focus in the following on this kind of systems, first, because of their strategic relevance for the BMW Group and, second, because of their distributed and heterogeneous nature, combined with widely shared resources, which is usually not compatible with common Cost Accounting approaches (see section 2.4).

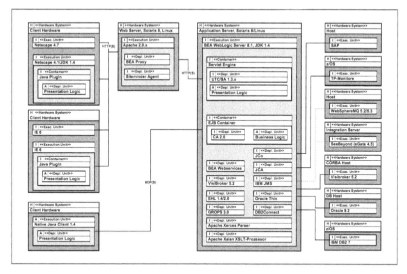

Figure 6.5: Master Solution Guideline J2EE/EJB (adapted from internal documentation)

6.3.1   Java/J2EE at the BMW Group

The basis for custom Java/J2EE-based applications systems are the master solution guidelines *J2EE/EJB* and *J2EE/Servlet*. The guidelines are mandatory for software projects and aim at standardizing system and software architectures as well as the necessary build and run processes (see section 6.2.2). For the documentation of guidelines and architectures the BMW Group uses a simple graphical notation similar to UML (see figures 6.5 and 6.6). In both master solution guidelines a Bea Weblogic Server (BEA, n.d.b) is used as Java application server. If the application system is accessed via web interfaces, an Apache HTTP Server (Apache, n.d.) delivers static web content and acts as proxy between client and application server. Web and application server run on shared or dedicated Unix or Linux (Intel) hardware. As database management systems, Oracle Database (HP-UX) and IBM DB2 (z/OS) are supported.

The J2EE/EJB master solution guideline is the basis for custom OLTP systems (see figure 6.5). Typical characteristics of such application systems are:

- complex business logic and multiple use cases

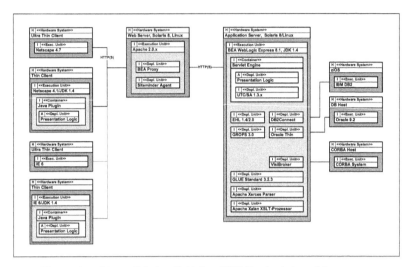

Figure 6.6: Master Solution Guideline J2EE/Servlet (adapted from internal documentation)

- high transaction volumes and complex transactions

- non-trivial data models

- read and write access to databases

- support for different client types (e.g., native clients and web clients)

- comprehensive integration of backend systems (e.g., using message-oriented middleware or web service technologies).

In contrast, the J2EE/Servlet master solution guideline (see figure 6.6) is used for simple information systems. A typical application scenario is the visualization of data from a database in a web browser. The business logic is implemented in neighbored systems or in the backend. Differentiating usage criteria to J2EE/EJB are:

- focus on presentation logic not on business logic

- no distributed transactions

- predominantly read access to databases (simple write operations allowed)

- only web clients supported

- backend integration is limited to database management and Corba systems.

Central IT offers standardized server environments either on shared or dedicated hardware for both kinds of application systems. For each server environment a single customer is defined, typically a Departmental IT or a business unit, to whom costs are allocated. If server resources are dedicated, incurred hardware and operations costs are passed on to this customer. If the resources are shared, a flat rate is charged per application system. Costs for databases are always fully allocated to a single application system, even if the database is used in different contexts. Resource consumption in a client/server environment such as network traffic, processor time or storage I/O, which drives new infrastructure investments, is not considered. So, for instance, if an application system uses a database running on a mainframe computer, the customer is charged for the processor time, while the processor time consumed by databases on Unix servers is "free". Although this cost allocation approach is quite efficient, such inconsistencies cause acceptance and free-rider problems (see section 6.2.4).

6.3.2 Integration into existing Processes

Resource profiles for cost accounting and capacity planning should be based on the final version of application system and infrastructure configuration. Thus, the optimal moment for their determination is after completed development and test phases, but before productive operations begins. For Java/J2EE-based application systems, Central IT conducts at that point in the lifecycle a mandatory *approval test*[1] (see figure 6.7). The project team in charge of the application system, typically consisting of Departmental IT, and business units' and external staff, hands over the final installation package to the approval test team (Central IT). They install the application system in a dedicated production-like environment, provided by the data center, and verify in a series of technical approval tests if it satisfies the following criteria:

- adherence to programming/architecture guidelines (manual)

- installation routines (manual)

---

[1] ITIL describes a similar process and therefore uses the term *acceptance test* (Office of Government Commerce, 2002a, ch. 5.3.4).

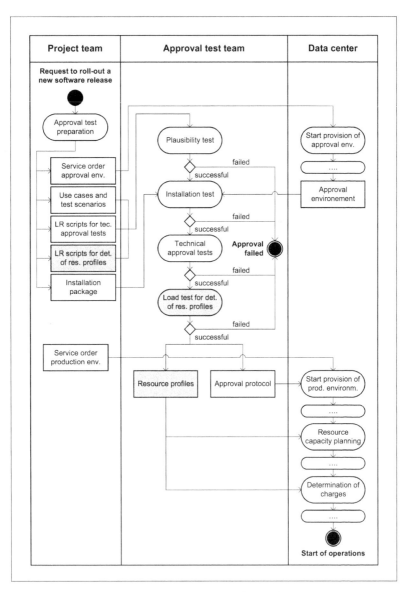

Figure 6.7: Integration into the Approval Process

- plausibility/completeness of load test scenarios (manual)

- robustness/stability/error tolerance (load test)

- processor and memory load (load test)

- response times (load test)

- dispatch and cluster capability (load test, manual intervention)

- database reconnect capability (load test, manual intervention)

The load tests are conducted with Mercury LoadRunner (see section 3.5.4). Both custom-built software and pure third party products must pass the approval process. If one or more of the above-mentioned criteria/preconditions fail, Central IT can reject productive deployment of the installation package. In that case the problems must be solved and the approval repeated. The approval is also repeated if at least one of the following changes occurs:

- change in the system architecture (e.g., use of new server components, communication protocols, interfaces)

- change in the software architecture (e.g., major changes to the user navigation, use of new software patterns)

- change of specifications (e.g., performance requirements, workload mix, system load)

The mandatory approval tests provide optimal occasions for the determination of resource profiles. We therefore analyzed during the feasibility study how the existing test procedures can be appropriately extended (see gray-shaded boxes in figure 6.7).

Once determined, services and resource profiles can serve as inputs for neighbored IT Service Management Processes (see figure 6.8). A stronger focus on services would primarily address shortcomings of the current IT Cost Accounting and Chargeback approach concerning *Planning and Control* (see section 6.2.5). Furthermore, the resource profiles would be valuable inputs for the alignment of business forecasting and IT Capacity Planning and thus support the *Capacity Management* process (*Service Delivery*). Finally, if the resource consumption per service and user becomes transparent during the approval test, it can be used as a criterion for the evaluation of software and for the specification of targets for developers and architects (*Solution Development*).

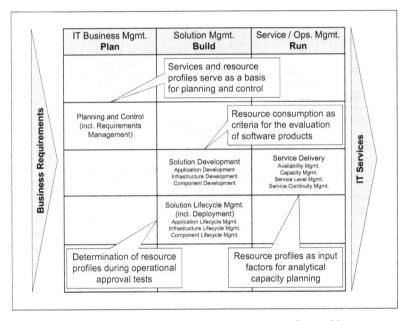

Figure 6.8: Integration into the IT Service Management Process Map (adapted from internal documentation)

6.3.3 Identification of Services

According to the concept description (see section 3.2.1), possible kinds of services could be the *execution of a business transaction* or the *access to an information system*. In the context of Java/J2EE at the BMW Group, we propose considering the access or the logon to an application system as default form of service invocation. The decision is based on three reasons:

1. The complexity of the considered Java/J2EE applications is very different. A common understanding of business transactions, as for instance in SAP systems, does not exist. We claim that services based on logons constitute a consistent and comprehensible accounting basis in this heterogeneous application landscape.

2. Compared to packaged application suites (e.g., for ERP, CRM, HR, SCM), the majority of the custom application systems are relatively small (for instance regarding

the number of concurrent users or the implemented use cases). We claim that one service per system is a reasonable granularity for cost allocation.

3. Most Java/J2EE applications use a central infrastructure service for user authentication and authorization. This component can be employed as a central meter for service invocations. No information from the application logs or operational databases must be analyzed to determine the internal cost shares.

However, this rule is not exclusive. In certain situations other forms of services might be more reasonable. Considering logon operations as service invocations is not trivial. Most Java/J2EE applications are interactive web applications. Users can interact with the system in different ways. For the approval tests the project team must provide load test scenarios (see section 3.5.4.2) which reflect typical user behavior. The test engineers only verify the plausibility and the completeness regarding component coverage. If the system under consideration has already been used, historical log files provide a solid basis for the determination of this "typical user behavior". Central IT offers several tools which automate the necessary log file analysis. In contrast, usage scenarios for new application systems are mainly based on the assumptions of the project team. According to the experiences of the load test engineers involved, these assumptions often do not match with reality. Charges based on these expected user behaviors would introduce additional bias and stimulate conflicts. In that case, we propose determining an interval instead of a discrete estimate of the expected resource consumption. We argue that is easier for new application systems to estimate different user profiles as the average user behavior. The information about scale and range of the resource consumption might be sufficient for a classification and the determination of charges.

6.3.4 Summary of Experiences

We applied the concepts and the software for the determination of resource profiles (see chapter 3) and analytical capacity planning (see chapter 5) to application systems in a data center of the BMW Group. In particular, we analyzed the extra efforts and the preconditions required for an integration of the approach into the existing approval tests (see section 6.3.2). To achieve significant results, we tried to adhere to all relevant process and architectural guidelines (see section 6.3.1). For the feasibility study and the experiments presented in chapters 4 and 5 we used the same infrastructure and example applications.

We could thus analyze during the experiments the viability of the concept and the software under realistic conditions. The test infrastructure follows the standards defined in the Java/J2EE master solution guidelines. We only replaced the operating system of the application server (Solaris 8/Linux) with a Microsoft Windows system (Windows 2000 Advanced Server) to integrate the three common types of client/server operating systems (Unix/Linux/Windows). A description and an exact specification of the environment is given in sections 4.1.1 and A.2. The experiments were conducted with two different application systems (see section 4.1.2). We intentionally chose one custom application system of the BMW Group (PASTA) to study the feasibility on a real-world example and one application system, which is freely available, to enable an external review of the results (Java Pet Store). The chosen application systems also represent the two kinds of master solution guidelines, J2EE/Servlet (PASTA) and J2EE/EJB (Java Pet Store).

In the previous section we proposed considering the logon to an application system as the default form of service invocation. PASTA as well as Java Pet Store are interactive web applications and we assumed that for both no historical usage data is available. Accordingly, we determined intervals instead of discrete estimates of the expected resource consumption (see section 6.3.3). For the feasibility of the approach it is crucial whether information about scale and range of the resource consumption is sufficient for the allocation of charges. In the experiments we therefore measured the resource consumption of two different PASTA user profiles and four different Java Pet Store user profiles (see section 4.1.2). The resulting intervals of the expected resource consumption are summarized in table 6.1. The complete resource profiles are provided in the appendix (see section A.3.1). The results were surprising. In the examples the impact of system and software design was far greater than the impact of different user behaviors. The systems could therefore be clearly attributed to different cost categories without any knowledge of the average user behavior.

Setting up an application system in a dedicated environment and preparing realistic load tests may require several days. The effort depends on aspects such as the ease of integration of backend systems, the complexity of server configurations or the use cases in the load test scripts. If this is already achieved, as in obligatory approval tests, the extra effort for the determination of resource profiles is acceptable. During the feasibility study we required approximately half a day for the adaption of an existing load test scenario ($\sim$ 1 h), the execution of the load test ($\sim$ 1-3 h) and the data analysis ($\sim$ 2 h).

Resource	PASTA		Java Pet Store	
	min	max	min	max
Database - Disk - SAN - Read/Write blocks	0	142,111	8,63	74,18
Database - Processor - all - Processor Time	2,672	7,337	0,00	0,07
App Server - Network - all - Bytes Total/sec	237.149	602.794	174.622	594.286
App Server - Processor - all - Processor Time	0,625	1,651	0,17	0,47
Client - Network - all - Bytes Total/sec	182.322	376.897	228.617	587.170
Web Server - Processor - all - Processor Time	0,028	0,08	0,01	0,03

Table 6.1: Example: Intervals of expected Resource Consumption

The load tests for the verification of QN models (see chapter 5) require a similar effort, but need more time and test runs for the optimization of the application system. During the study we found that a lot of potential bottlenecks are hidden in the system configuration (e.g., web server connections, session beans, database connection pool). As these software bottlenecks limit the throughput and thus the hardware utilization, the comparison with predicted values fails. For the determination of resource profiles those effects are less relevant, as they typically increase response times, but do not change the absolute resource consumption. However, the QN models cannot be validated until the configured bottlenecks are removed and the model hardware resources become the primary bottlenecks.

Overall, analytical capacity planning and the tuning efforts mentioned above are particularly reasonable for sizing dedicated computing or storage resources. At that point in time the hardware costs for the following years are typically determined. In contrast, it is less relevant for smaller application systems running on shared server hardware. A single application must not drive the hardware to its capacity limits and thus peril the availability of the neighbored applications. Nevertheless, it is a crucial factor for new investments whether an average application uses 1 % or 10 % of the processor or I/O capacity. Due to the difficulties of measuring and allocating the resource consumption in distributed environments, the BMW Group does not consider it for cost allocation keys. Here, resource profiles determined during obligatory approval tests could fill a gap.

6.3.5   Other Application Platform Technologies

Common application platforms at the BMW Group are, besides Java/J2EE, Microsoft/.NET, Mainframe (z/OS) and SAP. In the following we analyze whether and how the Java/J2EE-based experiences of the previous sections can be transferred to the other platforms.

Microsoft/.NET   The process and the software toolkit for the determination of resource profiles is directly applicable to Microsoft/.NET based application systems. Load test scripts for web-based applications can be recorded with the Virtual User Generator (see section 3.5.4.1). For Windows GUI applications Mercury offers the tool *WinRunner* (see Mercury, 2004, p. 967 et seqq.). The BMW Group uses Microsoft/.NET only for desktop integration. Accordingly, Microsoft/.NET-based systems are less distributed than Java/J2EE-based systems and cost allocation (e.g., direct costing) is easier.

Mainframe (z/OS)   Mainframe computers typically are not dedicated to a test environment or to a load test. The concept of measuring and allocating the total observed resource consumption to a specific service invocation is not applicable. However, the *Resource Measurement Facility* (RMF) shipped with the z/OS operating system enables a detailed analysis and allocation of resource consumption during a load test (see IBM, n.d.c). The data can be exported to common spreadsheet formats and thus integrated into the resource profiles. This is reasonable, for instance, when a Java/J2EE-based application system accesses a database running on a mainframe computer. If the mainframe is used as OLTP platform, the BMW Group already uses the information collected by the *System Management Facility* (SMF) (see IBM, n.d.b) for the determination of usage-based cost allocation keys. As the actual resource consumption can be efficiently measured and allocated, resource profiles with consumption estimates are not required.

SAP   From a technical point of view the process and the software toolkit is directly applicable to SAP systems. The LoadRunner toolkit supports web interfaces of SAP systems as well as the SAP GUI protocol. Compared to Java/J2EE application systems, the BMW Group has fewer, but larger, SAP-based OLTP systems. The server hardware is mostly dedicated. Furthermore, the SAP platform provides internal means to analyze system performance as well as executed business transactions. Accordingly, there is no immediate need for consumption estimates.

Beyond these technical considerations, an overall organizational problem is that for Microsoft/.NET, Mainframe (z/OS) and SAP-based application systems an approval test is not obligatory. This hampers the direct transfer of the concept and significantly increases the effort required for the determination of resource profiles.

6.4 Summary

During the proof of concept we analyzed whether the concept and the software for the determination of resource profiles and capacity planning is applicable in an industrial data center. Prior to a concrete feasibility study, we verified if the overall assumptions on requirements, objectives and practiced approaches of IT Infrastructure Cost Allocation are in accord with the situation of the BMW Group (see chapter 2). As this could be confirmed and customer-oriented services emerged as a promising complement to the existing planning and control perspectives, we tested the determination of adequate resource profiles by means of Java/J2EE-based application systems and proposed an integration of the concept into the existing IT Service Management Processes.

The majority of the considered application systems were relatively small, e.g., regarding the number of concurrent users or the implemented use cases, and ran on shared hardware. During the feasibility study most efforts were required for setting up the systems in a dedicated environment and preparing the load tests. If this is already achieved, e.g., for obligatory approval tests, the extra efforts for the determination of resource profiles are acceptable. Concerning the definition of services we introduced two simplifications. First, we considered the logon to an application system as the default form of service invocation. Thus, we could use the authentication and authorization infrastructure as a central meter for service invocation and avoided the analysis of application log files and operational databases. Second, we determined an interval instead of a discrete estimate for the expected resource consumption. In the example scenarios these simplifications turned out to be viable and significantly enhanced the practicability of the concept. However, for evaluating their general applicability more experiments are required.

Overall, we could demonstrate that resource profiles, acquired during obligatory approval tests, are an efficient possibility to incorporate the resource consumption into the determination of cost allocation keys. Furthermore, we identified a number of additional advantages of resource profiles, beyond cost accounting.

1. **Capacity planning for dedicated resources** In the experiments we could demonstrate that the resource profiles include valuable inputs for analytical capacity planning. While the motivating cost allocation concept mainly addresses shared resources, the support for capacity planning is particularly relevant for sizing dedicated resources. From the corporate perspective, at that point in time costs for the subsequent years are fixed, independent of their later apportionment.

2. **Evaluation of different IT architectures** The experiments illustrated the large impact of system and software architectures on the resource consumption (see for instance table 6.1). Today, the resource consumption can barely be considered in the early project phases when architectural alternatives are evaluated[2]. At the BMW Group the supported alternatives are specified by the Center of Competence IT Architectures in master solution guidelines. We recommend enhancing these guidelines with a section including example resource profiles to improve the basis for decision-making.

3. **Definition of targets for developers and architects** Once, resource profiles can be determined and appropriate benchmark values are specified in master solution guidelines, they can be used as targets for software developers and architects. Up to now, apart from response time behavior, it is only verified whether the average processor and memory utilization at the application server remains under certain absolute thresholds. The respective load tests are conducted with the expected number of concurrent users. The resource consumption is not analyzed on a per service or per user basis and the results are only relevant if the application system is installed on shared server resources. So, if the performance requirements are fulfilled, no more incentives for economic resource usage exist today. At that point an analysis of potential savings was out of scope, but we assume that the determination of resource profiles would already positively influence the cost consciousness of developers and architects.

Against this background, we propose the enhancement of the existing approval tests by the determination of resource profiles. More and more resource profiles of different application systems will then become available. On this basis our assumptions on services and on resource consumption can be verified. Depending on the operational experiences and the customer acceptance, the management can then decide whether further steps are taken toward an infrastructure cost allocation based on services and resource profiles.

---

[2] Scheeg (2005) analyzes this problem and proposes an alternative solution based on performance benchmarks (see section 3.7).

Chapter 7

Conclusions

7.1 Summary of Results

The starting point of this thesis was the question of how IT Service providers can determine usage-based cost allocation keys for shared IT infrastructures. We analyzed the question in the context of operational, interactive OLTP systems and proposed estimates for the expected resource consumption of customer-oriented services as a basis for cost allocation. In this way, we aimed to avoid elaborate and costly measurements during regular operations. For an assessment of the concept's technical viability, we developed a method and a software toolkit for the determination of consumption estimates (resource profiles) during standard load tests. The method is based on the hypothesis that the cumulated resource consumption increases linearly with the number of service invocations. In experiments with three-tier database applications we could confirm the hypothesis for computing resources (processor time) and communication resources (transferred bytes). We also analyzed the block transfer between a database server and a Storage Area Network (read/write blocks). There, high variations in the sample measurements complicated the determination of unbiased estimates.

Furthermore, we evaluated the method and the software toolkit with regard to four major requirements that we consider essential for the successful application in a professional IT Service Management organization:

1. **Accuracy** For computing and communication resources, we obtained in all experiments very precise and repeatable results. In particular, we verified in experiments with Queuing Network Models that the determined processor time estimates also hold in scenarios with varying system workloads and with multiple concurrently

active services. Nevertheless, the accuracy of the consumption estimates is subject to two major conditions: First, if a service requires interactions or parameters entered by the users, assumptions on the expected user behaviors must reflect reality. Second, resource profiles are always tied to a certain infrastructure configuration. If this configuration changes during regular operations (e.g., due to growing database sizes), the predictive accuracy of the consumption estimates can be biased. The concerned software architects and load test engineers must be aware of those effects and, if possible, anticipate them in the resource profiles.

2. **Consistency** The software toolkit fully relies on standard operating system tools for resource consumption measurements during the profiling process. It is therefore equally applicable to various kinds of hardware and software infrastructures without a need to change the respective systems or install additional software. We successfully verified this consistency concept in experiments with Windows, Unix and Linux operating systems.

3. **Capacity Planning** By means of Queuing Network Theory, we could demonstrate the appropriateness of processor time estimates as input parameters for analytical performance models. We compared forecasted server utilizations with measurements from a load test and determined a surprisingly high accuracy of the model predictions.

4. **Operating Efficiency** We analyzed in a proof-of-concept the integration of the approach for the determination of resource profiles into the existing IT Service Management processes at the BMW Group. In a feasibility study with Java/J2EE-based application systems, the most effort was required to fulfill preconditions such as setting up the systems in a dedicated environment and preparing the load tests. In professional IT organizations similar load tests are typically conducted prior to the roll-out of a new software release. If the determination of resource profiles could be combined with such obligatory approval tests, the extra efforts are acceptable. During the feasibility study we required approximately half a day for the adaption of an existing load test scenario, the execution of the load test and the data analysis.

There are two main advantages of the presented method and the software toolkit compared to related scientific work and commercial profiling tools. First, services can be defined according to customers' needs, irrespective of system boundaries. Resource profiles can be determined even if the service includes multiple user requests or causes complex interactions between distributed applications on different software and hardware platforms. Second, as the software toolkit fully relies on the standard performance monitors of operating systems, no additional measurement agents are required and new resources can be easily integrated.

Nevertheless, in spite of precise measurement and analysis techniques, uncertainties about the expected user behavior, variations as observed at the Storage Area Network and infrastructure changes such as growing database sizes can bias the consumption estimates. Against this background, we propose considering intervals rather than exact consumption estimates as the basis for cost allocation. We argue that intervals already allow for a classification of services. This might be sufficient for cost allocation. Furthermore, they could compensate to a certain degree variations of mean resource consumption values. So, extra analysis efforts can be reduced. At least in the experiments with two different application systems at the BMW Group, this simplification emerged as viable. However, such results are not generalizable. Further experiences with different kinds of applications are required.

The overall goal of this thesis was to contribute a viable alternative to existing cost allocation approaches. We claim that this has been achieved. The next step now is to gain more operational experiences with different kinds of application systems. On this basis, companies can then decide whether cost allocation based on services and resources profiles is an appropriate means to achieve their organization-level objectives on IT Cost Accounting and Chargeback.

7.2 Outlook

Topics such as IT Cost Accounting and Chargeback or IT Capacity Planning fall under the realm of IT Service Management. Despite the development of widely accepted standards such as ITIL or CobiT and the increasing importance of IT Service Management for the industry, little academic research has focused on this domain. Deficits of IT Service Management become apparent in a comparison with Operations Management. In the industrial production of physical goods and services it is for instance common practice that mathematical models and methods are used to optimize machine utilization, job scheduling or stock-keeping. Although most of these techniques would in principle be applicable to the production of digital goods and services, they are rarely used in today's data center.

In the adoption of respective models and methods, we see a large advancement potential for IT Service Management and interesting topics for future research.

Certainly, one may argue that data centers are not comparable to shop floors, the provision of IT services is often complex and hardware costs are less important than labor costs or costs for industrial production facilities. However, we observe that with rising budget pressure and competition on the outsourcing market, IT Service Providers are being forced to optimize their data center operations and resource utilization. Let us consider, for instance, the situation of dedicated application or database servers. Their initial sizing was typically based on estimated peak load requirements. During regular operations their mean utilization is often below 10 %. The industry has identified this as cost-saving potential and propagates the consolidation of servers by means of virtualization technologies (see also the discussion in section 2.5). The well-studied capacity planning methods from Operations Research could directly support the management of such shared resource pools and thus leverage the cost-savings. Example methods include combinatorial optimization techniques as generally applied to bin-packing problems or algorithms from Queuing Network Theory (see Bennani and Menascé, 2005; Chen et al., 2007; Urgaonkar et al., 2007, for example applications). However, this requires basic model input parameters such as the resource consumption of services or demand curves to become readily available. In the present work, we showed how resource profiles for customer-oriented services can be determined and demonstrated their appropriateness as input parameters for analytical performance models. This information on the resource consumption of services is applicable not only for IT Cost Accounting, but for various functions within IT Service Management. Until now, the resource profiles have been static and subject to certain assumptions, for instance on user behavior or infrastructure configuration. We claim that if that information could be determined in real-time, a vast potential for optimization of system and capacity management could be realized. There are recent developments in the domain of application transaction profiling tools, but these tools have not yet achieved a technology maturity level sufficient for a significant market penetration (see section 3.5.1).

Besides the shortcomings of monitoring tools, the optimization of resource utilization is often complicated by unpredictable and non-prioritized customer demands causing unnecessary peak loads on the components. For grid resources, researchers have proposed (market) mechanisms to regulate supply and demand (see for instance Kenyon and Cheliotis, 2004; Neumann et al., 2006). However, their concepts mainly apply to computing-

intensive jobs and not to the interactive workload of the online resources in today's data
centers. An efficient and effective demand control could be realized, for instance, by clas-
sifying and prioritizing customer requests. While in communication networks established
mechanisms allocate the available bandwidth to differently ranked customers and services,
there are few approaches to realize similar concepts for computing resources (see Bichler
and Setzer, 2007, for an admission control example).

Beyond all technical aspects, however, we consider the establishment of a common understanding of what the real end-products of data centers or IT units are to be the major
organizational challenge. While this question typically does not arise in the production of
physical goods, we regularly encounter different perceptions and discussions on the nature
of IT services. An IT unit considers, for instance, the provision of a server as an IT service, while its customers have support or automation of certain business processes in mind.
Generally, such misunderstandings complicate the communication between providers and
customers. We have discussed some of the arising problems against the background of
Cost Allocation and Capacity Planning. However, the underlying question affects IT Service Management as a whole. Uebernickel et al. (2006a,b) recently addressed this problem
and proposed a transfer of industrial product-engineering methods to IT Service Management. We claim that for an advancement of the discipline, further contributions in that
direction are required.

Bibliography

Aberdour, Mark. n.d. *Performance test tools*. URL http://www.opensourcetesting.org/performance.php. Viewed 2006-11-22.

Adobe. n.d. *Pet Market Blueprint Application*. Adobe Systems Incorporated. URL http://www.adobe.com/devnet/blueprint. Viewed 2007-03-12.

Albaugh, Virgil, Hari Madduri. 2004. The utility metering service of the Universal Management Infrastructure. *IBM SYSTEMS JOURNAL* **43**(1) 179–189.

Allen, Arnold O. 1990. *Probability, Statistics, and Queuing Theory With Computer Science Applications*. 2nd ed. Academic Press, San Diego, California.

Apache. n.d. *HTTP Server Project*. Apache Software Foundation. URL http://httpd.apache.org. Viewed 2007-02-26.

Appel, Andrew M., Neeru Arora, Raymond Zenkich. 2005. Unraveling the mystery of IT costs. *McKinsey on IT* (No. 5, Fall 2005) 12–17.

Aurenz, Heiko. 1997. *Controlling verteilter Informationssysteme. Client/Server-Architekturen*. Peter Lang, Frankfurt am Main.

Bard, Yonathan. 1979. Some Extensions to Multiclass Queueing Network Analysis. *The 3rd International Symposium on Modelling and Performance Evaluation of Computer Systems*. Vienna, Austria, 51–62.

Bartels, Andrew. 2006. Global IT Budget Composition: 2006. Tech. rep., Forrester Research, Inc. Published 2006-06-08.

Barton, Neil. 2006. Benchmarking, Outsourcing, And Evaluation In The IT Industry or "Commoditization Is In The Eye Of The Stakeholder". *The 13th European Conference on Information Technology Evaluation*. Genoa, Italy.

Baskett, Forest, K. Mani Chandy, Richard R. Muntz, Fernando G. Palacios. 1975. Open, Closed, and Mixed Networks of Queues with Different Classes of Customers. *Journal of the ACM* **22**(2) 248–260.

BEA. n.d.a. *BEA certified Petstore Demo (1.3.1 02)*. BEA Systems, Inc. URL https://petstore.projects.dev2dev.bea.com. Viewed 2007-03-12.

BEA. n.d.b. *BEA WebLogic Product Family*. BEA Systems, Inc. URL http://www.bea.com/weblogic. Viewed 2007-02-26.

Bennani, Mohamed N., Daniel A. Menascé. 2005. Resource Allocation for Autonomic Data Centers using Analytic Performance Models. *The 2nd IEEE International Conference on Autonomic Computing*. Seattle, Washington.

Bertleff, Claudia. 2001. Einführung einer IT-Leistungsverrechnung zur Unterstützung des strategischen IT-Controllings. Heidi Heilmann, ed., *Strategisches IT-Controlling*. HMD - Praxis der Wirtschaftsinformatik, dpunkt.Verlag, Heidelberg, 57–66.

Bertoli, Marco, Giuliano Casale, Giuseppe Serazzi. 2006. Java Modelling Tools: an Open Source Suite for Queueing Network Modelling and Workload Analysis. *The 3rd International Conference on the Quantitative Evaluation of Systems*. Riverside, California, 119–120.

Bichler, Martin, Thomas Setzer. 2007. Admission control for media on demand services. *Service Oriented Computing and Applications* **1**(1) 65–73.

Biethahn, Jörg, Harry Mucksch, Walter Ruf. 2004. *Ganzheitliches Informationsmangement - Band I: Grundlagen*. 6th ed. Oldenbourg, München.

Blosch, Marcus, Roger Woolfe, Jeremy Grigg. 2003a. Chargeback: How Far Should You Go? Tech. Rep. ID Number: G-11-4621, Gartner, Inc.

Blosch, Marcus, Roger Woolfe, Jeremy Grigg. 2003b. Chargeback: How Far Should You Go? (Executive Summary, freely available). Tech. Rep. ID Number: G-11-5501, Gartner, Inc.

BMW Group, ed. 2006. *Annual Report 2005*. Bayerische Motoren Werke Aktiengesellschaft, Munich.

Bolch, Gunter, Malte Gaebell, Hermann Jung. 1992. Analyse offener Warteschlangen-netze mit Methoden für geschlossene Warteschlangennetze. *Jahrestagung der Deutsche Gesellschaft für Operations Research*. Aachen, 324–332.

Bolch, Gunter, Stefan Greiner, Hermann de Meer. 2006. *Queueing Networks and Markov Chains*. 2nd ed. Wiley-Interscience, Hoboken, New Jersey.

Bolch, Gunter, Helmut Riedel. 1997. *Leistungsbewertung von Rechensystemen mittels analytischer Warteschlangenmodelle*. Teubner, Stuttgart.

Borland. n.d. *SilkPerformer*. Borland Software Corporation. URL http://www.borland.com/us/products/silk/silkperformer. Viewed 2006-11-18.

Brenner, Walter. 2004. Auf dem Weg zur Produktorientierung. *Computerwoche* (No. 45, published 2004-10-29) 38.

Bristol. n.d. *TransactionVision*. Bristol Technology Inc. URL http://www.bristol.com/transactionvision. Viewed 2006-12-21.

Buzen, Jeffrey P., Annie W. Shum. 1996. Beyond Bandwidth-Mainframe Style Capacity Planning for Networks and Windows NT. *The 22nd International Computer Measurement Group Conference*. San Diego, California, 479–485.

Carr, Nicholas G. 2003. IT Doesn't Matter. *Harvard Business Review* **81**(5) 41–49.

Carr, Nicholas G. 2005. The End of Corporate Computing. *MIT Sloan Management Review* **46**(3) 67–73.

Chang, Kay, Anthony Dasari, Hari Madduri, Alfredo Mendoza, John Mims. 2004. Design of an enablement process for on demand applications. *IBM SYSTEMS JOURNAL* **43**(1) 190–203.

Chaudhuri, Surajit, Umeshwar Dayal. 1997. An overview of data warehousing and OLAP technology. *SIGMOD Record* **26**(1) 65–74.

Chen, Yuan, Subu Iyer, Xue Liu, Dejan Milojicic, Akhil Sahai. 2007. SLA Decomposition: Translating Service Level Objectives to System Level Thresholds. Tech. Rep. HPL-2007-17, Hewlett-Packard Development Company.

Cherkasova, Ludmila, Diwaker Gupta, Amin Vahdat. 2007. When Virtual is Harder than Real: Resource Allocation Challenges in Virtual Machine Based IT Environments. Tech. Rep. HPL-2007-25, Hewlett-Packard Development Company.

CIMS Lab. n.d. *System Description Manual*. CIMS Lab, Inc. URL http://www.cimslab. com. Viewed 2006-06-01.

Controller Verein. 2004. *Unbekanntes Wesen IT-Kosten*. Internationaler Controller Verein. URL http://www.controllerverein.com/_cmsdata/_cache/cms_103944.html. Viewed 2007-08-01.

Cooper, Robin, Robert S. Kaplan. 1987. How Cost Accounting Systematically Distorts Product Costs. William J. Bruns, Robert S. Kaplan, eds., *Accounting and Management: Field Study Perspectives*. Harvard Business School Press, Boston, Massachusetts, 204–228.

Cooper, Robin, Robert S. Kaplan. 1988. Measure Costs Right. Make the Right decisions. *Harvard Business Review* **66**(5) 96–103.

DIN 66273. 1991. Messung und Bewertung der Leistung von DV-Systemen (DIN 66273 Part 1). Deutsches Institut für Normung.

Dirlewanger, Werner. 1994. *Messung und Bewertung der DV- Leistung. Auf Basis der Norm DIN 66273*. Hüthig, Heidelberg.

Drury, Donald H. 1997. Chargeback systems in client/server environments. *Information & Management* **32**(4) 177–186.

Econet. n.d. *cMatrix DataXRay*. Econet AG. URL http://www.econet.de/product/dataxray. Viewed 2006-07-13.

Erlang, Agner Krarup. 1909. The Theory of Probability and Telephone Conversations. *Nyt Tidsskrift for Matematik B* (20) 33–39.

Foster, Ian, Steven Tuecke. 2005. Describing the Elephant: The Different Faces of IT as Service. *ACM Queue* **3**(6) 26–34.

Fürer, Patrick J. 1994. *Prozesse und EDV-Kostenverrechnung. Die prozeßbasierte Verrechnungskonzeption für Bankrechenzentren*. Paul Haupt, Bern.

Friedman, Mark, Odysseas Pentakalos. 2002. *Windows 2000 Performance Guide*. O'Reilly, Sebastopol, California.

Frisch, Jürgen. 2002. Tools ordnen IT-Ausgaben ihrem Verursacher zu. *Computer Zeitung* (No. 35) 14.

Fujitsu Siemens. n.d. *RAV System Resource Accounting*. Fujitsu Siemens Computers GmbH. URL http://www.fujitsu-siemens.de/products/software/utilities/rav.html. Viewed 2006-07-29.

Funke, Harald. 1999. *Kosten- und Leistungsrechnung in der EDV. Stand und Entwurf einer prozeßorientierten DV-Kostenverrechnung*. Kassel University Press, Kassel.

Gadatsch, Andreas, Jens Juszczak, Martin Kütz. 2005. *Ergebnisse der Umfrage zum Stand des IT-Controlling im deutschsprachigen Raum, Schriftenreihe des Fachbereiches Wirtschaft Sankt Augustin*, vol. 12. Fachhochschule Bonn-Rhein-Sieg. Fachbereich Wirtschaft Sankt Augustin, Sankt Augustin.

Gadatsch, Andreas, Elmar Mayer. 2006. *Masterkurs IT-Controlling*. 3rd ed. Vieweg, Wiesbaden.

Gammel, Robert. 2005. Wer Agilität verliert, verpasst Chancen. Interview mit BMW CIO Jürgen Maidl. *Computerwoche* (No. 20, published 2005-05-12) 36.

Gartner. 2006. Hype Cycle for IT Operations Management 2006. Tech. Rep. ID Number: G00141081, Gartner, Inc.

Gerlach, James, Bruce Neumann, Edwin Moldauer, Martha Argo, Daniel Frisby. 2002. Determining the cost of IT services. *Communications of the ACM* **40**(9) 61–67.

Gerlinger, Annette, Alexander Buresch, Helmut Krcmar. 2000. Prozeßorientierte IV-Leistungsverrechnung - Der Weg zur totalen Transparenz? Helmut Krcmar, Alexander Buresch, Michael Reb, eds., *IV-Controlling auf dem Prüfstand*. Gabler, Wiesbaden, 105–142.

Godard, Sebastien. n.d. *Sysstat utilities*. URL http://perso.orange.fr/sebastien.godard. Viewed 2006-09-04.

Gomolski, Barbara. 2005. Selecting a Chargeback Method Depends on the Business Unit and IT Service. Tech. Rep. ID Number: G00126916, Gartner, Inc.

Gordon, William J., Gordon F. Newell. 1967. Closed queueing systems with exponential servers. *Operations Research* **15**(2) 254–265.

Gross, Donald, Carl M. Harris. 1998. *Fundamentals of Queueing Theory*. 3rd ed. John Wiley & Sons, New York.

Hamilton, George. 2005. Application Load Testing Market Is Poised for Growth. Tech. Rep. Pub ID: YANL1164955, Yankee Group Research, Inc.

Harvard Business Review. 2003. *Does IT Matter? An HBR Debate*. Harvard Business Review. URL http://harvardbusinessonline.hbsp.harvard.edu/b02/en/files/misc/Web_ Letters.pdf. Viewed 2007-01-14.

Haverkort, Boudewijn R. 1998. *Performance of Computer Communication Systems: A Model-Based Approach*. John Wiley & Sons, New York.

Hübner, Dirk G, Christoph Waschbüsch, Christof Weinhardt, Peter Bruhns, Markus Ko- erner. 1999. *Prozessorientiertes IT-Kostenmanagement in Banken. State-of-the-art, Trends, Strategien*. Fachverlag Moderne Wirtschaft, Frankfurt am Main.

Heilmann, Heidi, ed. 2001. *Strategisches IT-Controlling*. HMD-Praxis der Wirtschaftsin- formatik, dpunkt.verlag, Heidelberg.

Heine, Jack. 2006. Tiering Requirements Simplify Application Chargebacks. Tech. Rep. ID Number: G00143226, Gartner, Inc.

Heinrich, Lutz J. 2002. *Informationsmanagement*. 7th ed. Oldenbourg, München.

Hevner, Alan R., Salvatore T. March, Jinsoo Park, Sudha Ram. 2004. Design Science Research in Information Systems. *MIS Quarterly* **28**(1) 75–105.

Hewlett-Packard. n.d.a. *rstatd - Kernel Statistics Server (HP-UX Reference Release 11i)*. Hewlett-Packard Development Company. URL http://www.docs.hp.com/en/ B2355-90692/rstatd.1M.html. Viewed 2007-03-15.

Hewlett-Packard. n.d.b. *sar - System Activity Reporter (HP-UX Reference Release 11i)*. Hewlett-Packard Development Company. URL http://www.docs.hp.com/en/ B2355-90692/sar.1M.html. Viewed 2007-02-06.

Hlynka, Myron. n.d. *List of Queueing Theory Software*. URL http://www2.uwindsor.ca/~hlynka/qsoft.html. Viewed 2006-09-26.

Hochstein, Axel, Andreas Hunziker. 2003. Serviceorientierte Referenzmodelle des IT-Managements. Walter Brenner, Andreas Meier, Rüdiger Zarnekow, eds., *Strategisches IT-Management, HMD - Praxis der Wirtschaftsinformatik*, vol. 232. dpunkt.Verlag, Heidelberg, 46–56.

Hochstein, Axel, Rüdiger Zarnekow, Walter Brenner. 2004. ITIL als Common-Practice-Referenzmodell für das IT-Service-Management - Formale Beurteilung und Implikationen für die Praxis. *WIRTSCHAFTSINFORMATIK* **46**(5) 382–389.

Horngren, Charles T., Srikant M. Datar, George Foster. 2005. *Cost Accounting. A Managerial Emphasis*. 12th ed. Prentice Hall, Englewood Cliffs, New Jersey.

Horváth, Peter, Reinhold Mayer. 1989. Prozesskostenrechnung. Der neue Weg zu mehr Kostentransparenz und wirkungsvolleren Unternehmensstrategien. *Controlling* **1**(4) 214–219.

Horváth, Péter. 2006. *Controlling*. 10th ed. Vahlen, München.

Häusler, Oliver, Axel C. Schwickert, Sascha Ebersberger. 2005. IT-Service-Management : Referenzmodelle im Vergleich. Tech. Rep. 06/05, Professur für BWL und Wirtschaftsinformatik. Justus-Liebig-Universität Giessen.

IBM. 2004. *IBM Accelerates On Demand Initiative to Meet Growing Demand*. IBM Corporation. URL http://www-03.ibm.com/press/us/en/pressrelease/7313.wss.Viewed 2006-11-26.

IBM. n.d.a. *CIMS Chargeback System (now: Tivoli Usage and Accounting Manager)*. IBM Corporation. URL http://www.cimslab.com. Viewed 2006-07-13.

IBM. n.d.b. *Using System Management Facility*. IBM Corporation.URL http://publib.boulder.ibm.com/infocenter/wmqv6/v6r0/topic/com.ibm.mq.csqsav. doc/csq83aq.htm#csq83aq. Viewed 2007-01-18.

IBM. n.d.c. *z/OS Resource Measurement Facility*. IBM Corporation. URL http://www-03.ibm.com/servers/eserver/zseries/zos/rmf. Viewed 2007-02-27.

Ideal Observer. n.d. *Einkaufsführer Web Analytics*. Ideal Observer. URL http://www. idealobserver.de. Viewed 2006-09-04.

Intel. n.d. *Intel VTune Performance Analyzer*. Intel Corporation. URL http://www. intel.com/cd/software/products/asmo-na/eng/vtune/239144.htm. Viewed 2006-11-18.

ISO 14756. 1999. Measurement and rating of performance of computer-based software systems. International Organization for Standardization.

IT Governance Institute, ed. 2005. *COBIT 4.0*. Information Systems Audit and Control Association, Rolling Meadows, Illinois.

IT Governance Institute, ed. 2006. *IT Governance Global Status Report - 2006*. Information Systems Audit and Control Association, Rolling Meadows, Illinois.

ITFMA. n.d. *IT Financial Management Association*. IT Financial Management Association (ITFMA). URL http://www.itfma.com. Viewed 2006-08-06.

Jackson, James R. 1957. Networks of waiting lines. *Operations Research* **5**(4) 518–521.

Jackson, James R. 1963. Jobshop-Like Queueing Systems. *Management Science* **10**(1) 131–142.

JavaPerformanceTuning. n.d. *Tool reports*. JavaPerformanceTuning.com. URL http: //www.javaperformancetuning.com/tools. Viewed 2006-07-13.

Juse, Kai S., Samuel Kounev, Alejandro P. Buchmann. 2003. PetStore-WS: Measuring the Performance Implications of Web Services. *The 29th International Computer Measurement Group Conference*. Dallas, Texas, 113–123.

Kaplan, Robert S., Anthony A. Atkinson. 1998. *Advanced management accounting*. 3rd ed. Prentice Hall, Englewood Cliffs, New Jersey.

Kargl, Herbert. 1999. *DV-Controlling*. 4th ed. Oldenbourg, München.

Kemper, Alfons, André Eickler. 2006. *Datenbanksysteme*. 6th ed. Oldenbourg, München.

Kendall, David G. 1953. Stochastic processes occurring in the theory of queues and their analysis by the method of the imbedded Markov chain. *Annals of Mathematical Statistics* **24**(3) 338–354.

Kenyon, Chris, Giorgos Cheliotis. 2004. Grid Resource Commercialization. Jarek Nabrzyski, Jennifer M. Schopf, Jan Weglarz, eds., *Grid Resource Management: State of the Art and Future Trends*. Kluwer Academic Publishers, Norwell, Massachusetts, 465–478.

Kleinrock, Leonard. 1975. *Queueing Systems. Volume 1: Theory*. John Wiley & Sons, New York.

Kleinrock, Leonard. 1976. *Queueing Systems. Volume 2: Computer Applications*. John Wiley & Sons, New York.

Kounev, Samuel, Alejandro P. Buchmann. 2003. Performance Modeling and Evaluation of Large-Scale J2EE Applications. *The 29th International Computer Measurement Group Conference*. Dallas, Texas, 273–283.

Krcmar, Helmut. 2004. *Informationsmanagement*. 4th ed. Springer, Berlin.

Krcmar, Helmut, Alexander Buresch. 1994. IV-Controlling - Ein Rahmenkonzept für die Praxis. Tech. rep., Lehrstuhl für Wirtschaftsinformatik. Universität Hohenheim.

Krcmar, Helmut, Alexander Buresch, Michael Reb. 2000. *IV-Controlling auf dem Prüfstand*. Gabler, Wiesbaden.

Krüll, Jürgen. 1997. UNIX-Accounting als Datenbasis des IV-Controlling - Möglichkeiten und Grenzen. Tech. Rep. Diskussionspapier Nr. 345, Fakultät für Wirtschaftswissenschaften. Universität Bielefeld.

Lazowska, Edward D. 1984. *Quantitative System Performance. Computer System Analysis Using Queuing Network Models*. Prentice Hall, Englewood Cliffs, New Jersey.

Liebmann, Lenny. 1996. The Meter is running. *Communications Week* (Issue 1996-09-23) 50–55.

Liu, Xue, Jin Heo, Lui Sha. 2005. Modeling 3-Tiered Web Applications. *The 13th IEEE International Symposium on Modeling, Analysis, and Simulation of Computer and Telecommunication Systems*. Atlanta, Georgia.

Luftman, Jerry, Rajkumar Kempaiah, Elby Nash. 2006. Key Issues for IT Executives 2005. *MIS Quarterly Executive* **5**(2) 81–99.

MacDougall, Myron H. 1987. *Simulating computer systems: techniques and tools*. MIT Press, Cambridge, Massachusetts.

Mai, Jan. 1996. *Konzeption einer controllinggerechten Kosten- und Leistungsrechnung für Rechenzentren*. Peter Lang, Frankfurt am Main.

March, Salvatore T., Gerald F. Smith. 1995. Design and Natural Science Research on Information Technology. *Decision Support Systems* **15**(4) 251–266.

Marsan, Marco Ajmone, Gianfranco Balbo, Gianni Conte. 1984. A Class of Generalized Stochastic Petri Nets for the Performance Analysis of Multiprocessor Systems. *ACM Transactions on Computer Systems* **2**(2) 93–122.

McKinnon, William P., Ernest A. Kallman. 1987. Mapping Chargeback Systems to Organizational Environments. *MIS Quarterly* **11**(1) 5–20.

Menascé, Daniel A., Virgilio A. F. Almeida. 2000. *Scaling for E-Business: Technologies, Models, Performance, and Capacity Planning*. Prentice Hall, Upper Saddle River, New Jersey.

Menascé, Daniel A., Virgilio A. F. Almeida. 2002. *Capacity Planning for Web Services. Metrics, Models, and Methods*. Prentice Hall, Upper Saddle River, New Jersey.

Menascé, Daniel A., Virgilio A. F. Almeida, Larry W. Dowdy. 2004. *Performance by Design: Computer Capacity Planning by Example*. Prentice Hall, Upper Saddle River, New Jersey.

Mercury. 2004. *Mercury Virtual User Generator User's Guide (Version 8.0)*. Mercury Interactive Corporation, Sunnyvale, California.

Mercury. n.d.a. *Mercury LoadRunner*. Mercury Interactive Corporation. URL http://www.mercury.com/us/products/performance-center/loadrunner. Viewed 2006-07-13.

Mercury. n.d.b. *Mercury LoadRunner Data Sheet*. Mercury Interactive Corporation. URL http://www.mercury.com/us/pdf/products/datasheets/DS-0990-0506-loadrunner.pdf. Viewed 2006-01-31.

Mercury. n.d.c. *Mercury LoadRunner Protocols*. Mercury Interactive Corporation. URL http://www.mercury.com/us/pdf/products/loadrunner/1855-1006-loadrunner-protocols.pdf. Viewed 2007-01-31.

Michels, Jochen K. 2003a. *IT-Benchmarking*. 2nd ed. VDM Verlag Dr. Müller, Düsseldorf.

Michels, Jochen K. 2003b. *IT-Finanzmanagement*. 2nd ed. VDM Verlag Dr. Müller, Düsseldorf.

Michels, Jochen K. 2003c. *Pricing für SAP-Dienste*. 2nd ed. VDM Verlag Dr. Müller, Düsseldorf.

Michels, Jochen K. 2004. *IT-Betriebsabrechnung. Der BAB des Rechenzentrums*. VDM Verlag Dr. Müller, Düsseldorf.

Microsoft. n.d.a. *Microsoft .NET Pet Shop*. Microsoft Corporation. URL http://www.gotdotnet.com/team/compare/petshop.aspx. Viewed 2007-03-12.

Microsoft. n.d.b. *Overview of Performance Monitoring (Windows 2000 Server Resource Kit)*. Microsoft Corporation. URL http://www.microsoft.com/technet/prodtechnol/windows2000serv/reskit/prork/preb_mon_ofnh.mspx?mfr=true. Viewed 2007-02-05.

Miller, Jeffrey G., Thomas E. Vollmann. 1985. The Hidden Factory. *Harvard Business Review* **63**(5) 142–150.

Müller-Clostermann, Bruno. 2001. *Kursbuch Kapazitätsmanagement*. Books on Demand, Norderstedt.

Nagaprabhanjan, Bellari, Varsha Apte. 2005. A Tool for Automated Resource Consumption Profiling of Distributed Transactions. *The 2nd International Conference on Distributed Computing and Internet Technology*. Bhubaneshwar, India, 154–165.

Neumann, Dirk, Carsten Holtmann, Carsten Orwat. 2006. Grid-Economics. *WIRTSCHAFTSINFORMATIK* **48**(3) 206–209.

Neuse, Doug, K. Mani Chandy. 1981. SCAT: A heuristic algorithm for queueing network models of computing systems. *ACM SIGMETRICS Conference on Measurement and Modeling of Computer Systems*. Las Vegas, Nevada, 59–79.

Nicetec. n.d. *netinsight*. Nicetec GmbH. URL http://www.nicetec.de. Viewed 2006-07-13.

Object Refinery. n.d. *JFreeChart*. Object Refinery Limited. URL http://www.jfree.org/jfreechart. Viewed 2006-07-13.

Office of Government Commerce, ed. 2001. *Service Delivery*. IT Infrastructure Library (ITIL), Stationery Office Books, London.

Office of Government Commerce, ed. 2002a. *ICT Infrastructure Management*. IT Infrastructure Library (ITIL), Stationery Office Books, London.

Office of Government Commerce, ed. 2002b. *Planning to Implement Service Management*. IT Infrastructure Library (ITIL), Stationery Office Books, London.

Office of Government Commerce. n.d. *Glossary of Terms, Definitions and Acronyms*. Office of Government Commerce. URL http://www.best-management-practice.com/ gempdf/ITILGlossary.pdf. Viewed 2007-01-14.

Oleson, Thomas D. 1998. Price of precision. *CIO Magazine* (Issue 1998-02-15) 34–38.

OpTier. n.d. *CoreFirst*. OpTier, Inc. URL http://www.optier.com/Site/products/ technology.asp. Viewed 2006-12-21.

Owen, Gary, Jonathan Law. 2005. *A Dictionary of Accounting*. Oxford University Press, New York.

Padhye, Jitendra, Anirudha D. Rahatekar, Lawrence W. Dowdy. 1995. A Simple LAN File Placement Strategy. *The 21st International Computer Measurement Group Conference*. Nashville, Tennessee, 396–406.

Paul-Zirvas, Jana, Markus Bereszewski. 2004. Gründlich verrechnet. *Informationweek* (No. 5-6, published 2004-04-08) 12–14.

Quinlan, Terence A. 1989. *EDP cost accounting*. John Wiley & Sons, New York.

Redman, Bill, Bill Kirwin, Tom Berg. 1998. TCO: A Critical Tool for Managing IT. Tech. Rep. ID Number: R-06-1697, Gartner, Inc.

Reichmann, Thomas. 2006. *Controlling mit Kennzahlen und Management-Tools. Die systemgestützte Controlling-Konzeption*. 7th ed. Vahlen, München.

Reiser, Martin. 1981. Mean-Value Analysis and Convolution Method for Queue-Dependent Servers in Closed Queueing Networks. *Performance Evaluation* **1**(1) 7–18.

Reiser, Martin, Stephen S. Lavenberg. 1980. Mean-Value Analysis of Closed Multichain Queuing Networks. *Journal of the ACM* **27**(2) 313–322.

Riebel, Paul. 1994. *Einzelkosten- und Deckungsbeitragsrechnung.* 7th ed. Gabler, Wiesbaden.

Rolia, Jerome A., Kenneth C. Sevcik. 1995. The Method of Layers. *IEEE Transactions on Software Engineering* **21**(8) 689–700.

Ross, Jeanne W., Michael R. Vitale, Cynthia Mathis Beath. 1999. The untapped potential of IT chargeback. *MIS Quarterly* **23**(2) 215–237.

SAP. n.d.a. *SAP NetWeaver.* SAP AG. URL http://www.sap.com/platform/netweaver. Viewed 2006-01-19.

SAP. n.d.b. *SAP Standard Application Benchmarks.* SAP AG. URL http://www.sap.com/solutions/benchmark. Viewed 2006-12-11.

Schauer, Hanno. 2006. IT-Controlling. Vergleichende Buchbesprechung. *WIRTSCHAFTSINFORMATIK* **48**(3) 212–218.

Scheeg, Jochen Michael. 2005. *Integrierte IT-Kostentabellen als Instrument für eine effiziente IT-Leistungserbringung im Informationsmanagement: Konzeption und praktische Umsetzung.* Difo-Druck, Bamberg.

Schmitz, Ludger. 2005. Rechenleistung aus dem großen Topf. *Computerwoche* (No. 4, published 2005-01-27) 16.

Schweitzer, Paul J. 1979. Approximate analysis of multiclass closed networks of queues. *International Conference on Stochastic Control and Optimization.* Amsterdam, Netherlands, 25–29.

Schwichtenberg, Holger. n.d. *Tools and Software Components for the .NET Framework.* URL http://www.dotnetframework.de/dotnet/tools.aspx. Viewed 2006-07-13.

Siebertz, Jens. 2004. *IT-Kostencontrolling. Nutzenpotenziale von Controlling-Tools.* VDM Verlag Dr. Müller, Düsseldorf.

Simon, Herbert A. 1996. *The Sciences of the Artificial.* 3rd ed. MIT Press, Cambridge, Massachusetts.

Singh, Inderjeet, Beth Stearns, Mark Johnson. 2002. *Designing Enterprise Applications with the J2EE Platform.* Addison-Wesley, Boston, Massachusetts.

Son, Sertaç, Thomas Gladyszewski. 2005. *Return on IT-Controlling 2005. Eine empirische Untersuchung zum Einfluss des IT-Controllings auf die unternehmensweite IT Performance.* E-Finance Lab, Frankfurt am Main.

SourceForge. n.d. *Java Modelling Tools.* SourceForge.net. URL http://jmt.sourceforge. net. Viewed 2006-09-05.

SPEC. n.d.a. *CPU2000 (CPU Benchmark).* Standard Performance Evaluation Corporation. URL http://www.spec.org/cpu2000. Viewed 2006-08-31.

SPEC. n.d.b. *SPECjAppServer2002 (Java Application Server Benchmark).* Standard Performance Evaluation Corporation. URL http://www.spec.org/jAppServer2002. Viewed 2006-12-14.

Spitta, Thorsten. 2000. Kostenrechnerische Grundlagen für das IV-Controlling. *Kostenrechnungspraxis* **44**(5) 279–288.

Spitta, Thorsten, Fred G. Becker. 2000. Zeiterfassung in der IV - Personalkontrolle oder Transparenz? *WIRTSCHAFTSINFORMATIK* **42**(Sonderheft IT & Personal) 48–55.

Sun Microsystems. n.d.a. *Java Pet Store Sample Application.* Sun Microsystems, Inc. URL http://java.sun.com/blueprints/code/jps132/docs. Viewed 2006-07-13.

Sun Microsystems. n.d.b. *Sample Application Design and Implementation.* Sun Microsystems, Inc. URL http://java.sun.com/blueprints/guidelines/designing_enterprise_ applications_2e/sample-app/sample-app1.3.1.pdf. Viewed 2007-03-12.

Sun Microsystems. n.d.c. *The Java 2 Platform, Enterprise Edition (J2EE).* Sun Microsystems. URL http://java.sun.com/j2ee/1.3. Viewed 2007-03-10.

Symantec. n.d. *Application Performance Management.* Symantec Corporation. URL http: //www.symantec.com/Products/enterprise?c=prodcat&refId=1021. Viewed 2006-07-13.

Syskoplan. 2002. *Optimierung der Total Cost of Ownership in IT-Abteilungen scheitert an der fehlenden Leistungsverrechnung.* Syskoplan AG. URL http://www.syskoplan. de/content/pressemitteilungen/sysko_pres_260802.pdf. Viewed 2006-11-30.

TeamQuest. n.d. *TeamQuest Model.* TeamQuest Corporation. URL http://www. teamquest.com/solutions-products/products/model. Viewed 2006-09-05.

Teubner, Alexander, Stefan Klein. 2002. Informationsmanagement. Vergleichende Buchbesprechung. *WIRTSCHAFTSINFORMATIK* **44**(3) 285–299.

Tjims, Henk C. 1995. *Stochastic Models: An Algorithmic Approach*. John Wiley & Sons, New York.

TPPC. n.d.a. *TPC-App (Application server and web services benchmark)*. Transaction Processing Performance Council. URL http://www.tpc.org/tpc_app. Viewed 2006-06-26.

TPPC. n.d.b. *TPC-C (On-line transaction processing benchmark)*. Transaction Processing Performance Council. URL http://www.tpc.org/tpcc. Viewed 2006-12-11.

Uebernickel, Falk, Carlos Bravo-Sànchez, Rüdiger Zarnekow, Walter Brenner. 2006a. Eine Vorgehensmethodik für das IT-Produktengineering. *Multikonferenz Wirtschaftsinformatik*. Passau.

Uebernickel, Falk, Carlos Bravo-Sànchez, Rüdiger Zarnekow, Walter Brenner. 2006b. IS Service-Engineering: A process model for the development of IS services. *European and Mediterranean Conference on Information Systems*. Alicante, Spain.

University of Cambridge. n.d. *The Xen virtual machine monitor*. University of Cambridge Computer Laboratory. URL http://www.cl.cam.ac.uk/Research/SRG/netos/xen. Viewed 2006-08-29.

Urgaonkar, Bhuvan, Giovanni Pacifici, Prashant Shenoy, Mike Spreitzer, Asser Tantawi. 2007. Analytic Modeling of Multitier Internet Applications. *ACM Transactions on the Web* **1**(1).

USU. n.d. *Costing/Charging Manager*. USU AG. URL http://www.usu.de/it_management_solutions/finance_management/costing_charging_manager.html. Viewed 2006-07-13.

Verner, June M., Kranti Toraskar, R. Brown. 1996. Information systems chargeout: a review of current approaches and future challenges. *Journal of Information Technology* **11**(2) 101–117.

von Dobschütz, Leonhard, Manfred Barth, Heidi Jäger-Goy, Martin Kütz, Hans-Peter Möller, eds. 2000. *IV-Controlling. Konzepte - Umsetzungen - Erfahrungen*. Gabler, Wiesbaden.

Weill, Peter, Richard Woodham. 2002. Don't Just Lead, Govern: Implementing Effective IT Governance. Tech. Rep. MIT Sloan Working Paper No. 4237-02, Sloan School of Management.

Wheatley, Malcolm. 2003. Chargeback for good or evil. *CIO Magazine* (Issue 2003-03-01).

Woodside, C. Murray, J. E. Neilson, Dorina C. Petriu, Shikharesh Majumdar. 1995. The Stochastic Rendezvous Network Model for Performance of Synchronous Client-Server-like Distributed Software. *IEEE Transactions on Computers* **44**(1) 20–34.

Zhang, Qi, Ludmila Cherkasova, Guy Mathews, Wayne Greene, Evgenia Smirni. 2007. A Capacity Planning Framework for Multi-tier Enterprise Services with Real Workloads. *The 10th IFIP/IEEE International Symposium on Integrated Management.* Munich.

Ziehm, Oliver. 2004. Government on Demand. Neue Wege in der Projektfinanzierung. *7. Deutscher Verwaltungskongress Effizienter Staat.* Berlin.

Appendix A

Appendix

A.1 List of Symbols

a	Resource consumption of background activities
b	Baseline (load-independent) resource consumption of a service
i	Service ($i = 1 \ldots m$)
j	Resource ($j = 1 \ldots n$)
p_i	Resource profile of service i consisting of n values p_{ij}
p_{ij}	Estimate of the expected resource consumption of service i at resource j
r	Pearson product-moment correlation coefficient ($r \in [-1; 1]$)
t	Time (length of a measurement interval)
u	Load-dependent resource consumption of a service
$\bar{u}$	Constant approximation of u
x	Number of concurrent or subsequent service invocations
y	Total resource consumption

A.2 Test Infrastructure

	Load Generator	Web Server	Application Server	Database Server
Application	Vuser scripts and load test scenario	static web content (*.html, *.gif, *.jpg)	*.ear and *.war	Oracle tablespace
Software and Server Infrastructure	LoadRunner 8.0 JRE 1.5.0	Apache http 2.0.54	Bea Weblogic 8.1 JRE 1.3.1	Oracle 9.1
Operating Systems	Windows 2000 Advanced Server	Red Hat Linux Advanced Server 2.1 (Pensacola)	Windows 2000 Advanced Server	HP-UX 11.11
Number of CPUs	2	2	2	2
CPU Performance	1000 MHz	1400 MHz	1000 MHz	440 MHz
CPU Type	Intel x86 Pentium III Coppermine	Intel x86 Xeon MP	Intel x86 Pentium III Coppermine	PA 8500 CPU Module 2.3
CPU Architecture	CISC (32 bit)	CISC (32 bit)	CISC (32 bit)	RISC (64 bit)
Disk Storage	3 * 73 GB RAID 5	3 * 72 GB RAID 5	3 * 18 GB RAID 5	2 * 36,4 GB RAID 1 and 13 GB LUN on SAN (HP XP128) via FC
Network	100 Mbps	100 Mbps / 1Gbit	100 Mbps	100 Mbps and Fibre Channel
Memory	2 GB	2 GB	2 GB	2 GB
Server Type	HP DL360	IBM X360-03	HP DL360	HP N4000
Network Name	xxxxxx20	xxxxxx03d	xxxxxx15	xxxxxx01a

Table A.1: Overview of the Test Infrastructure

A.3 Experimental Results: Resource Profiles

A.3.1 Resource Profiles

A.3.1.1 PASTA

Experiment	PA01_1
Load test 1	2006-08-14 22:41:15.0 – 2006-08-14 23:53:12.0
Runtime (test 1)	1 h 11 min 57 sec
No. of users x	1 – 20 (20 steps)
No. of services i	2
No. of intervals	40 (20 per service)

Resource j	i	p	r
Application server - Network - all - Bytes Total	read_user	237,149	0.999
Application server - Network - all - Bytes Total	edit_user	602,794	1.000
Application server - Processor - all - Processor Time	read_user	0.625	0.990
Application server - Processor - all - Processor Time	edit_user	1.651	0.996
Client computer - Network - all - Bytes Total	read_user	182,322	0.998
Client computer - Network - all - Bytes Total	edit_user	376,897	0.995
Database server - Disk - SAN - Read/Write blocks	read_user	0	n/a
Database server - Disk - SAN - Read/Write blocks	edit_user	142.111	0.914
Database server - Processor - all - Processor Time	read_user	2.672	0.997
Database server - Processor - all - Processor Time	edit_user	7.337	1.000
Web server - Processor - all - Processor Time	read_user	0.028	0.925
Web server - Processor - all - Processor Time	edit_user	0.080	0.982

Table A.2: Resource Profile: PASTA – Services including multiple Client Requests

Experiment	PA03_1
Load test 1	2006-08-20 12:23:39.0 – 2006-08-20 13:45:53.0
Runtime (test 1)	1 h 22 min 14 sec
No. of users x	1 – 20 (20 steps)
No. of services i	13
No. of intervals	260 (20 per service)

Resource j	i	p	r
Application server - Network - all - Bytes Total	logon.do	3,023	0.998
Application server - Network - all - Bytes Total	actedit.do	54,584	1.000
Application server - Network - all - Bytes Total	statussave.do	28,339	1.000
Application server - Network - all - Bytes Total	statusedit.do	27,292	1.000
Application server - Network - all - Bytes Total	logon.do_submit	29,362	1.000
Application server - Network - all - Bytes Total	listsearch.do_submit	20,915	0.999
Application server - Network - all - Bytes Total	listsearch.do	10,831	0.999
Application server - Network - all - Bytes Total	listcurrent.do	12,581	1.000
Application server - Network - all - Bytes Total	frameset	4,493	0.996
Application server - Network - all - Bytes Total	actview.do	49,479	1.000
Application server - Network - all - Bytes Total	actitemsave.do	62,020	1.000
Application server - Network - all - Bytes Total	actitemedit.do	30,146	1.000
Application server - Network - all - Bytes Total	logout.do	12,381	1.000
Application server - Processor - all - Processor Time	listcurrent.do	0.043	0.720
Application server - Processor - all - Processor Time	logon.do	0.018	0.638
Application server - Processor - all - Processor Time	statussave.do	0.061	0.886
Application server - Processor - all - Processor Time	statusedit.do	0.061	0.795
Application server - Processor - all - Processor Time	logout.do	0.051	0.867
Application server - Processor - all - Processor Time	logon.do_submit	0.122	0.826
Application server - Processor - all - Processor Time	actedit.do	0.109	0.933
Application server - Processor - all - Processor Time	frameset	0.010	0.359
Application server - Processor - all - Processor Time	actview.do	0.111	0.964
Application server - Processor - all - Processor Time	actitemsave.do	0.135	0.969
Application server - Processor - all - Processor Time	actitemedit.do	0.075	0.855
Application server - Processor - all - Processor Time	listsearch.do	0.029	0.596
Application server - Processor - all - Processor Time	listsearch.do_submit	0.039	0.797
Client computer - Network - all - Bytes Total	actitemsave.do	29,195	0.999
Client computer - Network - all - Bytes Total	logout.do	5,511	0.995
Client computer - Network - all - Bytes Total	logon.do_submit	7,874	0.994
Client computer - Network - all - Bytes Total	logon.do	4,414	0.819
Client computer - Network - all - Bytes Total	listsearch.do_submit	16,721	0.999
Client computer - Network - all - Bytes Total	listsearch.do	44,206	0.836
Client computer - Network - all - Bytes Total	listcurrent.do	17,637	1.000
Client computer - Network - all - Bytes Total	actview.do	23,675	0.998
Client computer - Network - all - Bytes Total	actitemedit.do	16,019	0.999
Client computer - Network - all - Bytes Total	actedit.do	30,376	1.000
Client computer - Network - all - Bytes Total	statussave.do	27,838	0.999
Client computer - Network - all - Bytes Total	statusedit.do	22,874	1.000
Client computer - Network - all - Bytes Total	frameset	67,143	1.000
Database server - Disk - SAN - Read/Write blocks	logon.do	0	n/a
Database server - Disk - SAN - Read/Write blocks	actedit.do	2.518	0.326
Database server - Disk - SAN - Read/Write blocks	statusedit.do	1.123	0.156

continued next page

continued

Resource j	i	p	r
Database server - Disk - SAN - Read/Write blocks	logon.do_submit	29.462	0.842
Database server - Disk - SAN - Read/Write blocks	statussave.do	27.749	0.654
Database server - Disk - SAN - Read/Write blocks	listsearch.do_submit	0	n/a
Database server - Disk - SAN - Read/Write blocks	listsearch.do	0.866	0.306
Database server - Disk - SAN - Read/Write blocks	listcurrent.do	0	n/a
Database server - Disk - SAN - Read/Write blocks	frameset	1.651	0.258
Database server - Disk - SAN - Read/Write blocks	actview.do	0	n/a
Database server - Disk - SAN - Read/Write blocks	actitemsave.do	35.540	0.746
Database server - Disk - SAN - Read/Write blocks	actitemedit.do	0.878	0.085
Database server - Disk - SAN - Read/Write blocks	logout.do	5.086	0.539
Database server - Processor - all - Processor Time	listsearch.do	0.001	0.109
Database server - Processor - all - Processor Time	actitemedit.do	0.424	0.999
Database server - Processor - all - Processor Time	actitemsave.do	0.662	0.999
Database server - Processor - all - Processor Time	actview.do	0.440	0.999
Database server - Processor - all - Processor Time	frameset	0.003	0.382
Database server - Processor - all - Processor Time	listcurrent.do	0.212	0.999
Database server - Processor - all - Processor Time	statussave.do	0.218	0.999
Database server - Processor - all - Processor Time	listsearch.do_submit	0.710	1.000
Database server - Processor - all - Processor Time	logon.do	0	n/a
Database server - Processor - all - Processor Time	logon.do_submit	0.643	0.999
Database server - Processor - all - Processor Time	actedit.do	0.441	1.000
Database server - Processor - all - Processor Time	statusedit.do	0.211	0.999
Database server - Processor - all - Processor Time	logout.do	0.211	0.998
Web server - Processor - all - Processor Time	listcurrent.do	0.004	0.919
Web server - Processor - all - Processor Time	statussave.do	0.004	0.929
Web server - Processor - all - Processor Time	statusedit.do	0.004	0.950
Web server - Processor - all - Processor Time	logout.do	0.002	0.859
Web server - Processor - all - Processor Time	logon.do_submit	0.006	0.969
Web server - Processor - all - Processor Time	logon.do	0.001	0.494
Web server - Processor - all - Processor Time	listsearch.do	0.002	0.851
Web server - Processor - all - Processor Time	frameset	0.007	0.826
Web server - Processor - all - Processor Time	actview.do	0.006	0.931
Web server - Processor - all - Processor Time	actitemsave.do	0.006	0.962
Web server - Processor - all - Processor Time	actitemedit.do	0.006	0.793
Web server - Processor - all - Processor Time	actedit.do	0.005	0.934
Web server - Processor - all - Processor Time	listsearch.do_submit	0.004	0.933

Table A.3: Resource Profile: PASTA – Services including single Client Requests

A.3.1.2   Java Pet Store

Experiment   PE01_1
Load test 1   2006-10-06 13:29:32.0 – 2006-10-06 14:13:55.0
Runtime (test 1)   44 min 23 sec
No. of users x 10 – 100 (10 steps)
No. of services i 4
No. of intervals   40 (10 per service)

Resource j	i	p	r
Application server - Network - all - Bytes Total	determined_shopper	280,466	1.000
Application server - Network - all - Bytes Total	first_time_shopper	464,655	1.000
Application server - Network - all - Bytes Total	power_shopper	594,286	1.000
Application server - Network - all - Bytes Total	curious_visitor	174,622	1.000
Application server - Processor - all - Processor Time	curious_visitor	0.172	0.844
Application server - Processor - all - Processor Time	determined_shopper	0.252	0.945
Application server - Processor - all - Processor Time	first_time_shopper	0.461	0.958
Application server - Processor - all - Processor Time	power_shopper	0.473	0.912
Client computer - Network - all - Bytes Total	power_shopper	587,170	1.000
Client computer - Network - all - Bytes Total	curious_visitor	228,617	1.000
Client computer - Network - all - Bytes Total	determined_shopper	294,606	1.000
Client computer - Network - all - Bytes Total	first_time_shopper	476,526	1.000
Database server - Disk - SAN - Read/Write blocks	determined_shopper	50.198	0.916
Database server - Disk - SAN - Read/Write blocks	first_time_shopper	74.184	0.938
Database server - Disk - SAN - Read/Write blocks	power_shopper	54.138	0.917
Database server - Disk - SAN - Read/Write blocks	curious_visitor	8.628	0.417
Database server - Processor - all - Processor Time	power_shopper	0.073	0.993
Database server - Processor - all - Processor Time	curious_visitor	0.002	0.395
Database server - Processor - all - Processor Time	determined_shopper	0.046	0.992
Database server - Processor - all - Processor Time	first_time_shopper	0.064	0.976
Web server - Processor - all - Processor Time	curious_visitor	0.012	0.977
Web server - Processor - all - Processor Time	determined_shopper	0.017	0.992
Web server - Processor - all - Processor Time	first_time_shopper	0.026	0.994
Web server - Processor - all - Processor Time	power_shopper	0.032	0.997

Table A.4: Resource Profile: Java Pet Store – Services including multiple Client Requests

Experiment   PE03_1
Load test 1   2006-09-27 10:58:44.0 – 2006-09-27 13:00:32.0
Runtime (test 1)   2 h 1 min 48 sec

No. of users x 1 – 70 (70 steps)
No. of services i 13
No. of intervals   910 (70 per service)

Resource j	i	p	r
Application server - Network - all - Bytes Total	main.screen	13,654	1.000
Application server - Network - all - Bytes Total	cart.do	17,430	0.999
Application server - Network - all - Bytes Total	update_customer.screen	26,720	1.000
Application server - Network - all - Bytes Total	signon_welcome.screen	15,976	0.998
Application server - Network - all - Bytes Total	product.screen	15,122	1.000
Application server - Network - all - Bytes Total	j_signon_check	20,134	0.999
Application server - Network - all - Bytes Total	item.screen	15,102	0.999
Application server - Network - all - Bytes Total	enter_order_information.screen	22,099	1.000
Application server - Network - all - Bytes Total	customer.do_updated	25,132	1.000
Application server - Network - all - Bytes Total	customer.do	18,788	0.999
Application server - Network - all - Bytes Total	category.screen	15,089	1.000
Application server - Network - all - Bytes Total	cart.do_update	17,479	1.000
Application server - Network - all - Bytes Total	search.screen	14,984	1.000
Application server - Processor - all - Processor Time	enter_order_information.screen	0.015	0.981
Application server - Processor - all - Processor Time	main.screen	0.017	0.948
Application server - Processor - all - Processor Time	update_customer.screen	0.021	0.988
Application server - Processor - all - Processor Time	signon_welcome.screen	0.007	0.972
Application server - Processor - all - Processor Time	search.screen	0.013	0.984
Application server - Processor - all - Processor Time	product.screen	0.010	0.967
Application server - Processor - all - Processor Time	cart.do	0.017	0.977
Application server - Processor - all - Processor Time	customer.do_updated	0.026	0.993
Application server - Processor - all - Processor Time	customer.do	0.017	0.984
Application server - Processor - all - Processor Time	category.screen	0.010	0.979
Application server - Processor - all - Processor Time	cart.do_update	0.017	0.990
Application server - Processor - all - Processor Time	item.screen	0.013	0.989
Application server - Processor - all - Processor Time	j_signon_check	0.027	0.989
Client computer - Network - all - Bytes Total	category.screen	10,258	0.865
Client computer - Network - all - Bytes Total	search.screen	11,165	0.937
Client computer - Network - all - Bytes Total	product.screen	11,148	0.897
Client computer - Network - all - Bytes Total	main.screen	55,612	0.981
Client computer - Network - all - Bytes Total	j_signon_check	14,036	0.998
Client computer - Network - all - Bytes Total	item.screen	16,581	0.895
Client computer - Network - all - Bytes Total	enter_order_information.screen	17,386	0.956
Client computer - Network - all - Bytes Total	customer.do	14,940	0.983
Client computer - Network - all - Bytes Total	cart.do_update	11,761	0.898
Client computer - Network - all - Bytes Total	cart.do	20,195	0.959
Client computer - Network - all - Bytes Total	update_customer.screen	20,861	0.966

continued next page

continued

Resource j	i	p	r
Client computer - Network - all - Bytes Total	signon_welcome.screen	12,740	0.849
Client computer - Network - all - Bytes Total	customer.do_updated	18,575	0.989
Database server - Disk - SAN - Read/Write blocks	main.screen	0	n/a
Database server - Disk - SAN - Read/Write blocks	cart.do	0	n/a
Database server - Disk - SAN - Read/Write blocks	signon_welcome.screen	0	n/a
Database server - Disk - SAN - Read/Write blocks	product.screen	0	n/a
Database server - Disk - SAN - Read/Write blocks	update_customer.screen	0	n/a
Database server - Disk - SAN - Read/Write blocks	j_signon_check	0	n/a
Database server - Disk - SAN - Read/Write blocks	item.screen	0.007	0.076
Database server - Disk - SAN - Read/Write blocks	enter_order_information.screen	0	n/a
Database server - Disk - SAN - Read/Write blocks	customer.do_updated	0	n/a
Database server - Disk - SAN - Read/Write blocks	customer.do	0.013	0.077
Database server - Disk - SAN - Read/Write blocks	category.screen	0	n/a
Database server - Disk - SAN - Read/Write blocks	cart.do_update	0	n/a
Database server - Disk - SAN - Read/Write blocks	search.screen	0	n/a
Database server - Processor - all - Processor Time	item.screen	0.002	0.250
Database server - Processor - all - Processor Time	cart.do_update	0.002	0.747
Database server - Processor - all - Processor Time	category.screen	0.001	0.629
Database server - Processor - all - Processor Time	customer.do	0.002	0.171
Database server - Processor - all - Processor Time	customer.do_updated	0.004	0.883
Database server - Processor - all - Processor Time	enter_order_information.screen	0.001	0.517
Database server - Processor - all - Processor Time	update_customer.screen	0.003	0.858
Database server - Processor - all - Processor Time	j_signon_check	0.004	0.236
Database server - Processor - all - Processor Time	main.screen	0.000	0.019
Database server - Processor - all - Processor Time	product.screen	0.001	0.344
Database server - Processor - all - Processor Time	cart.do	0.002	0.238
Database server - Processor - all - Processor Time	signon_welcome.screen	0	n/a
Database server - Processor - all - Processor Time	search.screen	0.004	0.804
Web server - Processor - all - Processor Time	enter_order_information.screen	0.001	0.694
Web server - Processor - all - Processor Time	update_customer.screen	0.001	0.594
Web server - Processor - all - Processor Time	signon_welcome.screen	0.001	0.565
Web server - Processor - all - Processor Time	search.screen	0.001	0.592
Web server - Processor - all - Processor Time	product.screen	0.000	0.453
Web server - Processor - all - Processor Time	main.screen	0.004	0.911
Web server - Processor - all - Processor Time	item.screen	0.001	0.542
Web server - Processor - all - Processor Time	customer.do_updated	0.001	0.694
Web server - Processor - all - Processor Time	customer.do	0.001	0.659
Web server - Processor - all - Processor Time	category.screen	0.000	0.524
Web server - Processor - all - Processor Time	cart.do_update	0.000	0.513
Web server - Processor - all - Processor Time	cart.do	0.001	0.690
Web server - Processor - all - Processor Time	j_signon_check	0.001	0.801

Table A.5: Resource Profile: Java Pet Store – Services including single Client Requests

A.3.2 Background Activities

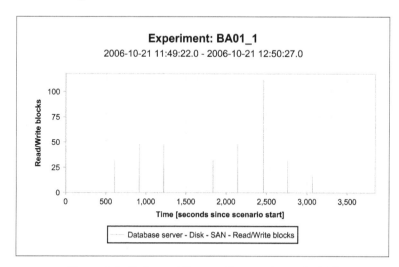

Figure A.1: Background Resource Consumption at the SAN

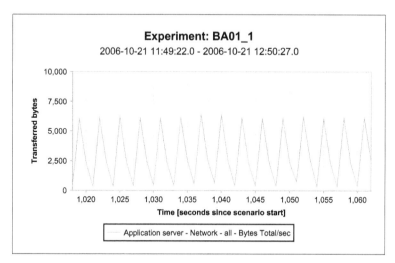

Figure A.2: Background Resource Consumption at the Network (excerpt showing 45 seconds)

A.3.3   Repeatability

A.3.3.1   Experiment PA01

Resource j	i	min	max	sd	cv
Application server - Network - all - Bytes Total	read_user	237,149	243,515	2,653	0.011
Application server - Network - all - Bytes Total	edit_user	602,794	613,230	4,637	0.008
Application server - Processor - all - Processor Time	read_user	0.591	0.631	0.017	0.027
Application server - Processor - all - Processor Time	edit_user	1.651	1.666	0.006	0.004
Client computer - Network - all - Bytes Total	read_user	175,744	189,366	6,759	0.037
Client computer - Network - all - Bytes Total	edit_user	376,897	404,564	11,442	0.029
Database server - Disk - SAN - Read/Write blocks	read_user	0	0	n/a	n/a
Database server - Disk - SAN - Read/Write blocks	edit_user	125.514	224.173	45.739	0.258
Database server - Processor - all - Processor Time	read_user	2.672	2.802	0.060	0.022
Database server - Processor - all - Processor Time	edit_user	7.337	7.440	0.040	0.005
Web server - Processor - all - Processor Time	read_user	0.026	0.030	0.001	0.051
Web server - Processor - all - Processor Time	edit_user	0.074	0.080	0.002	0.030

Table A.6: Repeatability: PASTA – Services including multiple Client Requests

A.3.3.2   Experiment PA03

Resource j	i	min	max	sd	cv
Application server - Network - all - Bytes Total	actitemsave.do	61,749	62,163	168.786	0.003
Application server - Processor - all - Processor Time	actitemsave.do	0.135	0.142	0.003	0.021
Client computer - Network - all - Bytes Total	actitemsave.do	29,195	29,973	332.671	0.011
Database server - Disk - SAN - Read/Write blocks	actitemsave.do	34.136	49.599	7.566	0.182
Database server - Processor - all - Processor Time	actitemsave.do	0.645	0.702	0.021	0.031
Web server - Processor - all - Processor Time	actitemsave.do	0.006	0.009	0.001	0.168

Table A.7: Repeatability: PASTA – Services including single Client Requests

A.3.3.3   Experiment PE01

Resource j	i	min	max	sd	cv
App - NW - all - Bytes Total	determined_shopper	280,004	280,721	298.276	0.001
App - NW - all - Bytes Total	first_time_shopper	464,501	465,401	393.261	0.001
App - NW - all - Bytes Total	power_shopper	593,405	594,286	478.314	0.001
App - NW - all - Bytes Total	curious_visitor	174,466	174,774	126.227	0.001

continued next page

continued

Resource j	i	min	max	sd	cv
App - Proc. - all - Proc. Time	curious_visitor	0.172	0.186	0.006	0.034
App - Proc. - all - Proc. Time	determined_shopper	0.252	0.268	0.007	0.027
App - Proc. - all - Proc. Time	first_time_shopper	0.461	0.541	0.035	0.068
App - Proc. - all - Proc. Time	power_shopper	0.461	0.473	0.005	0.011
Client - NW - all - Bytes Total	power_shopper	586,353	587,170	365.553	0.001
Client - NW - all - Bytes Total	curious_visitor	228,617	228,842	99.931	0.000
Client - NW - all - Bytes Total	determined_shopper	294,584	294,817	105.669	0.000
Client - NW - all - Bytes Total	first_time_shopper	476,104	476,526	193.669	0.000
DB - Disk - SAN - R/W blocks	determined_shopper	41.963	60.214	8.095	0.155
DB - Disk - SAN - R/W blocks	first_time_shopper	44.162	74.184	13.560	0.211
DB - Disk - SAN - R/W blocks	power_shopper	49.299	60.525	4.909	0.088
DB - Disk - SAN - R/W blocks	curious_visitor	0	0	n/a	n/a
DB - Proc. - all - Proc. Time	power_shopper	0.073	0.113	0.017	0.180
DB - Proc. - all - Proc. Time	curious_visitor	0	0	n/a	n/a
DB - Proc. - all - Proc. Time	determined_shopper	0.044	0.077	0.016	0.277
DB - Proc. - all - Proc. Time	first_time_shopper	0.064	0.105	0.018	0.202
Web - Proc. - all - Proc. Time	curious_visitor	0.010	0.014	0.001	0.111
Web - Proc. - all - Proc. Time	determined_shopper	0.016	0.017	0.000	0.029
Web - Proc. - all - Proc. Time	first_time_shopper	0.023	0.026	0.001	0.057
Web - Proc. - all - Proc. Time	power_shopper	0.028	0.032	0.002	0.055

Table A.8: Repeatability: Java Pet Store – Services including multiple Client Requests

A.3.3.4 Experiment PE03

Resource j	i	min	max	sd	cv
Application server - Network - all - Bytes Total	cart.do	17,430	17,978	240.046	0.014
Application server - Processor - all - Processor Time	cart.do	0.017	0.018	0.000	0.029
Client computer - Network - all - Bytes Total	cart.do	20,195	23,942	1,555	0.072
Database server - Disk - SAN - Read/Write blocks	cart.do	0	0	n/a	n/a
Database server - Processor - all - Processor Time	cart.do	0.002	0.002	0.000	0.047
Web server - Processor - all - Processor Time	cart.do	0.001	0.001	0.000	0.248

Table A.9: Repeatability: Java Pet Store – Services including single Client Requests

A.3.4 Load-dependent Behavior

A.3.4.1 Experiment PA02

Resource j	i	x=1	x=5	x=10	x=15	x=20
App - NW - all - Bytes Total	edit_user	660,617	618,110	615.329	614.377	611,402
App - Proc. - all - Proc. Time	edit_user	3.692	2.733	2.395	2.314	2.474
Client - NW - all - Bytes Total	edit_user	446,004	388,547	390,260	400,458	400,759
DB - Disk - SAN - R/W blocks	edit_user	151.900	258.600	162.325	168.483	167.002
DB - Proc. - all - Proc. Time	edit_user	7.508	7.417	7.462	7.520	7.485
Web - Proc. - all - Proc. Time	edit_user	0.209	0.086	0.082	0.077	0.082

Table A.10: Load-dependent Behavior: PASTA – Services including multiple Client Requests

A.3.4.2 Experiment PA04

Resource j	i	x=1	x=5	x=10	x=15	x=20
App - NW - all - Bytes Total	actitemsave.do	65,515	62,422	62,243	62,305	62,127
App - Proc. - all - Proc. Time	actitemsave.do	0.183	0.156	0.167	0.157	0.150
Client - NW - all - Bytes Total	actitemsave.do	34,686	30,463	30,122	30,072	29,847
DB - Disk - SAN - R/W blocks	actitemsave.do	14.632	10.560	21.485	23.310	18.403
DB - Proc. - all - Proc. Time	actitemsave.do	0.705	0.662	0.656	0.664	0.664
Web - Proc. - all - Proc. Time	actitemsave.do	0.020	0.008	0.007	0.007	0.006

Table A.11: Load-dependent Behavior: PASTA – Services including single Client Requests

A.3.4.3 Experiment PE02

Resource j	i	x=1	x=10	x=30	x=50	x=70
App - NW - all - Bytes Total	power_shopper	729,202	602,770	598,615	596,979	596,034
App - Proc. - all - Proc. Time	power_shopper	1.530	0.591	0.577	0.575	0.587
Client - NW - all - Bytes Total	power_shopper	715,437	593,885	590,265	589,083	588,531
DB - Disk - SAN - R/W blocks	power_shopper	10.353	43.232	53.323	59.518	69.726
DB - Proc. - all - Proc. Time	power_shopper	0.350	0.143	0.175	0.179	0.203
Web - Proc. - all - Proc. Time	power_shopper	0.344	0.048	0.039	0.036	0.034

Table A.12: Load-dependent Behavior: Java Pet Store – Services including multiple Client Requests

A.3.4.4   Experiment PE04

Resource j	i	x=1	x=10	x=30	x=50	x=70
App - NW - all - Bytes Total	cart.do	20,285	17,761	17,531	15,529	15,712
App - Proc. - all - Proc. Time	cart.do	0.052	0.027	0.021	0.017	0.018
Client - NW - all - Bytes Total	cart.do	18,983	22,552	19,276	17,915	22,316
DB - Disk - SAN - R/W blocks	cart.do	0	0	0	0	0
DB - Proc. - all - Proc. Time	cart.do	0.023	0.005	0.004	0.002	0.002
Web - Proc. - all - Proc. Time	cart.do	0.014	0.002	0.001	0.001	0.001

Table A.13: Load-dependent Behavior: Java Pet Store – Services including single Client Requests

A.3.5   Linear Regression

A.3.5.1   Experiment PA05

Resource	Service	tt=1s	tt=2s	tt=4s	tt=8s	tt=16s
App - NW - all - Bytes Total	edit_user	602,794	611,470	607,552	605,678	602,380
App - Proc. - all - Proc. Time	edit_user	1.651	1.652	1.505	1.594	1.831
Client - NW - all - Bytes Total	edit_user	376,897	399,086	392,452	378,885	388,361
DB - Disk - SAN - R/W blocks	edit_user	142.111	174.943	214.378	115.965	80.589
DB - Proc. - all - Proc. Time	edit_user	7.337	7.512	7.535	7.301	7.530
Web - Proc. - all - Proc. Time	edit_user	0.080	0.072	0.065	0.043	0.033

Table A.14: Linear Regression: PASTA – Services including multiple Client Requests

A.3.5.2   Experiment PA05

Resource	Service	tt=2s	tt=4s	tt=8s	tt=16s
App - NW - all - Bytes Total	power_shopper	594,695	595,566	595,787	593,441
App - Proc. - all - Proc. Time	power_shopper	0.524	0.510	0.544	0.583
Client - NW - all - Bytes Total	power_shopper	586,534	587,381	587,546	592,134
DB - Disk - SAN - R/W blocks	power_shopper	42.255	53.358	30.190	57.819
DB - Proc. - all - Proc. Time	power_shopper	0.283	0.296	0.308	0.308
Web - Proc. - all - Proc. Time	power_shopper	0.031	0.033	0.020	0.043

Table A.15: Linear Regression: Java Pet Store – Services including multiple Client Requests

A.3.6 Linear Regression (cross check)

A.3.6.1 Experiment PA06

Resource	Service	tt=1s	tt=2s	tt=4s	tt=8s	tt=16s
App - NW - all - Bytes Total	edit_user	614,192	613,690	618,423	631,138	662,395
App - Proc. - all - Proc. Time	edit_user	2.387	2.578	2.010	2.848	3.093
Client - NW - all - Bytes Total	edit_user	389,469	389,155	404,624	417,417	450,580
DB - Disk - SAN - R/W blocks	edit_user	162.165	156.745	160.680	160.190	125.759
DB - Proc. - all - Proc. Time	edit_user	7.429	7.570	7.575	7.608	7.706
Web - Proc. - all - Proc. Time	edit_user	0.081	0.087	0.086	0.138	0.241

Table A.16: Linear Regression (cross check): PASTA – Services including multiple Client Requests

A.3.7 Database Size

A.3.7.1 Experiment PE07

Resource j	i	p	r
Application server - Network - all - Bytes Total	determined_shopper	279,745	1.000
Application server - Network - all - Bytes Total	first_time_shopper	463,072	1.000
Application server - Network - all - Bytes Total	power_shopper	593,579	1.000
Application server - Network - all - Bytes Total	curious_visitor	174,544	1.000
Application server - Processor - all - Processor Time	curious_visitor	0.182	0.842
Application server - Processor - all - Processor Time	determined_shopper	0.250	0.943
Application server - Processor - all - Processor Time	first_time_shopper	0.487	0.976
Application server - Processor - all - Processor Time	power_shopper	0.470	0.895
Client computer - Network - all - Bytes Total	power_shopper	587,261	1.000
Client computer - Network - all - Bytes Total	curious_visitor	228,836	1.000
Client computer - Network - all - Bytes Total	determined_shopper	294,703	1.000
Client computer - Network - all - Bytes Total	first_time_shopper	477,865	1.000
Database server - Disk - SAN - Read/Write blocks	determined_shopper	26.307	0.823
Database server - Disk - SAN - Read/Write blocks	first_time_shopper	24.579	0.047
Database server - Disk - SAN - Read/Write blocks	power_shopper	39.870	0.790
Database server - Disk - SAN - Read/Write blocks	curious_visitor	0	n/a
Database server - Processor - all - Processor Time	power_shopper	0.412	0.992
Database server - Processor - all - Processor Time	curious_visitor	0.003	0.318
Database server - Processor - all - Processor Time	determined_shopper	0.343	0.986
Database server - Processor - all - Processor Time	first_time_shopper	0.387	0.979
Web server - Processor - all - Processor Time	curious_visitor	0.013	0.963
Web server - Processor - all - Processor Time	determined_shopper	0.017	0.994

continued next page

continued

Resource	Service	p	r
Web server - Processor - all - Processor Time	first_time_shopper	0.024	0.995
Web server - Processor - all - Processor Time	power_shopper	0.030	0.994

Table A.17: Resource Profile: Java Pet Store – Services including multiple Client Requests - 90% full Tablespace

A.4 Experimental Results: Analytical Models

A.4.1 Services including single Client Requests

Experiment	PE08_1
Load test 1	2006-10-22 17:51:13.0 – 2006-10-22 19:21:33.0
Runtime (test 1)	1 h 30 min 20 sec
Load test script	see section A.5.1
Number of users	10 – 180 (18 intervals)
Think time	outside classes: 1 sec (random range 50 %–150 %)
Interval length	5 min (first minute excluded from analysis)

QN Type	closed QN
No. of classes	13 (see table A.18)
No. of queues	4 (see figure 5.10)
Solution algorithm	Self Correcting Approximation Technique ($\varepsilon = 0.001$)

Mean absolute deviation of measured utilization and model predictions ($|u - u_{qn}|$):

Application Server	3.6 %	
Web Server	0.9 %	
Database Server	0.9 %	(see table A.19 for complete results)

Resource (queue)	Service (class)	p (sd)
Application server - Processor - all - Processor Time	cart.do_update	0.017
Application server - Processor - all - Processor Time	signon_welcome.screen	0.007
Application server - Processor - all - Processor Time	search.screen	0.013
Application server - Processor - all - Processor Time	product.screen	0.011

continued next page

continued

Resource (queue)	Service (class)	p (sd)
Application server - Processor - all - Processor Time	main.screen	0.017
Application server - Processor - all - Processor Time	j_signon_check	0.027
Application server - Processor - all - Processor Time	cart.do	0.017
Application server - Processor - all - Processor Time	item.screen	0.013
Application server - Processor - all - Processor Time	enter_order_information.screen	0.015
Application server - Processor - all - Processor Time	customer.do_updated	0.026
Application server - Processor - all - Processor Time	customer.do	0.017
Application server - Processor - all - Processor Time	update_customer.screen	0.021
Application server - Processor - all - Processor Time	category.screen	0.011
Database server - Processor - all - Processor Time	cart.do_update	0.003
Database server - Processor - all - Processor Time	category.screen	0.002
Database server - Processor - all - Processor Time	customer.do	0.002
Database server - Processor - all - Processor Time	customer.do_updated	0.005
Database server - Processor - all - Processor Time	update_customer.screen	0.003
Database server - Processor - all - Processor Time	enter_order_information.screen	0.000
Database server - Processor - all - Processor Time	item.screen	0.002
Database server - Processor - all - Processor Time	j_signon_check	0.005
Database server - Processor - all - Processor Time	main.screen	0.000
Database server - Processor - all - Processor Time	product.screen	0.002
Database server - Processor - all - Processor Time	search.screen	0.004
Database server - Processor - all - Processor Time	signon_welcome.screen	0
Database server - Processor - all - Processor Time	cart.do	0.002
Web server - Processor - all - Processor Time	j_signon_check	0.001
Web server - Processor - all - Processor Time	cart.do	0.001
Web server - Processor - all - Processor Time	cart.do_update	0.001
Web server - Processor - all - Processor Time	category.screen	0.001
Web server - Processor - all - Processor Time	customer.do	0.001
Web server - Processor - all - Processor Time	customer.do_updated	0.001
Web server - Processor - all - Processor Time	item.screen	0.001
Web server - Processor - all - Processor Time	main.screen	0.004
Web server - Processor - all - Processor Time	product.screen	0.001
Web server - Processor - all - Processor Time	search.screen	0.001
Web server - Processor - all - Processor Time	signon_welcome.screen	0.001
Web server - Processor - all - Processor Time	update_customer.screen	0.001
Web server - Processor - all - Processor Time	enter_order_information.screen	0.001

Table A.18: QN Model Input Parameter: Processors – Services including single Client Requests. Service demands (sd) taken from Experiment PE03_0

Column titles in tables A.19 and A.21:

u   Mean processor utilization during interval with a constant number of users

u_{qn} QN Model prediction for mean processor utilization during the interval

$u - u_{qn}$ absolute deviation

ε relative deviation $\left| \frac{u - u_{qn}}{u} \right|$

	Application Server				Database Server				Web Server			
user	u	u_{qn}	$u - u_{qn}$	ε	u	u_{qn}	$u - u_{qn}$	ε	u	u_{qn}	$u - u_{qn}$	ε
10	0.067	0.079	-0.013	18.8%	0.023	0.011	0.011	50.3%	0.008	0.006	0.002	23.1%
20	0.152	0.159	-0.007	4.5%	0.037	0.022	0.015	40.1%	0.012	0.012	-0.000	1.9%
30	0.231	0.238	-0.007	3.1%	0.040	0.034	0.006	15.2%	0.017	0.018	-0.001	7.3%
40	0.254	0.317	-0.063	24.8%	0.050	0.045	0.005	9.7%	0.020	0.024	-0.003	17.1%
50	0.444	0.397	0.047	10.5%	0.062	0.056	0.005	8.9%	0.025	0.030	-0.005	20.9%
60	0.344	0.475	-0.131	38.2%	0.070	0.067	0.003	4.5%	0.029	0.036	-0.007	25.0%
70	0.550	0.552	-0.001	0.2%	0.082	0.078	0.004	4.8%	0.034	0.042	-0.008	23.2%
80	0.574	0.627	-0.053	9.1%	0.096	0.089	0.008	7.8%	0.038	0.047	-0.009	23.9%
90	0.661	0.700	-0.039	5.8%	0.100	0.099	0.001	1.3%	0.043	0.053	-0.010	23.1%
100	0.819	0.768	0.051	6.3%	0.117	0.109	0.008	6.7%	0.045	0.058	-0.013	27.7%
110	0.809	0.826	-0.017	2.1%	0.131	0.117	0.014	10.7%	0.049	0.062	-0.013	26.7%
120	0.929	0.877	0.052	5.6%	0.133	0.124	0.009	6.8%	0.053	0.066	-0.013	25.1%
130	0.958	0.908	0.050	5.2%	0.140	0.129	0.012	8.3%	0.056	0.069	-0.013	22.9%
140	0.974	0.934	0.040	4.1%	0.148	0.132	0.016	10.7%	0.056	0.071	-0.014	25.0%
150	0.980	0.948	0.032	3.3%	0.147	0.134	0.013	8.9%	0.057	0.072	-0.014	24.8%
160	0.981	0.961	0.020	2.1%	0.148	0.136	0.012	8.0%	0.057	0.073	-0.015	26.7%
170	0.978	0.966	0.013	1.3%	0.152	0.137	0.016	10.3%	0.057	0.073	-0.016	29.0%
180	0.981	0.973	0.008	0.8%	0.143	0.138	0.005	3.6%	0.058	0.073	-0.015	26.6%

Table A.19: QN Model Validation: Processor Utilization – Services including single Client Requests

A.4.2   Services including multiple Client Requests

Experiment	PE09_1
Load test 1	2006-10-25 10:24:59.0 – 2006-10-25 12:05:46.0
Runtime (test 1)	1 h 40 min 47 sec
Load test script	see section A.5.2
Number of users	10 - 200 (20 intervals)
Think time	inside class: 40 x 1 sec (random range 50 %–150 %)
Interval length	5 min (first minute excluded from analysis)

QN Type	closed QN
No. of classes	1 (see table A.20)
No. of queues	4 (see figure 5.10)
Solution algorithm	Exact Mean Value Analysis

Mean absolute deviation of measured utilization and model predictions ($|u - u_{qn}|$):

Application Server	5.7 %	
Web Server	0.3 %	
Database Server	0.3 %	(see table A.21 for complete results)

Resource (queue)	Service (class)	p (service demand)
Application server - Processor - all - Processor Time	power_shopper	0.436
Database server - Processor - all - Processor Time	power_shopper	0.042
Web server - Processor - all - Processor Time	power_shopper	0.031

Table A.20: QN Model Input Parameter: Processors - Services including multiple Client Requests (values extracted from the resource profile of the adapted power_shopper user profile, see section A.5.)

user	Application Server				Database Server				Web Server			
	u	u_{qn}	$u - u_{qn}$	ε	u	u_{qn}	$u - u_{qn}$	ε	u	u_{qn}	$u - u_{qn}$	ε
10	0.052	0.054	-0.002	2.9%	0.008	0.005	0.003	35.2%	0.007	0.004	0.003	43.2%
20	0.109	0.108	0.001	1.3%	0.015	0.010	0.005	31.7%	0.010	0.008	0.002	24.1%
30	0.203	0.161	0.042	20.5%	0.018	0.016	0.002	12.7%	0.013	0.011	0.002	12.2%
40	0.155	0.215	-0.060	38.9%	0.023	0.021	0.003	11.2%	0.017	0.015	0.002	10.4%
50	0.377	0.269	0.108	28.7%	0.029	0.026	0.004	12.0%	0.021	0.019	0.001	7.1%
60	0.214	0.323	-0.108	50.6%	0.033	0.031	0.002	5.2%	0.025	0.023	0.002	8.3%
70	0.428	0.376	0.052	12.2%	0.038	0.036	0.002	4.6%	0.027	0.027	0.000	1.6%
80	0.436	0.430	0.007	1.5%	0.047	0.041	0.006	12.8%	0.031	0.031	0.001	2.5%
90	0.463	0.483	-0.020	4.4%	0.049	0.047	0.003	5.2%	0.034	0.034	-0.001	2.2%
100	0.701	0.536	0.165	23.5%	0.054	0.052	0.002	4.3%	0.037	0.038	-0.001	3.2%
110	0.532	0.589	-0.057	10.8%	0.061	0.057	0.005	7.7%	0.040	0.042	-0.002	3.9%
120	0.770	0.641	0.129	16.7%	0.058	0.062	-0.004	6.1%	0.044	0.046	-0.002	4.4%
130	0.694	0.693	0.000	0.1%	0.066	0.067	-0.001	1.4%	0.047	0.049	-0.002	4.0%
140	0.828	0.744	0.083	10.0%	0.080	0.072	0.009	10.8%	0.051	0.053	-0.002	4.4%
150	0.907	0.794	0.113	12.4%	0.076	0.077	-0.000	0.3%	0.055	0.056	-0.002	3.6%
160	0.910	0.843	0.068	7.4%	0.079	0.081	-0.002	2.2%	0.056	0.060	-0.004	7.9%

continued next page

												continued
user	u	u_{qn}	$u - u_{qn}$	ε	u	u_{qn}	$u - u_{qn}$	ε	u	u_{qn}	$u - u_{qn}$	ε
170	0.963	0.888	0.075	7.8%	0.092	0.086	0.006	6.7%	0.057	0.063	-0.006	9.9%
180	0.965	0.928	0.037	3.8%	0.090	0.089	0.000	0.2%	0.059	0.066	-0.007	12.3%
190	0.946	0.961	-0.015	1.6%	0.084	0.093	-0.009	10.2%	0.055	0.068	-0.013	24.0%
200	0.976	0.983	-0.007	0.7%	0.092	0.095	-0.003	3.0%	0.059	0.070	-0.011	18.2%

Table A.21: QN Model Validation: Processor Utilization – Services including multiple Client Requests

A.5 Example LoadRunner Scripts

The following LoadRunner scripts (Mercury LoadRunner 8.0) were used during the experiments with Java PetStore. To facilitate reading, we omitted code that solely triggers the transfer of static pictures (e.g., the Java PetStore logo).

Modifications of the scripts for experiments PE08 and PE09: Services including single client requests require a synchronous fulfillment of the requests. Those kinds of services are not applicable to asynchronous backend applications such as the order processing center in the Java Pet Store example (see section 4.1.2.2). Thus, the asynchronous "order.do" request could not be analyzed during experiment PE08 (script in section A.5.1). Hence, we removed in experiment PE09 this request from the power_shopper script (see section A.5.2). The intention was to use the same applications in both experiments and thus enable a mutual comparison of results. Furthermore, as we wanted to emulate unsynchronized service invocations, we omitted the rendezvous points in both scripts.

A.5.1 Services including single Client Requests

```
1
2   #include "web_api.h"
3   #include "lrw_custom_body.h"
4
5   vuser_init()
6   {
7           return 0;
8   }
9
10  #include "web_api.h"
11
12  Action()
13  {
14          web_reg_find("Text=petstore", LAST);
15          lr_rendezvous("main.screen");
16          lr_start_transaction("main.screen");
17
18          web_url("main.screen",
19                  "URL={url}/main.screen",
20                  "Resource=0",
```

```
21                "RecContentType=text/html",
22                "Referer=",
23                "Snapshot=t1.inf",
24                "Mode=HTTP",
25                LAST);
26
27   (... pictures ...)
28
29           lr_end_transaction("main.screen", LR_AUTO);
30
31           lr_think_time(7);
32
33           web_reg_find("Text=petstore", LAST);
34           lr_rendezvous("signon_welcome.screen");
35           lr_start_transaction("signon_welcome.screen");
36
37           web_url("Sign in",
38                "URL={url}/signon_welcome.screen",
39                "Resource=0",
40                "RecContentType=text/html",
41                "Referer={url}/main.screen",
42                "Snapshot=t2.inf",
43                "Mode=HTTP",
44                LAST);
45
46   (... pictures ...)
47
48           lr_end_transaction("signon_welcome.screen", LR_AUTO);
49
50           lr_think_time(7);
51
52           web_reg_find("Text=petstore", LAST);
53           lr_rendezvous("j_signon_check");
54           lr_start_transaction("j_signon_check");
55
56           web_submit_data("j_signon_check",
57                "Action={url}/j_signon_check",
58                "Method=POST",
59                "RecContentType=text/html",
60                "Referer={url}/signon_welcome.screen",
61                "Snapshot=t3.inf",
62                "Mode=HTTP",
63                ITEMDATA,
64                "Name=j_username", "Value={user}", ENDITEM,
65                "Name=j_password", "Value={password}", ENDITEM,
66                "Name=submit", "Value=Sign In", ENDITEM,
67                LAST);
68
69   (... pictures ...)
70
71           lr_end_transaction("j_signon_check", LR_AUTO);
72
73           lr_think_time(7);
74
75           web_reg_find("Text=petstore", LAST);
76           lr_rendezvous("customer.do");
77           lr_start_transaction("customer.do");
78
79           web_url("Account",
80                "URL={url}/customer.do",
81                "Resource=0",
82                "RecContentType=text/html",
83                "Referer={url}/signon_welcome.screen",
84                "Snapshot=t4.inf",
85                "Mode=HTTP",
86                LAST);
87
88   (... pictures ...)
89
90           lr_end_transaction("customer.do", LR_AUTO);
91
92           lr_think_time(7);
93
94           web_reg_find("Text=petstore", LAST);
95           lr_rendezvous("update_customer.screen");
96           lr_start_transaction("update_customer.screen");
97
98           web_url("Edit Your Account Information",
99                "URL={url}/update_customer.screen",
100               "Resource=0",
101               "RecContentType=text/html",
102               "Referer={url}/customer.do",
103               "Snapshot=t5.inf",
```

```
104            "Mode=HTTP",
105            LAST);
106
107  (... pictures ...)
108
109        lr_end_transaction("update_customer.screen", LR_AUTO);
110
111        lr_think_time(7);
112
113        web_reg_find("Text=petstore", LAST);
114        lr_rendezvous("customer.do_updated");
115        lr_start_transaction("customer.do_updated");
116
117        web_submit_data("customer.do",
118            "Action={url}/customer.do",
119            "Method=POST",
120            "RecContentType=text/html",
121            "Referer={url}/update_customer.screen",
122            "Snapshot=t6.inf",
123            "Mode=HTTP",
124            ITEMDATA,
125            "Name=action", "Value=update", ENDITEM,
126            "Name=given_name_a", "Value=XYZ", ENDITEM,
127            "Name=family_name_a", "Value=ABC", ENDITEM,
128            "Name=address_1_a", "Value=1234 Anywhere Street", ENDITEM,
129            "Name=address_2_a", "Value=Unit 555", ENDITEM,
130            "Name=city_a", "Value=Palo Alto", ENDITEM,
131            "Name=state_or_province_a", "Value=California", ENDITEM,
132            "Name=postal_code_a", "Value=94303", ENDITEM,
133            "Name=country_a", "Value=USA", ENDITEM,
134            "Name=telephone_number_a", "Value=555-16-48", ENDITEM,
135            "Name=email_a", "Value=reinhard.ba.brandl@bmw.de", ENDITEM,
136            "Name=credit_card_number", "Value=123456789", ENDITEM,
137            "Name=credit_card_type", "Value=California", ENDITEM,
138            "Name=credit_card_expiry_month", "Value=01", ENDITEM,
139            "Name=credit_card_expiry_year", "Value=01", ENDITEM,
140            "Name=language", "Value=en_US", ENDITEM,
141            "Name=favorite_category", "Value=REPTILES", ENDITEM,
142            "Name=mylist_on", "Value=on", ENDITEM,
143            "Name=banners_on", "Value=on", ENDITEM,
144            LAST);
145
146  (... pictures ...)
147
148        lr_end_transaction("customer.do_updated", LR_AUTO);
149
150        lr_think_time(7);
151
152        web_reg_find("Text=petstore", LAST);
153        lr_rendezvous("search.screen");
154        lr_start_transaction("search.screen");
155
156        web_submit_data("search.screen",
157            "Action={url}/search.screen",
158            "Method=GET",
159            "EncType=",
160            "RecContentType=text/html",
161            "Referer={url}/customer.do",
162            "Snapshot=t16.inf",
163            "Mode=HTTP",
164            ITEMDATA,
165            "Name=keywords", "Value=Test{zufall}", ENDITEM,
166            LAST);
167
168  (... pictures ...)
169
170        lr_end_transaction("search.screen", LR_AUTO);
171
172        lr_think_time( 7 );
173
174        web_reg_find("Text=petstore", LAST);
175        lr_rendezvous("category.screen");
176        lr_start_transaction("category.screen");
177
178        web_url("Birds",
179            "URL={url}/category.screen?category_id=BIRDS",
180            "Resource=0",
181            "RecContentType=text/html",
182            "Referer={url}/search.screen",
183            "Snapshot=t7.inf",
184            "Mode=HTTP",
185            LAST);
186
```

```
187  (... pictures ...)
188
189          lr_end_transaction("category.screen", LR_AUTO);
190
191          lr_think_time(7);
192
193          web_reg_find("Text=petstore", LAST);
194          lr_rendezvous("product.screen");
195          lr_start_transaction("product.screen");
196
197          web_url("Amazon Parrot",
198                  "URL={url}/product.screen?product_id=AV-CB-01",
199                  "Resource=0",
200                  "RecContentType=text/html",
201                  "Referer={url}/category.screen?category_id=BIRDS",
202                  "Snapshot=t8.inf",
203                  "Mode=HTTP",
204                  LAST);
205
206  (... pictures ...)
207
208          lr_end_transaction("product.screen", LR_AUTO);
209
210          lr_think_time(7);
211
212          web_reg_find("Text=petstore", LAST);
213          lr_rendezvous("item.screen");
214          lr_start_transaction("item.screen");
215
216          web_url("Adult Male Amazon Parrot",
217                  "URL={url}/item.screen?item_id=EST-18",
218                  "Resource=0",
219                  "RecContentType=text/html",
220                  "Referer={url}/product.screen?product_id=AV-CB-01",
221                  "Snapshot=t9.inf",
222                  "Mode=HTTP",
223                  LAST);
224
225  (... pictures ...)
226
227          lr_end_transaction("item.screen", LR_AUTO);
228
229          lr_think_time(7);
230
231          web_reg_find("Text=petstore", LAST);
232          lr_rendezvous("cart.do");
233          lr_start_transaction("cart.do");
234
235          web_url("Add to Cart",
236                  "URL={url}/cart.do?action=purchase&itemId=EST-18",
237                  "Resource=0",
238                  "RecContentType=text/html",
239                  "Referer={url}/item.screen?item_id=EST-18",
240                  "Snapshot=t10.inf",
241                  "Mode=HTTP",
242                  LAST);
243
244  (... pictures ...)
245
246          lr_end_transaction("cart.do", LR_AUTO);
247
248          lr_think_time(7);
249
250          web_reg_find("Text=petstore", LAST);
251          lr_rendezvous("cart.do_update");
252          lr_start_transaction("cart.do_update");
253
254          web_submit_data("cart.do",
255                  "Action={url}/cart.do",
256                  "Method=GET",
257                  "EncType=",
258                  "RecContentType=text/html",
259                  "Referer={url}/cart.do?action=purchase&itemId=EST-18",
260                  "Snapshot=t11.inf",
261                  "Mode=HTTP",
262                  ITEMDATA,
263                  "Name=action", "Value=update", ENDITEM,
264                  "Name=itemQuantity_EST-18", "Value=2", ENDITEM,
265                  LAST);
266
267  (... pictures ...)
268
269          lr_end_transaction("cart.do_update", LR_AUTO);
```

```
270
271        lr_think_time(7);
272
273        web_reg_find("Text=petstore", LAST);
274        lr_rendezvous("enter_order_information.screen");
275        lr_start_transaction("enter_order_information.screen");
276
277        web_url("Check Out",
278            "URL={url}/enter_order_information.screen",
279            "Resource=0",
280            "RecContentType=text/html",
281            "Referer={url}/cart.do?action=update&itemQuantity_EST-18=2",
282            "Snapshot=t12.inf",
283            "Mode=HTTP",
284            LAST);
285
286 (... pictures ...)
287
288        lr_end_transaction("enter_order_information.screen", LR_AUTO);
289
290        web_cache_cleanup();
291        web_cleanup_cookies();
292
293        lr_think_time(7);
294
295        return 0;
296 }
297
298 #include "web_api.h"
299
300 vuser_end()
301 {
302        return 0;
303 }
304
```

A.5.2   Services including multiple Client Requests

```
1
2  #include "web_api.h"
3  #include "lrw_custom_body.h"
4
5  vuser_init()
6  {
7         return 0;
8  }
9
10 #include "web_api.h"
11
12 Action()
13 {
14        lr_rendezvous("power_shopper");
15        lr_start_transaction("power_shopper");
16
17        web_url("main.screen",
18            "URL={url}/petstore/main.screen",
19            "Resource=0",
20            "RecContentType=text/html",
21            "Referer=",
22            "Snapshot=t59.inf",
23            "Mode=HTTP",
24            LAST);
25
26 (... pictures ...)
27
28        lr_think_time( 1 );
29
30        web_submit_data("search.screen",
31            "Action={url}/petstore/search.screen",
32            "Method=GET",
33            "EncType=",
34            "RecContentType=text/html",
35            "Referer={url}/petstore/main.screen",
36            "Snapshot=t60.inf",
37            "Mode=HTTP",
38            ITEMDATA,
39            "Name=keywords", "Value=iguna", ENDITEM,
40            LAST);
41
42 (... pictures ...)
```

```
43
44          lr_think_time( 1 );
45
46          web_submit_data("search.screen_2",
47              "Action={url}/petstore/search.screen",
48              "Method=GET",
49              "EncType=",
50              "RecContentType=text/html",
51              "Referer={url}/petstore/search.screen?keywords=iguna",
52              "Snapshot=t61.inf",
53              "Mode=HTTP",
54              ITEMDATA,
55              "Name=keywords", "Value=reptile", ENDITEM,
56              LAST);
57
58   (... pictures ...)
59
60          lr_think_time( 1 );
61
62          web_url("Venomless Rattlesnake",
63              "URL={url}/petstore/item.screen?item_id=EST-11",
64              "Resource=0",
65              "RecContentType=text/html",
66              "Referer={url}/petstore/search.screen?keywords=reptile",
67              "Snapshot=t62.inf",
68              "Mode=HTTP",
69              LAST);
70
71   (... pictures ...)
72
73          lr_think_time( 1 );
74
75          web_url("Add to Cart",
76              "URL={url}/petstore/cart.do?action=purchase&itemId=EST-11",
77              "Resource=0",
78              "RecContentType=text/html",
79              "Referer={url}/petstore/item.screen?item_id=EST-11",
80              "Snapshot=t63.inf",
81              "Mode=HTTP",
82              LAST);
83
84   (... pictures ...)
85
86          lr_think_time( 1 );
87
88          web_submit_data("cart.do",
89              "Action={url}/petstore/cart.do",
90              "Method=GET",
91              "EncType=",
92              "RecContentType=text/html",
93              "Referer={url}/petstore/cart.do?action=purchase&itemId=EST-11",
94              "Snapshot=t64.inf",
95              "Mode=HTTP",
96              ITEMDATA,
97              "Name=action", "Value=update", ENDITEM,
98              "Name=itemQuantity_EST-11", "Value={Zufallszahl}", ENDITEM,
99              LAST);
100
101  (... pictures ...)
102
103         lr_think_time( 1 );
104
105         web_url("Birds",
106             "URL={url}/petstore/category.screen?category_id=BIRDS",
107             "Resource=0",
108             "RecContentType=text/html",
109             "Referer={url}/petstore/cart.do?action=update&itemQuantity_EST-11=1",
110             "Snapshot=t65.inf",
111             "Mode=HTTP",
112             LAST);
113
114  (... pictures ...)
115
116         lr_think_time( 1 );
117
118         web_url("Finch",
119             "URL={url}/petstore/product.screen?product_id=AV-SB-02",
120             "Resource=0",
121             "RecContentType=text/html",
122             "Referer={url}/petstore/category.screen?category_id=BIRDS",
123             "Snapshot=t66.inf",
124             "Mode=HTTP",
125             LAST);
```

```
126
127   (... pictures ...)
128
129          lr_think_time( 1 );
130
131          web_url("Adult Male Finch",
132                 "URL={url}/petstore/item.screen?item_id=EST-19",
133                 "Resource=0",
134                 "RecContentType=text/html",
135                 "Referer={url}/petstore/product.screen?product_id=AV-SB-02",
136                 "Snapshot=t67.inf",
137                 "Mode=HTTP",
138                 LAST);
139
140   (... pictures ...)
141
142          lr_think_time( 1 );
143
144          web_url("Add to Cart_2",
145                 "URL={url}/petstore/cart.do?action=purchase&itemId=EST-19",
146                 "Resource=0",
147                 "RecContentType=text/html",
148                 "Referer={url}/petstore/item.screen?item_id=EST-19",
149                 "Snapshot=t68.inf",
150                 "Mode=HTTP",
151                 LAST);
152
153   (... pictures ...)
154
155          lr_think_time( 1 );
156
157          web_submit_data("cart.do_2",
158                 "Action={url}/petstore/cart.do",
159                 "Method=GET",
160                 "EncType=",
161                 "RecContentType=text/html",
162                 "Referer={url}/petstore/cart.do?action=purchase&itemId=EST-19",
163                 "Snapshot=t69.inf",
164                 "Mode=HTTP",
165                 ITEMDATA,
166                 "Name=action", "Value=update", ENDITEM,
167                 "Name=itemQuantity_EST-11", "Value={Zufallszahl}", ENDITEM,
168                 "Name=itemQuantity_EST-19", "Value={Zufallszahl}", ENDITEM,
169                 LAST);
170
171   (... pictures ...)
172
173          lr_think_time( 1 );
174
175          web_url("Fish",
176                 "URL={url}/petstore/category.screen?category_id=FISH",
177                 "Resource=0",
178                 "RecContentType=text/html",
179                 "Referer={url}/petstore/cart.do?action=update&itemQuantity_EST-11
180                 =1&itemQuantity_EST-19=1",
181                 "Snapshot=t70.inf",
182                 "Mode=HTTP",
183                 LAST);
184
185   (... pictures ...)
186
187          lr_think_time( 1 );
188
189          web_url("Goldfish",
190                 "URL={url}/petstore/product.screen?product_id=FI-FW-02",
191                 "Resource=0",
192                 "RecContentType=text/html",
193                 "Referer={url}/petstore/category.screen?category_id=FISH",
194                 "Snapshot=t71.inf",
195                 "Mode=HTTP",
196                 LAST);
197
198   (... pictures ...)
199
200          lr_think_time( 1 );
201
202          web_url("Adult Male Goldfish",
203                 "URL={url}/petstore/item.screen?item_id=EST-20",
204                 "Resource=0",
205                 "RecContentType=text/html",
206                 "Referer={url}/petstore/product.screen?product_id=FI-FW-02",
207                 "Snapshot=t72.inf",
208                 "Mode=HTTP",
```

```
209                    LAST);
210
211    (... pictures ...)
212
213           lr_think_time( 1 );
214
215           web_url("Fish_2",
216                    "URL={url}/petstore/category.screen?category_id=FISH",
217                    "Resource=0",
218                    "RecContentType=text/html",
219                    "Referer={url}/petstore/item.screen?item_id=EST-20",
220                    "Snapshot=t73.inf",
221                    "Mode=HTTP",
222                    LAST);
223
224    (... pictures ...)
225
226           lr_think_time( 1 );
227
228           web_url("Goldfish_2",
229                    "URL={url}/petstore/product.screen?product_id=FI-FW-02",
230                    "Resource=0",
231                    "RecContentType=text/html",
232                    "Referer={url}/petstore/category.screen?category_id=FISH",
233                    "Snapshot=t74.inf",
234                    "Mode=HTTP",
235                    LAST);
236
237    (... pictures ...)
238
239           lr_think_time( 1 );
240
241           web_url("Adult Female Goldfish",
242                    "URL={url}/petstore/item.screen?item_id=EST-21",
243                    "Resource=0",
244                    "RecContentType=text/html",
245                    "Referer={url}/petstore/product.screen?product_id=FI-FW-02",
246                    "Snapshot=t75.inf",
247                    "Mode=HTTP",
248                    LAST);
249
250    (... pictures ...)
251
252           lr_think_time( 1 );
253
254           web_url("Add to Cart_3",
255                    "URL={url}/petstore/cart.do?action=purchase&itemId=EST-21",
256                    "Resource=0",
257                    "RecContentType=text/html",
258                    "Referer={url}/petstore/item.screen?item_id=EST-21",
259                    "Snapshot=t76.inf",
260                    "Mode=HTTP",
261                    LAST);
262
263    (... pictures ...)
264
265           lr_think_time( 1 );
266
267           web_submit_data("cart.do_3",
268                    "Action={url}/petstore/cart.do",
269                    "Method=GET",
270                    "EncType=",
271                    "RecContentType=text/html",
272                    "Referer={url}/petstore/cart.do?action=purchase&itemId=EST-21",
273                    "Snapshot=t77.inf",
274                    "Mode=HTTP",
275                    ITEMDATA,
276                    "Name=action", "Value=update", ENDITEM,
277                    "Name=itemQuantity_EST-11", "Value={Zufallszahl}", ENDITEM,
278                    "Name=itemQuantity_EST-21", "Value={Zufallszahl}", ENDITEM,
279                    "Name=itemQuantity_EST-19", "Value={Zufallszahl}", ENDITEM,
280                    LAST);
281
282
283    (... pictures ...)
284
285           lr_think_time( 1 );
286
287           web_url("Bulldog",
288                    "URL={url}/petstore/product.screen?product_id=K9-BD-01",
289                    "Resource=0",
290                    "RecContentType=text/html",
291                    "Referer={url}/petstore/category.screen?category_id=DOGS",
```

```
292                "Snapshot=t79.inf",
293                "Mode=HTTP",
294                LAST);
295
296    (... pictures ...)
297
298        lr_think_time( 1 );
299
300        web_url("Male Adult Bulldog",
301                "URL={url}/petstore/item.screen?item_id=EST-6",
302                "Resource=0",
303                "RecContentType=text/html",
304                "Referer={url}/petstore/product.screen?product_id=K9-BD-01",
305                "Snapshot=t80.inf",
306                "Mode=HTTP",
307                LAST);
308
309    (... pictures ...)
310
311        lr_think_time( 1 );
312
313        web_url("Add to Cart_4",
314                "URL={url}/petstore/cart.do?action=purchase&itemId=EST-6",
315                "Resource=0",
316                "RecContentType=text/html",
317                "Referer={url}/petstore/item.screen?item_id=EST-6",
318                "Snapshot=t81.inf",
319                "Mode=HTTP",
320                LAST);
321
322    (... pictures ...)
323
324        lr_think_time( 1 );
325
326        web_submit_data("cart.do_4",
327                "Action={url}/petstore/cart.do",
328                "Method=GET",
329                "EncType=",
330                "RecContentType=text/html",
331                "Referer={url}/petstore/cart.do?action=purchase&itemId=EST-6",
332                "Snapshot=t82.inf",
333                "Mode=HTTP",
334                ITEMDATA,
335                "Name=action", "Value=update", ENDITEM,
336                "Name=itemQuantity_EST-11", "Value={Zufallszahl}", ENDITEM,
337                "Name=itemQuantity_EST-21", "Value={Zufallszahl}", ENDITEM,
338                "Name=itemQuantity_EST-19", "Value={Zufallszahl}", ENDITEM,
339                "Name=itemQuantity_EST-6", "Value={Zufallszahl}", ENDITEM,
340                LAST);
341
342    (... pictures ...)
343
344        lr_think_time( 1 );
345
346        web_url("Reptiles",
347                "URL={url}/petstore/category.screen?category_id=REPTILES",
348                "Resource=0",
349                "RecContentType=text/html",
350                "Referer={url}/petstore/cart.do?action=update&itemQuantity_EST-11
351                    =1&itemQuantity_EST-21=1&itemQuantity_EST-19=1&
352                    itemQuantity_EST-6=1",
353                "Snapshot=t83.inf",
354                "Mode=HTTP",
355                LAST);
356
357    (... pictures ...)
358
359        lr_think_time( 1 );
360
361        web_url("Iguana",
362                "URL={url}/petstore/product.screen?product_id=RP-LI-02",
363                "Resource=0",
364                "RecContentType=text/html",
365                "Referer={url}/petstore/category.screen?category_id=REPTILES",
366                "Snapshot=t84.inf",
367                "Mode=HTTP",
368                LAST);
369
370    (... pictures ...)
371
372        lr_think_time( 1 );
373
374        web_url("Green Adult Iguana",
```

```
375                    "URL={url}/petstore/item.screen?item_id=EST-13",
376                    "Resource=0",
377                    "RecContentType=text/html",
378                    "Referer={url}/petstore/product.screen?product_id=RP-LI-02",
379                    "Snapshot=t85.inf",
380                    "Mode=HTTP",
381                    LAST);
382
383    (... pictures ...)
384
385          lr_think_time( 1 );
386
387          web_url("Add to Cart_5",
388                    "URL={url}/petstore/cart.do?action=purchase&itemId=EST-13",
389                    "Resource=0",
390                    "RecContentType=text/html",
391                    "Referer={url}/petstore/item.screen?item_id=EST-13",
392                    "Snapshot=t86.inf",
393                    "Mode=HTTP",
394                    LAST);
395
396    (... pictures ...)
397
398          lr_think_time( 1 );
399
400          web_url("Cats",
401                    "URL={url}/petstore/category.screen?category_id=CATS",
402                    "Resource=0",
403                    "RecContentType=text/html",
404                    "Referer={url}/petstore/cart.do?action=purchase&itemId=EST-13",
405                    "Snapshot=t87.inf",
406                    "Mode=HTTP",
407                    LAST);
408
409    (... pictures ...)
410
411          lr_think_time( 1 );
412
413          web_url("Persian",
414                    "URL={url}/petstore/product.screen?product_id=FL-DLH-02",
415                    "Resource=0",
416                    "RecContentType=text/html",
417                    "Referer={url}/petstore/category.screen?category_id=CATS",
418                    "Snapshot=t88.inf",
419                    "Mode=HTTP",
420                    LAST);
421
422    (... pictures ...)
423
424          lr_think_time( 1 );
425
426          web_url("Adult Male Persian",
427                    "URL={url}/petstore/item.screen?item_id=EST-17",
428                    "Resource=0",
429                    "RecContentType=text/html",
430                    "Referer={url}/petstore/product.screen?product_id=FL-DLH-02",
431                    "Snapshot=t89.inf",
432                    "Mode=HTTP",
433                    LAST);
434
435    (... pictures ...)
436
437          lr_think_time( 1 );
438
439          web_url("Cats_2",
440                    "URL={url}/petstore/category.screen?category_id=CATS",
441                    "Resource=0",
442                    "RecContentType=text/html",
443                    "Referer={url}/petstore/item.screen?item_id=EST-17",
444                    "Snapshot=t90.inf",
445                    "Mode=HTTP",
446                    LAST);
447
448    (... pictures ...)
449
450          lr_think_time( 1 );
451
452          web_url("Manx",
453                    "URL={url}/petstore/product.screen?product_id=FL-DSH-01",
454                    "Resource=0",
455                    "RecContentType=text/html",
456                    "Referer={url}/petstore/category.screen?category_id=CATS",
457                    "Snapshot=t91.inf",
```

```
458                     "Mode=HTTP",
459                     LAST);
460
461  (... pictures ...)
462
463           lr_think_time( 1 );
464
465           web_url("Tailless Manx",
466                   "URL={url}/petstore/item.screen?item_id=EST-14",
467                   "Resource=0",
468                   "RecContentType=text/html",
469                   "Referer={url}/petstore/product.screen?product_id=FL-DSH-01",
470                   "Snapshot=t92.inf",
471                   "Mode=HTTP",
472                   LAST);
473
474  (... pictures ...)
475
476           lr_think_time( 1 );
477
478           web_url("Cats_3",
479                   "URL={url}/petstore/category.screen?category_id=CATS",
480                   "Resource=0",
481                   "RecContentType=text/html",
482                   "Referer={url}/petstore/item.screen?item_id=EST-14",
483                   "Snapshot=t93.inf",
484                   "Mode=HTTP",
485                   LAST);
486
487  (... pictures ...)
488
489           lr_think_time( 1 );
490
491           web_url("Persian_2",
492                   "URL={url}/petstore/product.screen?product_id=FL-DLH-02",
493                   "Resource=0",
494                   "RecContentType=text/html",
495                   "Referer={url}/petstore/category.screen?category_id=CATS",
496                   "Snapshot=t94.inf",
497                   "Mode=HTTP",
498                   LAST);
499
500
501  (... pictures ...)
502
503           lr_think_time( 1 );
504
505           web_url("Add to Cart_6",
506                   "URL={url}/petstore/cart.do?action=purchase&itemId=EST-17",
507                   "Resource=0",
508                   "RecContentType=text/html",
509                   "Referer={url}/petstore/item.screen?item_id=EST-17",
510                   "Snapshot=t96.inf",
511                   "Mode=HTTP",
512                   LAST);
513
514  (... pictures ...)
515
516           lr_think_time( 1 );
517
518           web_submit_data("cart.do_5",
519                   "Action={url}/petstore/cart.do",
520                   "Method=GET",
521                   "EncType=",
522                   "RecContentType=text/html",
523                   "Referer={url}/petstore/cart.do?action=purchase&itemId=EST-17",
524                   "Snapshot=t97.inf",
525                   "Mode=HTTP",
526                   ITEMDATA,
527                   "Name=action", "Value=update", ENDITEM,
528                   "Name=itemQuantity_EST-11", "Value={Zufallszahl}", ENDITEM,
529                   "Name=itemQuantity_EST-21", "Value={Zufallszahl}", ENDITEM,
530                   "Name=itemQuantity_EST-19", "Value={Zufallszahl}", ENDITEM,
531                   "Name=itemQuantity_EST-17", "Value={Zufallszahl}", ENDITEM,
532                   "Name=itemQuantity_EST-13", "Value={Zufallszahl}", ENDITEM,
533                   "Name=itemQuantity_EST-6", "Value={Zufallszahl}", ENDITEM,
534                   LAST);
535
536  (... pictures ...)
537
538           lr_think_time( 1 );
539
540           web_url("Check Out",
```

```
541              "URL={url}/petstore/enter_order_information.screen",
542              "Resource=0",
543              "RecContentType=text/html",
544              "Referer={url}/petstore/cart.do?action=update&itemQuantity_EST-11
545                  =1&itemQuantity_EST-21=1&itemQuantity_EST-19
546                  =1&itemQuantity_EST-17=1&itemQuantity_EST-13
547                  =1&itemQuantity_EST-6=1",
548              "Snapshot=t98.inf",
549              "Mode=HTTP",
550              LAST);
551  (... pictures ...)
552
553
554          lr_think_time( 1 );
555
556          web_submit_data("j_signon_check",
557              "Action={url}/petstore/j_signon_check",
558              "Method=POST",
559              "RecContentType=text/html",
560              "Referer={url}/petstore/enter_order_information.screen",
561              "Snapshot=t99.inf",
562              "Mode=HTTP",
563              ITEMDATA,
564              "Name=j_username", "Value={user}", ENDITEM,
565              "Name=j_password", "Value={password}", ENDITEM,
566              "Name=submit", "Value=Sign In", ENDITEM,
567              LAST);
568
569  (... pictures ...)
570
571          lr_think_time( 1 );
572
573          web_submit_data("order.do",
574              "Action={url}/petstore/order.do",
575              "Method=POST",
576              "RecContentType=text/html",
577              "Referer={url}/petstore/enter_order_information.screen",
578              "Snapshot=t100.inf",
579              "Mode=HTTP",
580              ITEMDATA,
581              "Name=given_name_a", "Value=XYZ", ENDITEM,
582              "Name=family_name_a", "Value=ABC", ENDITEM,
583              "Name=address_1_a", "Value=1234 Anywhere Street", ENDITEM,
584              "Name=address_2_a", "Value=Unit 555", ENDITEM,
585              "Name=city_a", "Value=Palo Alto", ENDITEM,
586              "Name=state_or_province_a", "Value=California", ENDITEM,
587              "Name=postal_code_a", "Value=94303", ENDITEM,
588              "Name=country_a", "Value=California", ENDITEM,
589              "Name=telephone_number_a", "Value=555-{Zufallszahl}-48", ENDITEM,
590              "Name=email_a", "Value=reinhard.ba.brandl@bmw.de", ENDITEM,
591              "Name=given_name_b", "Value=XYZ", ENDITEM,
592              "Name=family_name_b", "Value=ABC", ENDITEM,
593              "Name=address_1_b", "Value=1234 Anywhere Street", ENDITEM,
594              "Name=address_2_b", "Value=Unit 555", ENDITEM,
595              "Name=city_b", "Value=Palo Alto", ENDITEM,
596              "Name=state_or_province_b", "Value=California", ENDITEM,
597              "Name=postal_code_b", "Value=94303", ENDITEM,
598              "Name=country_b", "Value=California", ENDITEM,
599              "Name=telephone_number_b", "Value=555-{Zufallszahl}-48", ENDITEM,
600              "Name=email_b", "Value=reinhard.ba.brandl@bmw.de", ENDITEM,
601              LAST);
602
603  (... pictures ...)
604
605          lr_think_time( 1 );
606
607          web_url("Sign out",
608              "URL={url}/petstore/signoff.do",
609              "Resource=0",
610              "RecContentType=text/html",
611              "Referer={url}/petstore/order.do",
612              "Snapshot=t101.inf",
613              "Mode=HTTP",
614              LAST);
615
616  (... pictures ...)
617
618          lr_think_time( 1 );
619
620          web_url("Java Pet Store Demo logo",
621              "URL={url}/petstore/main.screen",
622              "Resource=0",
623              "RecContentType=text/html",
```

```
624                "Referer={url}/petstore/signoff.do",
625                "Snapshot=t102.inf",
626                "Mode=HTTP",
627                LAST);
628
629    (... pictures ...)
630
631            lr_end_transaction("power_shopper", LR_AUTO);
632
633            web_cleanup_cookies();
634            web_cache_cleanup();
635
636            lr_think_time(15);
637
638            return 0;
639    }
640
641    #include "web_api.h"
642
643    vuser_end()
644    {
645            return 0;
646    }
647
```

Von der Promotion zum Buch

GPSR Compliance
The European Union's (EU) General Product Safety Regulation (GPSR) is a set
of rules that requires consumer products to be safe and our obligations to
ensure this.

If you have any concerns about our products, you can contact us on

ProductSafety@springernature.com

In case Publisher is established outside the EU, the EU authorized
representative is:

Springer Nature Customer Service Center GmbH
Europaplatz 3
69115 Heidelberg, Germany